THE ETHICAL TRAVEL GUIDE

THE ETHICAL TRAVEL GUIDE

Your passport to exciting alternative holidays

Polly Pattullo with Orely Minelli for Tourism Concern

London • Sterling, VA

First published by Earthscan in the UK and USA in 2006
Reprinted 2006

ISBN-13:   978-1-84407-321-4
ISBN-10:   1-84407-321-1

Typesetting by MapSet Ltd, Gateshead, UK
Printed and bound in the UK by Bath Press
Cover design by Susanne Harris
Index by Indexing Specialists (UK) Ltd

For a full list of publications please contact:

Earthscan
8–12 Camden High Street
London, NW1 0JH, UK
Tel: +44 (0)20 7387 8558
Fax: +44 (0)20 7387 8998
Email: earthinfo@earthscan.co.uk
Web: www.earthscan.co.uk

22883 Quicksilver Drive, Sterling, VA 20166–2012, USA

Earthscan is an imprint of James and James (Science Publishers) Ltd and publishes
in association with the International Institute for Environment and Development

A catalogue record for this book is available from the British Library

Library of Congress Cataloging-in-Publication Data

Pattullo, Polly.
  The ethical travel guide : your passport to alternative holidays / by Polly Pattullo
with Orely Minelli for Tourism Concern.
    p. cm.
  ISBN-13: 978-1-84407-321-4 (pbk.)
  ISBN-10: 1-84407-321-1 (pbk.)
    1. Tourism – Moral and ethical aspects. 2. Tourism – Social aspects. I. Minelli,
Orely. II. Title.
  G155.A1P353 2006
  910.46 – dc22

                                                                2005034320

The text pages and cover of this book are
FSC certified. FSC (the Forest Stewardship
Council) is an international network to promote
responsible management of the world's forests.

Mixed Sources
Product group from well-managed
forests and other controlled sources
www.fsc.org Cert no. SGS-COC-2121
© 1996 Forest Stewardship Council

CONTENTS

Foreword   *vii*
Acknowledgements   *ix*

Under an Ethical Sky   1
by Polly Pattullo

——————DIRECTORY——————

AFRICA

EAST

Ethiopia	57
Kenya	58
Madagascar	63
Rwanda	64
Tanzania	64
Uganda	68
Zanzibar	71

NORTH

Egypt	72
Morocco	73

SOUTHERN

Botswana	75
Lesotho	77
Malawi	78
Mozambique	78
Namibia	80
South Africa	81
Swaziland	88
Zambia	89

WEST

The Gambia	91
Ghana	93
Nigeria	95
Senegal	96

THE AMERICAS

CARIBBEAN

Cuba	99
Dominica	100
Dominican Republic	102
Haiti	103
Jamaica	104

CENTRAL

Belize	106
Costa Rica	107
Guatemala	113
Honduras	117
Mexico	118
Nicaragua	120

NORTH

Hawai'i	122
USA	123

SOUTH

Bolivia	125
Brazil	128
Colombia	132
Ecuador	134
Peru	139
Venezuela	144

ASIA

CENTRAL

Kazakhstan	148
Kyrgyzstan	149
Mongolia	150

SOUTHEAST

Cambodia	151
Indonesia	152
Laos	154
Malaysia	156
Thailand	157
Vietnam	160

SOUTH

Bhutan	161
India	162
Nepal	168
Sri Lanka	172

SOUTHWEST

Jordan	175
Palestine	176

OCEANIA

Australia	181
Fiji	187
New Zealand	188
Solomon Islands	190

EUROPE

Bosnia & Herzegovina	193
Croatia	194
Greece	195
Italy	197
Portugal	198
Russia	199
Serbia & Montenegro	200
Slovakia	201
Sweden	202

TOUR OPERATORS

UK OPERATORS	204
US OPERATORS	210
NON-UK/US OPERATORS	212
VOLUNTEERING	213

Resources   217

BOXES

Feedback   x
The way to go   2
Preparing for your trip   6
Tourism Concern's travel code   9
The ethical tourist goes to Thailand   11
The ethical tourist goes to Jamaica   14
Survival for tribal peoples   19
The ethical tourist goes to Ethiopia   22
The ethical tourist goes to Bolivia   25
The ethical tourist goes to Zambia   28
Ethical tourism: A growing concern   32
The ethical tourist goes to Cambodia   34
Climate change and travel   38
The ethical tourist goes to Sri Lanka   43
Trekking wrongs: Porters' rights   47
The ethical tourist goes to southern India   49
The Himalayan Tourist Code   167

MAPS

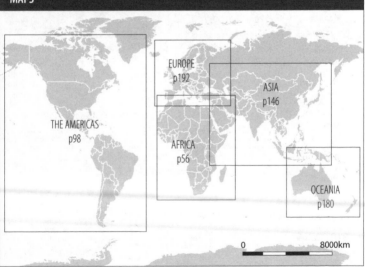

FOREWORD

Tricia Barnett

I often wonder if it's all my fault and whether I work for Tourism Concern to absolve my guilt! Travelling around the world for several years, often feeling I was a genuine adventurer as I veered off to the most seemingly remote of places, I had no thought for the future. How would I have known when, 30 years ago, a Thai friend took me to his village in Northeast Thailand, that now half a million tourists a year would go trekking in the area? I was the first white woman to set foot in the village, and to celebrate my arrival I was given a wonderful length of silk that my friend Charn's family had woven. I still have it. We went for rides on the village elephant, bathed with the women in a leech-filled pool and ate and slept beside his family. Can it really be half a million?

Although I feel blessed by such experiences, by the extraordinarily hospitable people that I met and stayed with, I also feel anxious about how much people like me contributed to an unhealthy change.

But then perhaps that's always the way: thinking it was better in the past. The importance of this book is that it's looking forward, not back – reclaiming the experience that was so important to me and helping to create a more positive future.

First-footers, like me, wander in without a thought of the morrow, fascinated by 'the other' and hooked into satisfying our own needs. We see wonders and meet a true welcome. Then we tell our friends, and, a little like the feature film *The Beach*, it becomes something many others want to tick off their list.

And in so doing, the interaction shifts from free, warm hospitality and cultural exchange to one where the locals can become entrepreneurs and profit from new money relationships. And next, the big developers move in. We, unknowingly, were the scouts for those whose eyes are on the next good place to exploit.

Tourism Concern, a membership organization, has always worked to raise awareness of exploitation in tourism and has more recently campaigned successfully for change. It has a unique position in the UK as an advocacy organization for people whose voices would not be heard by the global tourism industry.

So how do you get the world's fastest growing industry to develop in a way that brings benefits to local people rather than exploiting them and their environment? This is particularly a problem when holidays are about our own needs and pleasures. All too often the problems are also well hidden. How would you know that this beautiful hotel is on land snatched from fishermen, for which they weren't compensated? How would you know that the water in the pool and shower are depleting local people's resources and that their access to water is limited to two hours a day, as in villages in Goa? And we certainly don't ask waiters how much they're earning, and whether it's enough to help them climb out of poverty.

This book is part of the change that needs to happen and a challenge to the status quo. Local people, in environments however remote, are not fools. They know that there is money in the tourism business. It's evident all around them, but they scarcely even access the trickle down, even if their cultures are used in marketing the holiday and are the reason the visitors have come.

In order to access the tourists themselves the locals must develop and create something their potential visitors would enjoy. All over the world, as this book's listings show, people have worked hard to produce accommodation and activities for travellers. They have been resourceful, often driven by the idea that they can bring income into the community. They are delighted when they receive guests. They are thrilled that outsiders value their cultures, enjoy their food and respect them. But, unfortunately, they often don't have the capital to market themselves. That's why this book is important.

The Ethical Travel Guide lists over 300 places for us to visit in over 60 countries. It is a tribute to enterprising people all over the world and a fulfilment of Tourism Concern's commitment to ensure that people in all destinations benefit from tourism. If you decide to visit one of these hotels, guest houses, lodges or villages you will know that your money will go to people directly and not be lost to outsiders. You can then have a great holiday and not take a guilt trip!

These listings are groundbreaking. You can stay in very simple, local style accommodation; more sophisticated, with western plumbing; or the very luxurious. You can stay with people who are doing it alone or who are working closely with an outsider who has made a commitment to develop tourism that the locals can benefit from, or go through tour operators who are in partnership with locals. Perhaps a visit to one of these initiatives will form a short break or a day's outing in a longer holiday (for example, in South Africa or Costa Rica or Australia or Greece). There is a large and growing choice – which will continue to grow as we support the alternative, fair trade, ethical holiday. Enjoy!

Taking one of these holidays is an important and enjoyable way to contribute, but you can also join Tourism Concern and help end exploitation in tourism. See the last page of this guide for details.

www.tourismconcern.org.uk

Fighting Exploitation in Tourism

TourismConcern

A ride on a traditional ox-cart through one of Cambodia's national parks

DEBBIE WATKINS, CARPE DIEM TRAVEL

ACKNOWLEDGEMENTS

This book is a successor to Tourism Concern's previous book, *The Good Alternative Travel Guide*, conceived and written by Mark Mann.

Tourism Concern has been blessed with the following skilled and supportive contributors, without whom there would have been no book: Paul Smith and Lee Viesnik (who gave invaluable support with the listings, bibliography and photos); Corinne Attwood, Rosalina Babourkova, Chris Ball, Tim Clancy, Stroma Cole, Alison Crowther, Shirley Eber, Nigel Hetherington, Patrick Hourmant, Angela Kalisch, Michael Lomotey, Paul Miles, Claire Milne, Polly Pattullo, Diane Scott, Victoria Tongue, Monica Vecchi, Rachel Walmsley and Nigel Watt (who wrote the informed country introductions); and Roy de Graff, who supplied suggestions about how we should prepare for our travels.

Other backstage help has come from Roger Diski, Tony Janes and Chris McIntyre, who checked Africa out for us; also Emma Collins and Rana Torsun for advertising sales and Maria de Gysser for design help.

Last, but not least, many thanks too to the Tourism Concern members who wrote in about their holiday experiences.

FEEDBACK

The enterprises listed in this book are the result of exhausting, but not exhaustive research. If we have missed anything, please forgive us and let us know about it. We also welcome your comments and feedback on all the issues addressed in the guide. Please contact us by letter, phone or email at:

TOURISM CONCERN

Stapleton House	**Tel: +44(0)20 7133 3330**
277–281 Holloway Road	**Fax: +44(0)20 7133 3331**
London N7 8HN	**Email: info@tourismconcern.org.uk**
UK	**Web: www.tourismconcern.org.uk**

All listings and prices are correct at the time of going to press. We cannot take any responsibility for changes that might occur. We have tried our utmost to ensure that each tour or holiday is beneficial to local people – not just because they're being employed, which we take for granted – but because they actually get something positive in return. It can be the opportunity to get proper career training, get paid fair wages or that their children will get an education, that they'll get some health services or get to share in the profits and decide for themselves where the money is best placed for the community to profit as a whole. We strongly believe that the most authentic, genuine experience comes from people who welcome you because they've been part of the development of the project. They have either some ownership or community investment. But again, we cannot guarantee that this is the case. Please do tell us if there are issues around community benefits that have concerned you.

Tourism Concern offers a free service to all those enterprises that are listed. No one has paid to be included. But neither do we endorse any of those who are listed here because we do not have the capacity to inspect every one. What we have done instead is to send each initiative a very extensive questionnaire which looks in depth at their ownership structure, contribution to the local community and partnerships, as well as what they are offering visitors. We've only included those that show the highest standards of commitment to ethical tourism. So there is no Tourism Concern kitemark – just our hope that you will get pleasure from the commitment, passion and energy that is often behind the projects included in this book.

The exciting fact is that the majority of the listings have websites. This is a revolution for many of them that are remote and have no other marketing budgets. They are an invaluable asset and can give you far more information than we are able to, so please use them.

Luxurious rooms at Lewa House, Kenya, where the owners reinvest all profits into the community

GUSTAVO D. ROMANO OLIVERA, LEWA ENTERPRISES

UNDER AN ETHICAL SKY

Polly Pattullo

A morality tale

Once, when Europeans went on holiday to The Gambia, they all stayed on the coast near the capital, Banjul. With its wide, sandy beaches bordering the Atlantic Ocean, the 'Smiling Coast', as it was known, welcomed tourists to its manicured resorts. The hotels looked like any other hotel the tourists might have visited in say Florida or Spain, and provided food just like the tourists ate at home. The visitors rarely left the beach. Sometimes they complained about the young men, the bumsters, who chatted up the women; sometimes they bought carvings from the endless craft stalls clustered around the resorts, alongside bars advertising roast beef specials. They would never get to see anything that was 'real' about The Gambia although once a week they would get a bizarre glimpse of reality when their hotels offered an 'African buffet' and put on a folkloric evening of drumming and dancing.

Much money was spent, but Gambians rarely saw it. From airport to hotel, to trips on the river or to Joffre, the ancestral home of *Roots* author Arthur Haley, the package-greedy, foreign-controlled tourist industry retained an iron grip

When local people tried to break into the tourist industry, they found their paths blocked; the foreigners had it all sewn up. No one bought their products or their services – the big boys would not take the risk. They tried to leaflet the hotels but no one seemed interested; they went to the airport to find business but the arriving package-tour visitors would be hustled away by the tour reps.

Recently, however, things have been changing. Some tourists have begun to choose another sort of holiday, while Gambians – from guides to guesthouse owners, from fruit-sellers to farmers – have begun to gain a foothold in their own tourist industry.

One model initiative is the Tumani Tenda ecotourism camp, a collection of earth-coloured cottages overlooking a creek on the River Gambia. The idea evolved when the villagers of Tumani Tenda won an award for conserving their forest in a sustainable way. The villagers decided that the best investment would be to build a camp and offer the forest as part of the attraction for tourists. Helped by a Norwegian couple who had built their own camp and encouraged Tumani Tenda to do the same, the village did just that. They also consulted Gambia Tourism Concern on getting things right. The camp at Tumani Tenda opened its doors in 1999.

To get to Tumani Tenda, leave the coast behind and take a bus to the market town of Brikama and then a bush-taxi. Then, leaving the main road, follow a sandy track to the village. There, as you pass, adults wave in welcome as they go about their daily business in family compounds, homes of mud and straw separated by sisal wicker fences. There's a village bakery, a one-storey school; chickens and goats forage, women pump water from the well – the ubiquitous sights and sounds of a Gambian village. Mango trees abound – a green canopy shading the sun-scorched earth.

And then, some 500 metres from the village, lies the camp. 'It's the most peaceful place on earth', said one visitor. Facing a mangrove-edged river creek and backed by a forest of indigenous trees, accommodation is in huts built in a traditional style. The rooms are all simply and appropriately furnished: the wooden beds have palm-frond slats and foam mattresses covered in tie-dye sheets. There are mosquito nets, and fresh water comes from the village well. Visitors eat at a palm-thatched restaurant, known as the *bantaba* (meeting place) – there might be smoked oyster stew, fish or chicken, with rice and vegetables for dinner, alongside beer and wine (although this is, typically, a Muslim village).

Visitors get a chance to experience village life: they can admire the neat, well-organized garden plots where cassava, tomatoes, eggplants, herbs and fruits are grown; walk in the award-winning community forest; go on a canoe trip with the women to collect oysters from the mangroves; fish, swim, birdwatch, learn about salt-making, soap-making or dyeing, or simply laze in a hammock and gaze at the sleepy life of the river.

THE WAY TO GO

Why does an ethical holiday make sense?

For the host, an ethical holiday makes sense because:

- it can help alleviate poverty by putting our money into local hands;
- it can give back a sense of pride to marginal communities;
- it can contribute to community needs such as schools and clinics;
- it gives a more central role to women;
- it stops the flight to the cities from rural areas;
- it does not destroy the environment;
- happy hosts equal happy tourists.

For the tourist, an ethical holiday makes sense because:

- it allows us to get closer to other cultures – we're invited to experience them;
- it makes us feel a bit better rather than a lot worse about the 'footprint' we leave at our holiday destination;
- it can be great fun;
- it does not have to be expensive;
- it can be as luxurious – or as simple – as you want it to be;
- it benefits our hosts;
- it safeguards the future of our holiday destinations;
- happy tourists equal happy hosts.

To sum up: everyone gets a cut of the action on an ethical holiday.

Tumani Tenda itself is anything but sleepy. With a population of some 300 people from seven families, its gardens and forest, livestock and rice and millet fields are owned and worked communally. Although the people are very poor, they are enormously productive and sensitive to the importance of a sustainable lifestyle. Profits from tourism have gone into community needs: the money has helped build a school, a bakery, a poultry project, and in providing the village with electricity. Without tourism, life would be even tougher.

What the people of Tumani Tenda have done is to create a community tourism that is compatible with village life. As Sulayman Sonko, a villager closely involved in the camp, told the *Guardian* newspaper in 2004: 'We don't want visitors handing out sweets and pens. It's a Jola tradition to control our own destiny and not depend on charity.' At the same time, they are fulfilling a need for the growing numbers of visitors who want to leave – mentally and physically – the familiar beat of the coast for a more discerning and stimulating holiday in the hinterland.

The tourist camp has proved that holidaymakers can do that. Visitors admire the kindness and friendliness, as well as the achievement, of the village in this ambitious and unique project. As Adama Bah, the founder of Gambian Tourism Concern, says, 'Tumani Tenda has made me feel optimistic that tourism can be made better – it's tourism with a soul and a human face'.

New role for consumers

A variety of terms is now used to describe the type of holiday experienced by visitors to Tumani Tenda: 'alternative', 'responsible', 'fair trade' or 'ethical' tourism. Hard and fast definitions may not exist, but, at their core, such holidays are all concerned about an interaction between guests and host countries, and the impact that this can have on the social, political, economic and environmental well-being of the host countries – the places where we take our holiday. Essentially, such holidays seek to minimize the negative impacts of tourism and maximize the potential economic (and other) benefits to hosts.

Sometimes this might sound sanctimonious or a bit po-faced. Those who use the phrase 'politically correct' to denigrate 'eco-experiences' like to sneer at the terms 'ethical' or 'responsible' tourism. Critics say that those who promote ethical tourism are backward-looking elitists, that they are idealizing some pristine age, before Tuscany, Barbados, or 'that little place in Kerala' had been 'ruined' by 'ordinary people'. The implications are that the holidaymakers who try to be a bit ethical are holier than thou and that their holidays are not really holidays at all but some sort of wearisome social work project disguised as pleasure.

This could not be further from the truth. Holidays such as those at Tumani Tenda are as much fun and can provide as much excitement and wonder as any other sort of holiday. As the website responsibletravel.com says: 'If you travel for relaxation, fulfilment, discovery, adventure and to learn – rather than simply to tick off "places and things" then responsible travel is for you.' This British-based website also maintains that responsible tourists can make a difference by doing what they want to do, to 'cut loose and experience their world', by getting closer to local cultures and environments by involving local people.

Travelling to benefit the destination as well as the traveller is fast becoming a talking point. It's not looking backwards, but represents the cutting edge of thinking. The *Observer* newspaper, during the G8 conference between the world's eight largest economies at Gleneagles, Scotland, in July 2005, ran a piece on what it called 'trips with a conscience'; it headlined the piece 'You may not be St Bob but you can help fight poverty in Africa simply by choosing the right holiday'.

Choosing the right holiday in Rwanda – with a chance to glimpse the rare mountain gorillas

MICHAEL, AMAHORO TOURS

This is a powerful message. As the *Observer* commented: 'Go on holiday and save the world may sound like a title of a Ben Elton sketch, but the idea seems to be catching on.'

This brand-new role for consumers in the tourism market has emerged from two trends: first, there is a thirst for different and more 'exciting' holidays; second, there is a growing realisation of the negative impacts of tourism – its clodhopping footprints in other people's homes in the deserts, forests, seashores, mountains of the world. These two moods have come together to build a demand for a new type of holiday.

However, the ideas behind ethical tourism are also part of something broader – a global consumer movement, which is strengthening as people begin to flex their muscles and make thoughtful choices about what they spend their money on and why.

The fair trade movement is part of this new wave of people power, designed to provide producers in developing countries with a fair share of the returns from the sale of their produce. Just as more consumers are choosing fairly traded coffee or bananas because they know that this simple (if sometimes slightly more expensive) act supports a small coffee grower or banana farmer rather than a multinational company, so they are beginning to choose a fair trade holiday rather than a mass-market and mass-marketed one.

While fair trade products benefit the producers on the ground so fair trade tourism maximizes the benefits to the host countries and their workers. The fact that you can now not only read about 'fair trade' holidays, 'responsible' holidays or 'ethical' holidays but go on one shows how far tourism has been changing for the better.

Bigger than ever

Holidays such as those at Tumani Tenda – and the other holidays featured in this book – are very special; they do not represent a typical pattern of a holiday, either for the guests at the feast or for the tourism providers. Most tourists are the willing participants in mass tourism, the traditional arm of what has become the world's largest service industry and the fastest growing.

What does this mean? It means that more than 700 million tourist trips are taken each year – and every year more people go on more holidays. In 2000, nearly 50 million more people went on holiday (the same number as visit Spain each year) than they had done the previous year. In 2010 there will be one billion and in 2020 half as many again.

Yet at present, only a tiny percentage of the world's population goes abroad on holiday and most of them come from the developed world. So tourism has virtually only just begun.

World tourism generated around US$474 billion (£265 billion) in earnings in 2002, far more than the international reserves of Japan, China and the United States put together. Tourism provides more than 215 million jobs, with a third of those people working directly in the industry. In fact, one in every 12 of the world's workers is to be found in travel and tourism.

Before the 1960s, travel to places far flung from western capital cities was an elite pursuit, often an extension of colonial connections. The British upper class, for example, would be seduced by advertisements to 'winter in the West Indies'. Then, as the cost of flying decreased, more and more people could afford package holidays, first to Spain or Greece, and, later, to further away places such as Florida, Barbados or Bangkok.

At the same time, as more of us want – and have the money – to travel, the world has become more accessible. Nowadays, you don't have to be a hairy-chested, adventurer anorak to have a holiday in a remote part of the world. 'Ordinary people', who only a generation ago would have spent two weeks enjoying tea and egg sandwiches in their own backyard, are now white-water rafting in the Rockies, birdwatching in the Arctic or trekking in Laos.

In the mid-20th century, Western Europe and North America attracted nearly all the world's tourists, but by the end of the century tourists were busy searching out the 'long-haul' destinations: by 1999, for example, only 62 per cent of holidays were taken in the developed world (the 'north'); most countries of the developing world (the 'south') had increased their market share and were continuing to do so.

In the UK, for example, at the turn of the 21st century, we took 60 million trips abroad: 12.5m to Spain, with France not far behind. But more and more of us are going further afield: in 2002, the most popular long-haul destinations were the Caribbean (779,000), India (465,000) and South Africa (397,000). Growth rates to places in east Asia and the Pacific are high, and long-haul destinations in general are likely to see growth rather than those closer to home.

This ease of travel can take us to every nook and cranny of

PREPARING FOR YOUR TRIP

Here is a list of simple guidelines and useful tips that can save you money either directly into your pocket or indirectly by reducing the invisible costs of environmental and cultural damage. They are 'dos' rather than 'don'ts' that aim to help you make the most of your trip while also making it better for your hosts.

THE PLANNING STAGE: WHERE TO GO AND HOW TO GET THERE

The entire world (almost) is now open to travellers. We can make a difference, both for good (putting money into local pockets) or bad (propping up oppressive regimes; overloading the environment). Where you go depends on your passions and your finances, but it's worth thinking about your touristic footprints before you go – although there are no easy answers.

Try to learn something about the history, culture, society and politics of the place, before you go. Knowledge is power and can open doors for you. Read up on recent local news and pick up tips from other travellers through websites and internet forums.

If you book a package tour through a mainstream operator, consider that this normally maximizes profit for the tour operator and hotel at the expense of local people and small businesses. Some independent UK tour operators now incorporate responsible policies into their brochures, so it is worth shopping around. If booking a package through a mainstream tour operator, ask them how they monitor treatment and conditions of local staff, and whether they support local communities and help preserve the environment.

With a little bit of research it will be cheaper and more fun to go independently. This book is, of course, packed with ideas. Look for a hotel or project that is owned and/or managed by the local community.

Carbon-neutral flights. You can neutralize your own 'CO$_2$ emissions' by paying online via Climate Care or the Carbon Neutral Company (see page 38). Your money goes to plant trees or provide low-energy light bulbs to rural communities. Or you could even go by train, bicycle, two feet or donkey!

PACKING LIST – THE ESSENTIALS

Pack the minimum you can, and buy what you need along the way. Leave room for locally produced clothes and souvenirs.

Trousers with zipped bottoms (they turn into shorts) are great for warm climates as you get two for the price of one. Look for clothes made from fibres that can be hand washed and dry quickly. Natural fibres feel better close to the skin if you wear them for a long time and are cooler in hot climates.

Fair trade clothes can be bought in many places now and are normally of good quality and good value. Buying fair trade means the manufacturers get a fair price for their work.

Sunglasses should cover your eyes well and be of high quality and very durable. Get a hard case for them and always put them in the case when not on you – glasses are the first thing to get lost or broken on a trip.

A toothbrush made from natural rubber, or one with replaceable heads, saves on resources and waste.

Soap from natural oils biodegrades naturally with no harmful affects, and is gentle on your skin. A gentle, all-purpose liquid soap saves space and money: it can be used for the body, face, hair, shaving, washing clothes and disinfecting fruit and vegetables. Try to use your own toiletries rather than the disposable packets given at hotels, as hotel toiletries are usually cheap and full of chemicals, not to mention the waste of packaging.

Mosquito repellent – think twice before you buy chemical repellents based on DEET. It is harmful for your skin and for the environment. There are natural substances that repel mosquitoes – if you're lucky – effectively (lemon-grass oil extract, citronella or eucalyptus oil) when mixed with a gentle oil like coconut or your body cream. The best way to avoid getting bitten is to stay away from stagnant water and wear long-sleeved clothes in the evenings.

Purify your own water and help reduce the amount of plastic being thrown each day into landfills. In developing countries, plastic is a huge problem and tourists only make it worse. Aquapure Traveler is a handy bottle with a filter built into the cap. All you do is fill it up from any fresh water source, leave it to stand for 15 minutes and the water comes out clean and pure from the top. The filter contains a physical and chemical barrier to block almost all bacteria and pollutants. One filter cap supplies 350 litres of drinking water. This is a good alternative to buying bottled water as the industry is reaping huge rewards by purifying water, putting it in plastic bottles and selling for high profit.

Use a cloth bag for dirty laundry rather than litterbugging plastic bags.

For all electrical gadgets use Ni-Mh rechargeable batteries. You will save money and prevent thousands of your old batteries going into landfills and discharging chemicals into the soil. Battery chargers are small and efficient these days, so they're easy to travel with. You can even get a solar battery charger if you go to a very sunny place.

ON THE ROAD

When you get to your destination, use local knowledge. Ask local people where to go and what to do rather than relying on outdated guide books that encourage a herd mentality.

Giving photographs to people can be a great gift: a Polaroid camera like the iZone comes in handy.

If you buy plastic bottled water look out for recycling bins; remember to crush the bottle to conserve on space in the landfill.

If you stay at guesthouses, find out if they provide purified drinking water refills.

YOUR TRIP STARTS NOW

Awareness of these issues will help to enhance your experience wherever you are going. Of course, different countries have different cultures, which means being aware of local cultural, religious and political issues, and giving real thought as to how you might observe them.

our world. We can go almost anywhere, under conditions of safety (despite terrorism) and comfort and without having to plan too much for ourselves except the journey to the airport: tour operators, travel agents, ground handlers, tour guides, hotel receptionists do the rest.

We have a sense that the world is ours to explore, that we have a right to go anywhere we want, that is part of our freedom. Yet our ability to go anywhere and to do anything can, in some ways, diminish our enjoyment. So much is now researched, parcelled up, organized, analysed for us; little is unpredictable or open-ended in our travelling. This can sometimes leave us frustrated, with desires to push the boundaries of our experiences further.

Why be a host?

So, what has this exciting new world of travel possibilities done for the south? The answer is that while tourism can create enormous opportunities, it has also plunged the south into debt and dependency, and caused pain to many people. How has this happened?

At first, earning dollars from tourism appeared to be a terrific idea. The south has, after all, spectacular, ready-made natural resources and many magic cultural carpets to sell.

As a result, many developing countries turned to tourism as a way out of poverty. They saw tourism as an engine of development; international organizations also thought that tourism was a good thing. It was seen as a way to attract investment and stimulate the economies of struggling third-world countries; in 1967, for example, the Organisation for Economic Co-operation and Development (OECD) declared that tourism was 'a promising new resource for economic development'. Money poured into mainstream tourism projects. Later, bodies such as the World Bank and the International Monetary Fund expressed their support and provided funds, often linking tourism aid to debt repayment strategies.

Tourism generated foreign exchange. At the same time, income from traditional occupations such as agriculture was in decline so tourism became an attractive option. Indeed, tourism beckoned the poor: being a waiter in an air-conditioned restaurant, for example, seemed more desirable than working all day in sun-baked fields.

So, in a highly interdependent world, poor countries came to believe that tourism could help them out of their misery. Indeed, on the surface, the figures would suggest that too, for tourism now features abundantly in the GDP statistics of many countries.

In the last 30 years, third-world countries attracted tourists in their millions: they laid them out on their coral-edged beaches and piled them into their newly built hotels, which looked the same whether in Thailand or, half a world away, in Tobago. But by the mid-1990s, mass tourism had begun to lose some of its appeal; it also began to lose its economic edge for host nations. In some places, within a generation, the beaches had filled up, the resorts had become a bit tacky, the coastline blighted and the entertainments somewhat hackneyed.

TOURISM CONCERN'S TRAVEL CODE

Being sensitive to the following ideas means getting more out of your travels – and giving more back to the people you meet and the places you visit.

- **Learn about the country you're visiting**

  Start enjoying your travels *before* you leave by tapping into as many sources of information as you can. A trip to your local library to explore books on the culture, religion, environment, history and politics of a country can be rewarding, and knowing a few basic words of the language is always appreciated when you get there. For more current information try the BBC's World Service radio station (now also with an informative website at www.bbc.co.uk/worldservice/index.shtml as well as newspapers.

- **The cost of your holiday**

  Think about where your money goes – be fair and realistic about how cheaply you travel. Try and put money into local people's hands; drink local beer or fruit juice rather than imported brands and stay in locally owned accommodation.

  Haggle with humour and not aggressively. Pay what something is worth to you and remember how wealthy you are compared to local people.

- **Culture**

  Open your mind to new cultures and traditions – it will transform your experience. Think carefully about what's appropriate in terms of your clothes and the way you behave. You'll earn respect and be more readily welcomed by local people.

  Respect local laws and attitudes towards drugs and alcohol, which vary in different countries and communities. Think about the impact you could have:

  > *The effect on the local community of travellers taking drugs when visiting the hilltribes of Thailand can be devastating. People become trapped into selling drugs to travellers and become addicted themselves, especially young people who want to be like the travellers.* Jaranya Daengnoy, REST

- **How big is your footprint?**

  Minimize your environmental impact. Think about what happens to your rubbish – take biodegradable products and a water filter bottle. Be sensitive to limited resources like water, fuel and electricity. Help preserve local wildlife and habitats by respecting rules and regulations, such as sticking to footpaths, not standing on coral and not buying products made from endangered plants or animals.

- **Guidebooks**

  Use your guidebook as a starting point, not the only source of information. Talk to local people, then discover your own adventure!

- **Photography**

  Don't treat people as part of the landscape, they may not want their picture taken. Put yourself in their shoes, ask first and respect their wishes.

The ideas expressed in this code were developed by and for independent travellers. They show what individuals can do to play their part towards Tourism Concern's goal of more ethical and fairly traded tourism. For more information visit www.tourismconcern.org.uk or call +44 (0)20 7133 3330

The evidence indicated a swing away from the mass, packaged, beach holiday and towards a new trend – ecotourism. This, at its simplest, means 'responsible travel to natural areas that conserves the environment and improves the well-being of local people' (the definition of the Ecotourism Society). Ecotourism, which utilizes the hinterlands as well the beaches, also became an attractive possibility for countries that had never thought they had anything to offer the tourist. Cloud forests and boiling lakes, sizzling deserts and empty tundra regions began to be opened up to tourism. Ecotourism, it was claimed, satisfied the desires of the growing numbers of 'discerning' tourists who wanted to get-away-from-the-hordes.

So, in its different forms, tourism remains an attractive source of wealth: it uses the natural skills and attractions of people and places, it replaces traditional and often waning sources of wealth, it provides jobs, it builds roads and airports. Madagascar, for example, the fourth largest island in the world and a place of diverse beauty and cultural complexity, had no tourism industry until 1990; now tourism is the second largest source of revenue after coffee. If tourism can generate foreign exchange in Madagascar, one of the world's poorest and unknown countries, it might be argued, it can do so anywhere. The news spread.

In Dominica, for example, an exquisite island of rainforest, mountains and rushing rivers in the eastern Caribbean, tourism has been slow to develop. But for many years, the people of the village of Vieille Case have been looking forward to the tourists, only to see the tour buses from the cruise ships pass them by. Its people are self-sufficient farmers and fishermen; its community is based around the church, local societies and cultural groups. They have been tourists themselves, on holidays or working trips to St Maarten or Antigua, and they believe that their community, too, has something to offer visitors. And when the man from the tourist board paid a visit and said that tourism would help to sustain the economy and raise foreign exchange, the villagers were enthusiastic. 'We have the people who would make the tourists' time enjoyable so we can take advantage of tourism', said one villager. Even a few extra dollars would help in times of economic pressure and the collapse of the banana industry. The anticipation remains that tourism will make a difference.

From his home in Khayelitsha township, Golden Nongawuza runs a thriving business making flowers from recycled tin cans and bottletops

ROGER DISKI, RAINBOW TOURS

THE ETHICAL TOURIST GOES TO THAILAND

Linda Barrett stayed at Lamai Homestay, Ko Phet village, Isand.

'The Lamai homestay is run by Lamai, who was born in Ko Phet, and her husband Jimmy. It is a great example of a very small enterprise helping to support the local community. All visitors (maximum of six) are taken to local cafes and food shops to spend money. I was taken to visit the local silk village (not a tourist village). Here I spent a day learning the rudimentaries of silk making. I followed the process from the growing of the silk worms to the finished garment. I did some spinning and some weaving and found the whole process fascinating. Several of the local women benefited financially from this experience.

'I walked through the rice fields and visited the various houses in the village where the rice is processed. There, too, the locals were paid for their participation. I bought a bag of Ko Phet rice to take home.

'I visited Lamai's family home where her mother and aunt spent a day showing me how to make baskets – some for catching fish, others for collecting produce. I made one to take home. We also made a small rug out of the reeds collected from the lakeside.

'The following day, we visited the village noodle-maker. She showed me how to make delicious Thai noodles. Back in the homestay, Lamai gave me a half-day cookery course where I learned how to make the most delicious meals from simple local ingredients.

'Finally, my favourite day was a 'food-foraging' day when I accompanied one of the village elders out and about to search for traditional food. This included net-fishing on the lake, digging for roots in the fields and catching frogs, fresh water crabs and grubs in the paddy fields. At dusk, we donned "miners' helmets" with torches on the front and took nets out into the fields to catch flying insects. Everything was then added in various ways to the staple diet of rice.

'I have been to Thailand many times in the past and had no idea that this kind of community still existed. It was fascinating and at the end of it I felt that I had contributed to the survival of the village people. There was no contrived pageant; I just joined in with normal village life. On top of that, I was provided with extremely comfortable accommodation, Western standard toilet/bathroom facilities and wonderful food.

'I came away wanting others to know that such holidays exist (because of the high cost of advertising, they are hard to find). I would like more people to know about a way of having tremendous fun but also to contribute to the local economy in a very personal way.'

Globalization: A new trip

The people of Vieille Case are not alone in thinking that tourism will provide. All over the world communities are being urged to turn to tourism. The world's tourist industry is on speed; the only thing that appears to stop it is an apocalyptic event such as the tsunami that swept across the Indian Ocean on Boxing Day 2004 or the urban devastation of 9/11.

Such events may keep people at home, but only for a time. Then, it's all go again: back to old places, exploring new places. The extraordinary expansion of tourism has not just happened because of cheap airfares. Another reason is that we live in an economically interconnected world, which fans out from the rich metropolitan centres in Europe and North America.

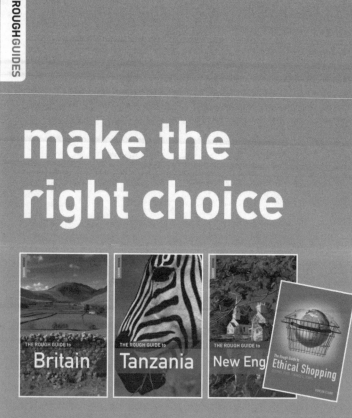

The age of globalization has arrived. This is the term used to describe the way in which multi-national corporations do business across the boundaries of nation states; global capitalism has shown that borders have little meaning when it comes to international trade. And in a climate of free trade, the major corporations can run roughshod over the countries and peoples of the poor south. This happens in tourism as it does for other services and products.

This economic invasion of vulnerable countries by multinational companies is one aspect of globalization. But as the protestors against global capitalism have shown, globalization has also made us aware of our responsibilities as global citizens. Global warming is one pressing example of the fact we all live in a 'global village' and that what we do can affect others living thousands of miles away from us, both now and in the future.

The concept of the global village has triggered an interest in the idea of global citizenship and shared responsibilities. As the Earth Charter states, its mission is to 'establish a sound ethical foundation for the emerging global society and to help build a sustainable world based on respect for nature, universal human rights, economic justice and a culture of peace'. Much of this new thinking has come from a growing concern about what the rich north has done to the poor south.

Tourism is a case in point. While those at the cutting-edge of the tourist industry – thoughtful travellers, campaigning NGOs, farsighted tour operators and radical organizers – in both the north and south, first discussed the uncomfortable impacts of tourism in the 1960s, the bureaucratic world has taken a lot longer to take action.

Recognition of how tourism should be managed was first formally expressed at the first Earth Summit in Rio in 1992 in its Agenda 21. This stated that 'environmental protection should constitute an integral part of

Interior of a restored Cretan settlement in a sustainable community

VASILLIS KOTROTSOS, MILIA. RESTORED TRADITIONAL CRETAN SETTLEMENTS the tourism development process' and that 'tourism development should recognize and support the identity, culture and interests of indigenous people'. This was a commitment from 182 governments. Later, the conservative World Tourism Organization also adopted a global code of ethics, which addresses such issues as preventing the exploitation of women and children. More recent initiatives have included such events as the Year of Ecotourism in 2002 and programmes such as a 'pro-poor tourism' policy developed by the UK's department for international development.

These initiatives reflect the thinking of the ethical pioneers: that while tourism can be a force for economic good, in many instances it is seriously damaging the health of peoples and places. The potential for good – putting money in the hands of those who work for it and need it, in return for a great holiday – has in many cases turned sour.

Smile please, we're tourists

Tourists have a good idea about what could be called the sliding scale of the smile. When we book a holiday abroad we delight in hearing that the people of that place are friendly, smiling and welcoming. But this is not a commodity that anyone gets paid for. It is a human response to a human encounter; it is best when it comes unexpectedly and unsolicited.

The manufactured smile, however, when tourist 'providers' have been trained to smile for the tourists, has a different context. 'Smile. You are a walking tourist attraction' was one slogan used in the Caribbean many years ago. That approach may be outdated but the requirement remains and it takes its toll on the workers. In the Dominican Republic, a country that now welcomes more than three million tourists a year, one hotel worker said: 'We

THE ETHICAL TOURIST GOES TO

The poet Benjamin Zephaniah visited Mandeville and stayed at the Astra Country Inn Hotel where its pioneering manager, Diana McIntyre-Pike, is chairwoman of the Rural and Community-based Tourism network, and an important mover in the Sustainable Communities Foundation.

'Mandeville has no formal museum but it does have many "home museums" where you see the town's history through the history of its residents. Diana keeps talking about "community tourism". She can set you up with a family, on a farm, get you married in a sustainable forest, or simply send you to another hotel. Hotels work together here, tourists blend in and workers in the tourist industry don't put on strange American accents.

'At Diana's house, I meet her extended family. When I perform for them, I'm told that a poet should be prepared to perform anywhere. They clap for me and then I'm given a history lesson I will never forget. This is a home museum, a collection of family memorabilia, paintings and photographs that go back generations, even to their distant Scottish relatives. Where there are no photos or paintings, I'm given the oral history. I leave uplifted, saying "community tourism" and "organic family farming" every time I speak. But these are not new-age hippies. The people behind this movement are, on average, 60 years old, they are Christians and they want me to tell the world that tourism doesn't have to mean beaches and large hotels; it can mean villages, farms and staying with someone who reminds me of my mother.'

JAMAICA

Liz Angus visited Mandeville and Treasure Beach. Here is an extract from her letter to Diana McIntyre-Pike.

'Dear Diana,

'What a pleasure, to say the least, to meet you and be so deliciously hosted for our few extraordinarily eventful days in Mandeville. We were very comfortable at the Astra and slept extremely well in pleasant surroundings and were spoiled rotten by the outstanding Jefferson, whom we miss.

In just a few short days, we were made to feel quite at home by your staff, friends & family and must thank you for your lovely welcome and hospitality.

'From Mandeville, we went to Ital Rest, Treasure Beach on the south coast, where we stayed for five days in such unexpected company that we felt we were becoming Treasure Beach nationals. The owners of Ital Rest are very hospitable and on our first morning we breakfasted with them and spent many pleasant hours in their company (one night playing very bad Scrabble). We walked all over Treasure Beach and met many residents; Jeanne Genus took us under her wing and also off to Sunday morning at the bakery where she sang and played the guitar. (Jeanne was a political activist in the way back when in the US.) She's also president of the Treasure Beach Women's Group, which has just built a super new centre.

'We lived in sarongs and bare feet and read by candlelight. (Hurricane Ivan made a dent in this paradise – the beach was clawed away and swimming dicey. This was an education for us – tourism crisis in action.)

'Jamaican people are the most genuine souls I have found anywhere in the world – proud, sophisticated and beautiful. For a first-time visitor – the good mightily outweighs the bad (which we did not see). We only found a staggeringly beautiful country, and such hospitality that neither of us wanted to leave – and that hasn't happened before.'

have to smile to the tourists but it is not what we are feeling in our souls. We want to work and we want to make your holidays happy. But it is difficult.'

And then, if the tourists behave as new colonialists and come like invaders trampling over everything you hold dear, the smiles can fade away entirely. As the writer Martin Amis recognized when he visited a village in St Lucia: 'We stop for a can of orange juice and are unsmilingly overcharged. Although you wouldn't call them hostile, they are no more friendly than I would feel, if a stranger drove down my street in a car the size of my house.'

Perhaps then we need to ask: why should 'they' smile at 'us'? Have they anything to smile about? Not if they don't benefit from tourism and not if they have no real stake in its future and how it is managed.

That is why, just occasionally, from different corners of the world, comes the call: 'stay away' – don't get out that backpack, don't buy a ticket, don't get on a plane and visit us, however beautiful our home is, however delightful our people, however delicious our food, however spectacular our sunsets. These people are not diseased, crazy or criminal; their demand comes from a recognition that tourists make life worse, not better. 'To all the tourists, visitors, travellers or whatever other name you are called: I beg you, please don't come [here]... Tourism is killing us. It is literally sucking the life out of us. We are running out of sweet water. Our lands have been sucked dry. When once there were taro fields and fishponds today there are golf courses, hotels and urban sprawl'. That call came from Hawai'i, one of the most tourist-drenched places in the world, in the mid 1990s. Much earlier, in the

1970s, a young Caribbean politician had announced at a conference: 'tourism is whorism'.

In Hawai'i, the concern was about what millions of visitors had done to the environment and its culture. In the Caribbean, also a region of vulnerable islands, the hostility came from the sense that offering your home up to visitors was a recipe for exploitation and servility, and an echo of slavery.

Not much, however, happened to affect the flow of tourists when those appeals were made. Holidaymakers continue to flock to Hawai'i while tourism has become the lifeblood of the Caribbean. Then, we didn't take much notice of what was being said.

Now, it may be different. We may not be staying at home, but we are beginning to think about how we can do things differently when it comes to our holidays. Gradually, a consumer awareness is building about the damage that our blissful worldwide holidays can cause the planet and its people. We are recognizing that an equal opportunities policy just does not operate when it comes to tourism.

Who gets the dosh?

'Tourism makes some people extremely rich, but most of them live in the places from where the tourists come', the director of Tourism Concern once said. For tourism has not only become big in numbers, but sophisticated in organization. For the most part, the industry is based not in the countries where it operates but in the great metropolitan centres of the north. In the UK, for example, four companies (TUI UK, First Choice, My Travel Group and JMC) control most of the UK package market. Some tour companies, such as the German TUI, are not only tour operators, but also own airlines and hotels. TUI, for example, owns the leading UK operator Thomson, which owns an airline, Thomson Flights, and the largest

travel agent Lunn Poly. This is known as vertical integration. TUI is now the largest travel company in the world. Little escapes its grasp.

The way the industry is organized means that, for the most part, consumers spend much of their holiday cash in buying the package – before they leave home. Much of the rest goes into the pockets of foreign-owned companies in the host countries – not many nationals of poor countries get to own marble-floored hotels, shopping chains or flashy restaurants serving fusion food. Statistics vary, but some people argue that what is known as economic 'leakage', the extent to which local economies lose – or never receive – the revenue generated by tourism, can be as high as four-fifths the cost of a holiday. Even when it's not that high, leakage remains a serious problem for most host countries.

Studies have shown how this works. For example, you decide to go on holiday in Kenya, a country famous for its tourism (wildlife safaris, glorious Indian Ocean beaches). Kenya is glad to welcome you for tourism is its biggest foreign exchange earner. You book through your local, high street UK travel agent. All well and good, and certainly very convenient for you, the customer.

Your holiday costs £1500 (around US$2650). Of that, 40 per cent goes to the airline and 20 per cent to the tour operator. That leaves Kenya with 40 per cent. But that is not the end of the story because a quarter of that 40 per cent goes on imports (essential for keeping the tourists in the manner to which they have become accustomed) while nearly a third is

Kasbah Du Toubkal recently funded the building of a community hammam in Imil Village

KASBAH DU TOUBKAL

used to service Kenya's debt. Your £1500 holiday leaves Kenya just £225 (or US$400) richer. None of this, however, reaches the Maasai, the pastoralist people who have lived for generations alongside the elephants and lion, wildebeests and antelopes, the animals you have come to see. But, in fact, many Maasai no longer tend their cattle on the great grasslands. Displaced from their land to create wildlife parks, they live on the margins. The only way they can benefit from tourism is to give up their culture and go to work as waiters, dancers or souvenir-makers.

Or how about an all-inclusive holiday to the Dominican Republic? On an all-inclusive holiday (as little as £499/US$885 for two weeks in 2005), you pay for everything – flight, hotel, food, drink, entertainments, sports – upfront. That's great for the customer but not so good for those bars, restaurants, food stalls and guides outside the hotel premises. Because, once you have paid for 'everything', you may not want to spend any more money in the local craft shops, the bars, the roadside food stalls. And while all-inclusives – very popular, in particular, in the Caribbean – have been a successful and well-run sector of the industry, the grass roots see things rather differently. By and large, locals feel bitter about the glittering ghettos that have opened in their midst – for local businesses only get the crumbs of the crumbs from those all-inclusive customers who have 'left their wallets behind'.

We might expect tourism to generate benefits across the economy. After all, tourists are demanding: they need feeding and watering and entertaining. They need someone to grow the food, make the furniture, bottle the beer and so on. But too often, in poor countries, tourists eat imported food and sleep in rooms where nothing has been made locally. They demand their cornflakes and steaks, their cheeses and crisps – as if they were at home; and they drink imported beers rather than try the local brands. All this contributes to leakage. So many tourism earnings are either retained by the tourist-sending countries, or repatriated to them in some way. Somehow or other, it ends up with our hosts – not us – picking up much of the bill.

The Maldives, for example, is a scattering of 87 resort islands in the Indian Ocean. In 2005, it came top of a UK poll as the world's most desirable destination; perhaps this was because it was the honeymoon choice of the celebrity model Jordan or perhaps because its One & Only Reethi Rah resort is man-made, shaped like an octopus, and sells US$300 flip-flops. Whatever the reason, many of its hotels bask in unimaginable luxury. However, all that the islands contribute for the tourists are a gorgeously benign climate and some swaying palm trees. Nearly everything else that a tourist needs is imported (including much of the labour) by a repressive regime, which keeps its tourists segregated from its people. Your food, for example, like the beefburgers made from Japanese cows, on the Reethi Rah menu, is largely imported. There is ample fish in the sea around the Maldives – before tourism, fishing was the main occupation – but no refrigeration. This means that the catch

SURVIVAL FOR TRIBAL PEOPLES

Tourism need not be a destructive force for tribal peoples. But unfortunately it usually is. Any tourism that violates tribal people's rights should be opposed. Tourism must be subject to the decisions made by tribal peoples themselves.

Don't bring in disease. Care must be taken in areas where tribal peoples' immunity to outside diseases may be poor. Some contagious disease (such as colds, influenza, etc.), which affect tourist only mildly, can kill tribespeople. Please also remember that AIDS kills.

Do recognize land rights. Tribal peoples' ownership of the lands they use and occupy is recognized in international law, and should be respected regardless of whether the national government applies the law or not (governments are amongst the principal violators of tribes' rights). When in tribal lands, tourists should behave as they would on any other private property.

Do ask permission. The lands lived in or used by tribes should never be entered without the free and informed consent of the tribal peoples themselves. Obtaining this consent may be a lengthy process, requiring respect, tact and honesty. Bribery should never be used.

Don't demean, degrade, insult or patronize. All tourism and advertising that treats tribal peoples in an insulting, degrading or patronizing manner (for example, references to 'stone-age cultures', 'untouched by time' etc.) should be opposed. It is demeaning and quite simply untrue.

Do pay properly. Tribespeople should be properly rewarded for their services and the use of their territory. Payment should be agreed in advance with their legitimate representatives (bribery should never be used). Where profits arise from the use of tribal areas, this should be properly explained to the tribes, who may want a share. Anyone who does not accept tribal peoples' own terms for payment should not be there.

Do be respectful. Tour operators should ensure that their staff and clients behave respectfully towards tribal peoples. Any false stereotypes the tourists may harbour should not be reinforced.

cannot be stored. Hotels need fish as and when they need it – they cannot be dependent on a poor catch day. So fish has to be imported; as does practically everything else. Meanwhile, its people live in poverty – up to 42 per cent on just over a dollar a day, with more than 30 per cent of children under five suffering from malnutrition, according to the United Nations.

Working at the table

One of the great defences of tourism is that it creates jobs. This is true. But what sort of jobs? Joshua, for example, works in a hotel on the Swahili coast in Kenya. 'I work 10–12 hour shifts and am paid 219 shillings [£1.75/US$3] a day, but not if you are sick or have a rest day. We are only meant to work eight hours a day but if you don't do overtime then there is no point coming back tomorrow. The managers tell the tour operators we are earning a good wage because the operators don't want their clients to have to pay tips…Only the managers eat the food the tourists don't finish. We are given poor food and if you are found with a glass of orange juice you are charged a full breakfast of 600 shillings. They treat us very badly. They make us show how much we have in our pockets to stop us keeping tips.'

Joshua is one of millions of hotel workers. Not all, of course, suffer such bad pay and conditions. However, the tourist industry is notorious for being unorganized and exploitative. In much of the developing world, jobs in the tourist sector, many of which are casual, as they are in the UK and Europe, are characterized as being seasonal and part-time, with a high turnover of staff.

Jobs in tourism are also very vulnerable to external events, such as hurricanes or terrorism. Tourists do not take risks: they do not travel to what they perceive to be dangerous places; they can always go elsewhere. When the tourists do not arrive, jobs are lost. The tsunami of 2004, which killed hundreds of thousands of people in Asia and Africa, also destroyed livelihoods when hotels, bars and restaurants were washed away.

MILIA RESTORED TRADITIONAL SETTLEMENTS

'Peace and quiet in prodigious amounts' in Crete

In 2003, the International Labour Organization estimated that 2.8m jobs were lost in the Asia–Pacific region as a result of the war in Iraq and the brief SARS virus scare. Workers in Bali reported to Tourism Concern, before the second terrorist attack in 2005, that they still had to smile and pretend nothing was wrong even though their working hours and salaries had been cut in half. They said that tourists thought that because the workers were 'still smiling so they must be happy'.

Beyond those who work within the hotel walls are unknown numbers of workers in the informal economy. These are taxi drivers, shoeshine boys, the vendors, tour guides, part-time prostitutes – all desperate to pick up the odd 'tourist dollar'. Millions of those working in the informal sector depend on tourists who are prepared to 'freelance' – to break away from the all-inclusive hotels or the cruise-ship day trips, and put some money directly into the pockets of local people.

Even so, wages and conditions are hard. Porters, for example, work in some of the harshest tourism conditions in the world, carrying tourists' backpacks. From Machu Picchu, to the Himalayas, to Kilimanjaro, Tourism Concern discovered that porters earned poor wages in poor working conditions. In Nepal, the porters are poor farmers from lowland areas, 'as unused to the high altitudes and harsh conditions as western trekkers'. They wear thin jackets and inadequate footwear. Yet they are expected to be super strong. The reality is that they suffer four times more accidents and illnesses than western trekkers.

Cruise-ship tourism is often associated with glamour, even if it has lost its upper-crust ambience. But for the workers on the cruise ships, life has never been cool. In the Caribbean, for example, which is the world's busiest cruise zone, many cruise lines employ European officers, with North

THE ETHICAL TOURIST GOES TO ETHIOPIA

Marisa Astill-Brown took a trek in the Meket area of North Wollo, northern Ethiopia. The trek was organized by a local NGO called Tourism in Ethiopia for Sustainable Future Alternatives (TESFA), which is part of a rural development programme. Two communities have developed sites offering accommodation, food, drink, guides and pack animals.

'Having left the road we bumped over dried muddy soil and rock for a while in a flat and apparently featureless landscape, and then at random (or so it seemed) we stopped. This was where the walk was to begin. We got out, happy to stretch our legs after several hours in the car. Our guide set off and we followed him.

'Within two minutes we had reached the edge of the world. The flat ground abruptly stopped as we found ourselves on the edge of a precipice so high and beholding such a vast panorama that we could do nothing but gape, awestruck, at villages thousands of feet below us, mountains stretching out to the horizon.

It was an unforgettable moment. The sun was low in the sky, casting a pale orange glow on the mountains, the smoke from cooking fires drifting up into misty sheens around settlements far below. We looked along the edge of the precipice, stretching as far as the eye could see in both directions, and saw where we were to stay that night.

'Stone, thatched *tukuls* or huts provided bedrooms and dining room some steps from the edge, a toilet just feet from the precipice, with a view that would win awards were they given for dramatic locations, and even a shower *al fresco* – a bamboo cubicle with heated water poured into a bag above a shower head. On arrival we were given delicious snacks washed down with ginger tea. Then we simply gawped at the view as the sun sank behind the mountains. We were served gin and tonics as we watched a majestic sunset, convinced there could be no place nor any moment more beautiful.

'At sunrise we opened the door of our *tukul* to find a tray of steaming ginger tea in the morning chill, and the silhouettes of the *zabagnas* (night watchmen) crouched on the edge of the abyss against the glow of the dawn sky. After breakfast we set off for the second village, some six hours' walk distant. We had a horse accompany us, to rest any tired limbs, and we walked the paths used by the communities to travel between settlements or to market. Our guides provided thought-provoking information and discussion about the TEFSA project, the community, its aspirations and how it fitted into the wider development debate.

'After a while we left the edge of the precipice and crossed a relatively flat plateau before the land suddenly opened out again, this time without the precipice but with equally dramatic vistas. We wound our way down the mountainside to reach another cliff-side spot for the night.

'This time the second of the two sleeping *tukuls* was only being finished as we arrived. Our arrival was, however, a cause for much interest; we sensed our fascination with the view was paralleled by the local community's curiosity about us.

'In a place where life is a daily struggle and physically gruelling, the chasm between us was palpable. We had chosen to come and marvel at the scenery and experience a little window on life in the Ethiopian Highlands, whilst our hosts, surrounded by magnificent beauty, were trapped in a life of grinding poverty and hardship. Their dignity and resilience was humbling even as it masked the gulf between us and our different lives.

'More fine food and ginger tea and we left the following day for a short climb to where our Land Rover awaited us. It was a rare window on a unique culture and landscape.'

American and western European staff in the business and entertainment jobs, supported by a third-world crew. Crew members, often from the poorest parts of the third world, are paid low wages, labour in shoddy working conditions and endure an authoritarian management code, according to a 2002 study. 'Conditions for workers below deck haven't improved in decades', said an inspector with the International Transport Workers Federation. 'Many are reluctant to come forward and complain. To most people, workers on cruise liners are nonentities. They have an almost invisible existence.'

Losing your home and your job

While tourism has brought opportunities and routes out of poverty, for some, it has destroyed jobs and denied people the means to continue their traditional livelihoods.

One of the most alarming negative effects of tourism is the displacement of peoples from their homes to make way for tourism developments. These are often multimillion dollar projects backed by powerful investors and local governments. Local people have little say in what happens.

Pastoralist groups in East Africa, for example, have been victims of a tourism policy that has promoted safari tourism at the expense of people. The Maasai have been one of the groups worst affected by displacement – thrown off the land that they and their animals have inhabited for centuries. Conservationists defended their policy of creating national parks and evicting people by arguing that nomadic groups like the Maasai were responsible for over-grazing and the over-hunting of wildlife. The effect has been devastating. George Monbiot, the environmentalist, has argued that the Maasai have lost 'all but two of their major dry season pastures and drought reserves'. Now they are confined to spaces that cannot support their herds and their growing populations. In Northern Kenya, the Samburu district used to provide fertile grazing during the dry season for its pastoralists. Now, two national reserves have been created and the Samburu are forbidden to enter. Their watering-hole, which provided them with the only pure water in the region, is now a turquoise blue swimming pool in the grounds of the Sarova Shaba Hotel. While tourists frolic, the Samburu have to rely on an inadequate water supply from the Uaso River for their cattle, which graze on land bare of grass. 'The plight of the Samburu is desperate...They were always self-sufficient in food, but without access to their dry-land grazing their cattle are dying. The Samburu are now dependent on food aid to stay alive', wrote Jean Keefe, a writer on displacement in tourism. As one hunter-gatherer from Mau Forest, Kenya, commented: 'When the whites first arrived in this area, they thought we were wild animals and chased us into the forest. Now that they have found out that we are people they are chasing us out again.'

One of the most notorious examples of how people have been displaced to make way for tourism has been in Myanmar (formerly Burma) where organizations such as Amnesty International have commented on the disturbing connection between tourism development and human rights abuses. In Myanmar, this has also involved forced labour. Tourists have witnessed thousands of people – manacled prisoners, women and children – being forced to help clean the Mandalay Palace moat so that the military junta could promote the palace for tourists. In another part of Myanmar, at

KURT HOLLE, PERU RAINFOREST EXPEDITIONS

Excellent observation facilities at the Amazonas Lodge, Peru

the ancient capital of Pagan, founded in the 9th century and adorned with pagodas and shrines, more than 5000 people who lived inside its walls were told to pack their bags ready for removal to Pagan new town, a parched-earth site, some five kilometres from the old town. Their homes were destroyed to make way for tourism and the resort hotels that now promote their charms online.

The journalist John Pilger, writing on the gross abuses of the military regime, quoted Myanmar's director of tourism: 'At last the doors to Myanmar, the magic golden land, are open', boasted Dr Naw Angelene in an official handout. 'Roads will be wider, lights will be brighter, tours will be cleaner, grass will be greener, and with more job opportunities, people will be happier.'

Tourism development does not have to be as ruthless as that in Myanmar to cause hardships to local people. The building of land-guzzling golf courses, particularly in Asia, has denied local people their land and their jobs, as investors have gobbled up land for the golf craze, while paying very little in compensation. Chee Yoke Ling of the Global Anti-Golf Movement in Malaysia wrote: 'The golf business dramatically widens the gap between the rich and poor. Contrary to the principle of sustainable development, the game, through alliances between politicians and developers, contributes to the conversion of livelihood-sustaining resources of the poor to opulence-sustaining resources for the rich.'

A decade ago, the golfing craze prompted the United Nations Economic and Social Commission for Asia and the Pacific (UNESCAP) to comment on the practice: 'Golf course construction has created widespread negative social, cultural and environmental impacts, particularly in the developing countries of the region. Typical impacts include forest destruction and air, water and soil pollution caused by the excessive use of chemicals.'

THE ETHICAL TOURIST GOES TO BOLIVIA

Bruce Olson visited Chalalan Ecolodge in Madidi National Park in the Amazon rainforest. The lodge is the product of years of hard work by the nearby indigenous community and the commitment of two foreign aid organizations who supported the community's initiative. It is owned and managed by the indigenous Quechuas.

'My trip to the Bolivian Amazon rainforest was the adventure of a lifetime.

'My visit to Chalalan, the eco-friendly safari lodge deep within the rainforest, was a truly authentic and enchanting adventure in this remote area. The lodge has been built and run by the people of the Tacana village of San Jose de Uchupiamonas, a village with over 390 years of history. They make all the visitors to Chalalan feel extremely welcome with their warm and friendly hospitality and professional customer service expertise. They have created a well-supplied camping area in the middle of Madidi National Park, which their village controls under a title granted by the national government.

'The entire Chalalan experience was set up so as to give us the greatest possible exposure to the surrounding rainforest and its animal and plant life. Our guides were the most knowledgeable wildlife experts imaginable, with an uncanny knack at finding the wildlife we were most interested in seeing. From tracing down a herd of over 100 wild boars to naming and explaining the medicinal use of virtually every plant in sight, our guide never ceased to amaze us with his knowledge of the rainforest all around us. His greatest accomplishment may have been finding a 300lb tapir and its cub along the Rayamalya River. As the tapir broke through the brush a mere five metres from our guide's shoulder he threw himself to the ground so as not to startle the animals and also to give us a great view for picture shots.

'I could not recommend an adventure trip more highly than this excursion into the beautiful country of Bolivia. This is the trip for anyone who wants to experience the rainforest from the eyes of the people who have lived there for centuries.'

Water rations

But golf courses do not just use up and pollute the land, they consume vast quantities of water. And so do tourists. The United Nations has claimed that 'The average tourist uses as much water in 24 hours as a third-world villager would use to produce rice for 100 days.' Tourists need unlimited supplies of water – they are used to it at home and desire copious amounts on holiday: for drinking, baths and showers, swimming pools, overflowing fountains and green, manicured lawns. But water in developing countries is often a precious commodity. More than two billion people lack access to clean water and sanitation and 80 per cent of all deaths in the developing world are water-related.

Put a hotel near a local community and the pressure on the water supply is acute. A Goan cartoonist, Alexyz, depicted the situation with these words: 'Goa has been declared a drought area', says one local. 'Except the areas of tourist hotels, tourist spots and ministers' bungalows', says another. As the concreted world of tourism creeps over more coastal land, the water table is lowered; and water that once went back into the soil now pours off straight into the sea.

Land grab

The natural as well as the man-made landscape relies on water for its well-being. And tourism wallows in the delights of the environment. It has become a key element of what, for many people, makes a good holiday. No longer are holidaymakers satisfied with a packed stretch of beach under a cloudless sky, with wall-to-wall entertainment. They are stretching their wings, and seeking the 'unspoiled' places. Inevitably, this trend towards ecotourism has been picked up by tour operators and travel agents: packaging the wild has become big business, and, as we have seen, welcomed by destinations that have landscapes rather than built environments to offer.

But tourists can wreck the environment, too. There is a horrendous United Nations list of the environmental damage caused by coastal tourism. This includes: destruction of mangrove swamps (which protect the land and provide nurseries for fish), destruction of coral reefs (other factors are also to blame), erosion of beaches, sand mining and pollution from water sports.

Community tourism village at the mouth of the Quolora River, Wild Coast, South Africa

ROGER DISKI, RAINBOW TOURS

Perhaps the greatest culprit of all is the gigantic cruise-ship industry. Its waste-dumping practices can create pressure on beaches in small countries with limited refuse sites; while dumping at sea contaminates the sea. According to the Bluewater network (www.bluewaternetwork.org), a typical one-week cruise generates 50 tons of garbage, one million gallons of graywater (waste from sinks and showers and so on), 210,000 gallons of sewage, 35,000 gallons of oil-contamination and unknown amounts of hazardous water. Almost all is dumped, some is treated, some is not, says Bluewater. While the powerful cruise companies claim they have done much to reduce pollution, the laws are lax, regulations often ignored and records show that the majority of the big companies have convictions for dumping even as they claim to be addressing the problem.

Ecotourism has also contributed to environmental damage. It's the sort of tourism, which, as we have seen, sounds like apple pie – as good as it gets – but the pitfalls have become obvious. Many claims for ecotourism experiences are not much more than 'green wash'. Setting a hotel in the middle of a forest by a river does not qualify for an ecotourism badge if the sewage from the hotel goes straight into the river, forests get cut down to build the property and people lose their homes and livelihoods.

Cultural loss

Closely linked to the damage that tourism can do to the environment is the damage to the human environment. As we have extended the scope of our holidays into remote places, we now see 'remote people' as part of our holiday landscape. Our interest in other people's cultures is not always sensitively approached. What are the implications, for example, of tourists photographing tribal peoples who now demand payment in exchange for a quick bit of modelling in their festivals' finery?

Performing for tourists has become an income earner for tribal groups all over the world. But the income comes with a price. In Peru, for example, a representative of the Yagua tribe writes that one community is made to 'perform dances on no matter what day, which is contrary to our customs, since with us each dance would be performed at a particular time of the year, times which are festivals for us. Our brothers are exhibited to the tourists like animals, and have to be at their disposal so that they can take photos.'

Tourists are also shoppers and love to buy souvenirs. Craft markets spring up to serve the tourists; they make money for locals but sometimes what is sold is not local at all but made on a different continent, despite the logo on the candlestick, the T-shirt or the basket. What academics call 'authenticity', the true representation of a people's material culture, is subverted by tourism; reality gets lost to the retail therapy demands of the tourists.

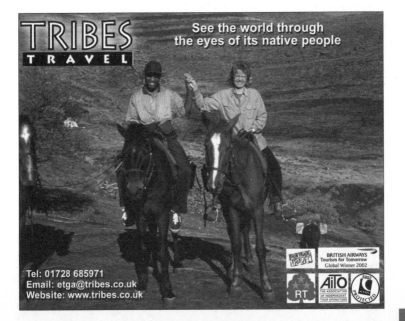

Sun, sea, sand — and sex

The Dominican Republic, Thailand and the Philippines are where tourists go most readily and most often for sex. Their young girls (and boys) leave villages for the resorts, and the vagaries of a life of prostitution, whether highly organized or casual. The international sex industry flourishes when first-world punters holiday in faraway playgrounds and look for cheap sex – doing what they would not do at home – in a fantasy world of moonlit nights on hot beaches.

HIV infection rates are also sometimes attributed to tourism. Tourists bring infection to remote places; infection rates flourish alongside sex tourism. Similarly, the tourist trade provides an infrastructure in which the drugs trade can flourish. Good communications systems provided by tourism make life convenient for drug traffickers.

The social impact of tourism goes beyond the crude effects of drugs and sex. The arrogance of Western tourists who bring their own moral codes on holiday with them and expect locals to embrace them can create serious dislocation to distant cultures. Just seeing tourists wear inappropriate clothes can make local people feel marginalized. 'Like an alien in we own land' is the way one Caribbean calypsonian described his feelings about tourism in general, and all-inclusive hotels in particular.

Who cares?

We have spelled out above the dismal indicators – economic, environmental, social, cultural – of what can go wrong with tourism. It is a chronicle that builds into an unsustainable world of greedy tourists and helpless hosts, with the tourists setting the pace in their quest for ever cheaper holidays.

THE ETHICAL TOURIST GOES TO

Sue Wheat visited Kawaza village, South Luangwa, Zambia. The villagers work closely with safari operators, particularly Robin Pope Safaris and Expert Africa, who helped them set up the business and now market it to their clients.

'I stood in a thatched rondavel and watched a traditional healer dressed in a white smock with a red cross on it go into a trance and invoke spirits to keep me healthy. It was an utterly surreal experience and one that I would never have had if I hadn't visited Kawaza. Zambia is famous for its spectacular wildlife, and incredible though that was, I remember my time with the villagers of Kawaza far more clearly than the animals I saw on safari.

'Kawaza, which lies about 10km outside the South Luangwa national park, is home to around 40–50 people, living a subsistence farming life. The villagers have set up a community-run tourism business, using the income to fund their school, provide water and community facilities.

'My village guides were Meya and David, who both spoke good English. They gave me a friendly briefing about what was and wasn't appropriate to do: women should wear a *chitenje* (local sarong) while they are walking around, men and women eat separately, and they ask you not to give money or gifts to children, but to make a donation to the community if you want to.

'For 24 hours I experienced everyday Zambian life as realistically as I think it's probably possible to do while still being a tourist on a short visit. We walked through cotton farms to the connecting villages and watched a blacksmith make a fire with two sticks and then expertly shape a piece of metal. We passed through a family yard and talked to the children plaiting each other's hair while their mother made dinner.

'We visited the school where the whole project had started and met the headmaster – a man thoroughly impassioned by the potential of the Kawaza community tourism project to transform the lives of the village's children through the income it generates. Then we returned and I sat and ate *nshima* (ground maize that sets like polenta) with peanut and spinach relish with the local women, while they quizzed me good-humouredly through Meya about my life.

'After a warm bath in the privacy of a simple bamboo cubicle for visitors, I went with David to the campfire where people come from surrounding villages to dance and tell stories – Kawaza, it seems, is a local social hub. The energy from their performances was amazing. Then to sleep in a hut identical to those of the other villagers – except they give visitors a bed with mattress, a mosquito net and more blankets for the cool nights.

'The noises here at night were different to in the national park – no throaty serenades by the local hippos on the riverbank, just the occasional murmur of a child waking momentarily from their sleep. Then around 5am a rhythmic thump, thump, thump marked the beginning of the new day – sorghum being pounded for the next day's meals. I left itching to see more – I hadn't been fishing in the lagoon, been into the forests to collect honey, made medicinal herbs with the healer or spent enough time with the children. Twenty-four hours at Kawaza had definitely not been enough.'

But as the holidays in this book show it doesn't have to be like that. And as more people realize that the traditional profile of tourists and tourism needs to change, so we are beginning to ask questions and to modify our behaviour. An 'understanding and knowledge of the perceived inequity of mass tourism', wrote Clare Weeden, a lecturer at the University of Brighton, England, is 'an important factor in tourist decision-making'.

But how far are we along that road? A focus group, set up by Weeden and recruited through Tourism Concern, discussed how the group had come to understand the impact of tourism on the destinations they had visited. It was a shock, they said, when they first realised that tourism was not always 'a good thing'. One member of the group, a geography teacher, remembered a holiday in Southeast Asia: 'There was a lady cutting rice with a little implement so I thought this was a good photograph and I took her photograph. She was very sweet and I gave her some cigarettes for it and I overpaid her and it changed her instantly into a beggar... It really was a shock.' It was this sort of culture shock and the experience of seeing widespread poverty ('I felt quite embarrassed about being there') that triggered awareness in this group, a key stage along the road towards becoming an 'ethical tourist'.

Leo Hickman, who spent a year living the 'good life' for the *Guardian* newspaper, described this new awareness as the 'mangetout moment'. He explained it as 'the rush of guilt that tells you that what you're doing – buying, say, a small pack of mangetout that's been air-freighted out of season from a field in Kenya to the supermarket shelf before you – is somehow a negative force on the world'.

But what are we doing about it? Can we, the consumers, do anything about it? The answer is 'yes'. As consumers, not just of holidays but also of products and other services, we are beginning to be aware of our power. In 1999, *Ethical Consumer* magazine recorded that nearly half of us had a 'I do what I can' attitude when it came to making 'ethical' consumer decisions. While only 5 per cent of us were hardline 'global watchdogs', 18 per cent were 'conscientious consumers', classified as more affluent than the 'do what I can' group. The least ethically aware were those with the lowest incomes: 22 per cent had an 'I look after my own' attitude. The problem, however, is that while some of us are concerned about ethical issues, far fewer of us actually behave ethically when it comes to our purchases.

The most 'ethical' of us in the UK tend to be middle-aged, relatively affluent, and well educated. Internationalist in outlook they are interested in how companies operate in developing countries. These activists may be a niche market of some six million people, but they are also recognized as trendsetters, with money to spend. *Ethical Consumer* summed up this group as: 'potentially important as an engaged consumer group, more likely to act on ethical considerations in purchasing and in other relationships with companies they become potential advocates of those they consider ethical' and 'potential critics of those companies they perceive to be unethical'.

AFRICAN HEARTLAND JOURNEYS

Community horse trail on Wild Coast, South Africa

Ethical tourism: Does anyone care?

These consumers have, as it were, seen the ethical light. Not only are they likely to buy a fairly traded banana but they are also likely to care about their holidays and the implications of how they spend their holiday cash.

The tourism guru Jost Krippendorf predicted these activists in his book *The Holidaymakers*, published nearly 20 years ago. He foresaw a new kind of holidaymaker. Once our basic holiday needs – eating, drinking, sleeping – had been met, he argued, we would become more adventurous, we would have what he called social needs, we would want to be fulfilled on holiday. To this end, Krippendorf foresaw 'an independent and emancipated tourist, a critical consumer not only at home but also when travelling'.

Krippendorf was right. According to Justin Francis of responsible-travel.com 'there is a trend for more "experiential" tourism that provides more "authentic" experiences… tourists want to be more like travellers and want to immerse themselves in local cultures and places – even if for just part of their holiday'. This is one aspect of another trend, away from ready-made package holidays bought from the big tour operators and towards do-it-yourself holidays, often thoroughly researched and bought over the internet.

Allied to these trends towards 'authenticity' is a new – if slowly growing – anxiety about the effects of mass travel. In 2003, research by Mintel, the UK market researchers, revealed that the 'concerned tourist' had emerged from its subculture niche – beyond groups such as Tourism Concern – into the consciousness of the general public. Mintel declared: it is 'only a matter of time before public awareness of the impacts of tourism increases further'.

Indeed, the World Tourism Organization has also registered this trend. It recognized that an increasing percentage of people who cared about the strain that tourism put on developing countries and that 'the requirement [for tourism] to be sustainable will be more than ever decisive'.

The marketing men and women in suits have also noticed a new trend in holidaymaking. Echoing Krippendorf, words such as 'lifestyle' and 'personal enhancement' have entered their vocabulary. 'Lifestyle' decisions may or may not incorporate 'ethical' ones but what is important to notice is that consumer power now features on the stylists' radar. Could ethical holidays become as trendy as hip hotels? Could we be witnessing the emergence of 'etho-chic' holidays?

What exactly are we, the consumers, thinking about our holidays? Where do we stand when it comes to buying a holiday? In 2003, Mintel asked more than 2000 people what were important factors for an enjoyable holiday (see box overleaf). While good accommodation and sunshine came top of the poll, statements with an ethical content featured with a small group of people. Mintel expected this category to grow. Mintel also asked about attitudes towards ethical issues and holidaymaking. It showed a small but significant minority clearly aware and concerned about ethical tourism. More women than men are making the connections between

ETHICAL TOURISM: A GROWING CONCERN

In 2003, Mintel, the market research company, asked 2000 people what were important factors for enjoying a holiday abroad. These are their answers.

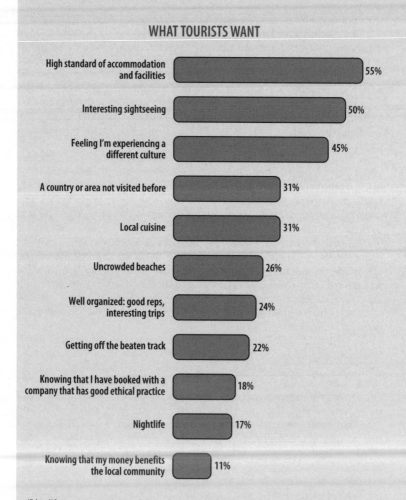

WHAT TOURISTS WANT

High standard of accommodation and facilities — 55%

Interesting sightseeing — 50%

Feeling I'm experiencing a different culture — 45%

A country or area not visited before — 31%

Local cuisine — 31%

Uncrowded beaches — 26%

Well organized: good reps, interesting trips — 24%

Getting off the beaten track — 22%

Knowing that I have booked with a company that has good ethical practice — 18%

Nightlife — 17%

Knowing that my money benefits the local community — 11%

'Ethical' factors are not at the top of the list, but they do feature. Mintel demonstrated that a trend towards ethical good practice on holiday existed; the group was small, said Mintel, but was expected to grow in importance.

Mintel also asked the same people about their attitudes towards ethical issues connected with going on holiday. The results (summarized below) again bore out the impression that ethical tourists form a significant, and growing, minority.

ATTITUDES

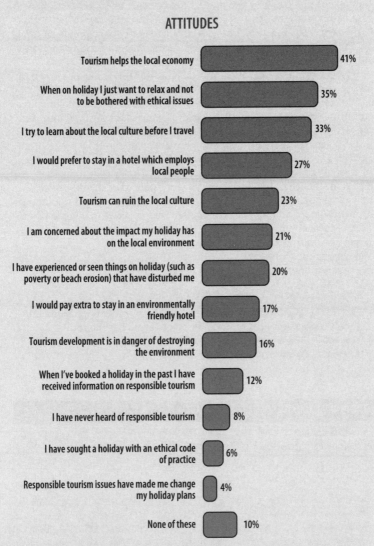

Tourism helps the local economy	41%
When on holiday I just want to relax and not to be bothered with ethical issues	35%
I try to learn about the local culture before I travel	33%
I would prefer to stay in a hotel which employs local people	27%
Tourism can ruin the local culture	23%
I am concerned about the impact my holiday has on the local environment	21%
I have experienced or seen things on holiday (such as poverty or beach erosion) that have disturbed me	20%
I would pay extra to stay in an environmentally friendly hotel	17%
Tourism development is in danger of destroying the environment	16%
When I've booked a holiday in the past I have received information on responsible tourism	12%
I have never heard of responsible tourism	8%
I have sought a holiday with an ethical code of practice	6%
Responsible tourism issues have made me change my holiday plans	4%
None of these	10%

tourism and ethics, as are older (rather than younger) people, affluent urbanites and professionals. These are the same sort of people who are the flag bearers for all sorts of consumer awareness campaigns.

Another study, by the development agency Tearfund showed an even more distinctive trend towards ethical holidays. In 1999, 45 per cent of respondents in a poll said that they would be more likely to book a holiday with a company having an ethical policy; in 2001, this figure had risen to 52 per cent. Tearfund also discovered that a majority of respondents would pay more if their holidays guaranteed decent wages, working conditions and good environmental practices.

The Association of British Travel Agents (ABTA) has noted a trend towards a more engaged attitude towards our holidays in two polls (2000 and 2002). Although our top anxieties remain dirty beaches, polluted seas and crime, more than half of the respondents said that food and water shortages for local communities mattered a great deal to them (an increase from 51 per cent to 59 per cent between 2000 and 2002).

Other changes indicated by the ABTA polls revealed an increasing concern about the well-being of local people: 30 per cent thought it very important that their holiday should benefit people of the destination; 45 per cent thought it very important that their holiday should not damage the environment and 42 per cent wanted their holiday to include experiences of local culture and food. All these figures are for 2002 and showed an increase on the earlier poll.

Focus groups, organized by Tourism Concern, in 2002, revealed that the five most important factors for a fair trade holiday were:

- local involvement, consultation and control
- fair wages, good working conditions and employment opportunities
- local products/services given a fair price (avoid haggling)
- respect for the environment
- respectful consumer behaviour.

THE ETHICAL TOURIST GOES TO CAMBODIA

Helen Hoare went with the tour operator, Carpe Diem, on a 14-day, small group holiday. This is an extract from her 'thank you' to Carpe Diem.

'I have travelled the world extensively but in truth I think my visit to Cambodia in 2003 was one of the best trips I have ever been on in my life.

'I was instantaneously attracted to your trip by virtue of the wonderful ingredients contained in it. For me it was a winning combination – interesting and excellent tourist sites, combined with local hands-on experiences and an insight in to the difficulties being suffered by the people and country in their attempts to rebuild their lives. I was deeply moved by my experience and will simply never forget it. I enjoyed every single moment of it and through your wonderful guidance and experience I believe that I did succeed in connecting with the country and the people in a way that is and will have a lifelong effect on me.'

These groups also wanted high quality products and services (for example, expert guiding) and reported that tour operators should provide guidelines for responsible behaviour and information about the local culture. And, of course, they wanted the sort of experiences that everyone wants – excitement, freedom, relaxation, good friends, healthy food, clean water, clean toilets – and 'not too many other tourists (particularly if they are badly behaved)'. Such studies point to a growing unease about using other people's homes as a playground without a backward glance at their needs and desires.

Oh to be an ethical tourist!

Now, whether any of us do what we say we'll do when it comes to choosing our holidays is another matter. We can aspire to do 'the right thing' but often our aspiration does not quite match the reality. Sometimes it seems to be difficult to know how to do the right thing, or the enthusiasm to go to a particular place overrides our concerns about our impact as a tourist. We feel ethically challenged but don't know how to make a difference – even if we can.

Even members of the focus group recruited through Tourism Concern, well aware of the issues around tourism, were confused. Not only did they find the concept of ethical tourism itself confusing, they also admitted to feeling guilty if their behaviour fell short of their good intentions. Ethical tourism is 'a goal, set up in lights, which is difficult to achieve', said one participant in a focus group discussion on ethical tourism.

In his book, *A Life Stripped Bare*, journalist Leo Hickman recorded letters from readers who were also trying to live 'ethically'. What these letters show, as does Hickman's own honest assessment of the challenge, are that our actions are not based on a strict list of do's and don'ts, but are shaped by something more abstract: a sense of trying to make the world a better place even though, as one letter writer noted, 'one sometimes feels that the odds are overwhelmingly against'.

PETER RICHARDS, REST

Peter Richards of REST discusses the benefits of community based tourism with Thai operators, guides and communities' representatives

The need to know

One of the problems is that we're not sure how to be ethical. Consumer research shows that those who care are crying out for information about what we are buying. 'Three quarters of the public agree that their purchasing decisions would be influenced if they had more information on companies' ethical behaviour', said the *Ethical Consumer*. And although it is getting easier to source fair-trade coffee or tea in the supermarket, finding a fair-trade holiday is trickier.

We are still left largely in the dark when it comes to making ethical decisions about our holidays. This is not, as we have seen, because we are lazy or grouchy, uncaring or sloppy: it is because the tourism industry has – until very recently – been happy to leave us ignorant and powerless.

So who in the tourism industry is making a contribution to fairer tourism by giving us even some basic information? Back in 1993, when ethical tourism was barely a whisper in even the most radical of salons, Tourism Concern, together with the WWF, conducted a survey of 69 companies and institutions from all sectors of the UK tourism industry. It found that the industry was 'generally aware' that 'long-term environmental and social problems can result from certain types of tourism, and that these can damage the business success of tourism'. In response, sections of the industry had adopted practices such as recycling and waste reduction, educating tourists with tips and advice on sustainable practices, or creating partnerships with local charities and groups. These were positive moves.

However, there were obstacles to further progress. Large operators are committed to filling charter flights. This encourages a short-term perspective and allows the market to be dominated by customers who go abroad because it is cheap, rather than from a desire to experience foreign cultures and environments. Since then, cheap overseas holidays for UK tourists have become the norm (adding urgency to one of the fundamental debates for the ethical tourist, concerning the effects of CO_2 emissions from air travel – see box overleaf for more about this issue).

The survey concluded that sustainable tourism was seen as an 'expensive niche product' and that many companies felt that it was not their responsibility to review their corporate behaviour. The companies put the burden on local governments and/or consumers. 'It's what the consumer wants' (cheap holidays in Bali) or 'these local governments don't have proper planning regulations, so you can get away with building a resort on the last remaining mangrove swamp', were some of the arguments offered. But, as commentators have pointed out, Body Shop and B&Q thrive on socially responsible policies in the retail business – if they can do it, so can the tourist business.

Winds of change

Now, more than ten years on, there is a shift from that it's-nothing-to-do-with-us attitude. Winds of change are in the air. Ian Reynolds, the former chief executive of ABTA, which represents all the major stakeholders in the tourism business, told Tourism Concern that while 'initially it was just specialist tour operators who took an interest in this [responsible tourism]...now the major tour operators are showing a much greater interest because they see the benefits'. And it's not just because of saving costs, but 'because it's a good point to make with consumers who are beginning to appreciate this, and it's a good point to make locally – to be seen to be a good citizen and more welcoming at the destination'.

CLIMATE CHANGE AND TRAVEL

Half the population of the UK now flies at least once a year; low cost air travel makes it easy. There are even tour operators promoting weekends to South Africa and Dubai. But air travel is the fastest-growing source of greenhouse gas emissions, with the world's 16,000 commercial jet aircraft creating more than 600 million tonnes of CO_2 annually – nearly the same amount as all of Africa. And while technological advances may, in the future, cut aircraft pollution, the increase in air traffic will, it is argued, offset any of the benefits brought about by technological change. The Institute for Public Policy Research, a UK think tank, predicts that air travel will be responsible for a third of the UK's total greenhouse gas emissions by 2030, making flying by jet plane 'the least environmentally sustainable way to travel'.

So what to do? Our CO_2 reduction checklist, below, offers practical advice about action individuals can take to help cut carbon emissions. Clearly, only the most committed of us will stay at home, or holiday by train or by bicycle every time, and most of the holidays offered in this guide would scarcely be possible without air travel. There is no simple solution, but it can only be good that interest in the climate impact of air travel is gathering momentum amongst travellers, ensuring that debate will continue.

The Ethical Traveller's CO_2 Reduction Checklist

- **Avoid air travel where possible.** Boats, trains, bicycles or foot travel are often more scenic and adventurous alternatives. You may not get to your once-in-a-lifetime safari in Kenya other than by air, but much of Europe is easily accessible from the UK thanks to the Channel Tunnel, while domestic flights should be as a last resort.
- **Research your carrier.** If possible choose one which recognizes its responsibility to work towards lower emissions. British Airways began to encourage its passengers to pay a 'green fee' in 2005, and joined forces with Virgin Atlantic, EasyJet, First Choice and Flybe in forming the Sustainable Aviation Group, whose members take voluntary measures to minimize noise, pollution and emissions.
- **Offset your carbon emissions.** You can do this by registering with one of the companies that works out your own contribution to global warming for each flight you take. The schemes charge you according to the share of carbon dioxide emitted by your aircraft and send your money to support projects such as installing solar power lighting in poor rural communities and restoring rainforests. While carbon offsetting could be seen as a stop-gap on the long road to a low-consumption, low-carbon, sustainable world, for today's ethical traveller it is a tool worth considering for the travel kit. Websites that make offsetting simple for you include www.carbonneutral.com and www.climatecare.org.
- **Support the Emissions Trading Scheme.** The EU ETS is a policy to reduce emissions of CO_2 and combat climate change. The scheme requires net carbon polluters such as airlines to buy carbon credits to offset their emissions, the funds raised then being used (as in carbon offsetting) to support low carbon and renewable energy projects. To keep informed about progress – or lack of it – in years to come, www.uketg.com, www.defra.gov.uk and www.stopclimatechaos.org are good starting points.

Flying is, of course, only one part of this global problem. The growth of economies such as China and India, which replicate the unsustainable patterns of our own society, is a major contributor. But there is much that the individual can do to reduce carbon emissions in their everyday activities, no matter how insignificant these actions seem – visit www.cred-uk.org, www.est.org.uk or www.greenpeace.org for a wealth of ideas. Also, you can get the facts on climate change by looking at any of the thousands of websites addressing climate change. Some to get you started include: http://climatechange.unep.net/, www.ipcc.ch and www.realclimate.org.

Join the debate on climate change and ethical travel on the Earthscan website – simply visit www.earthscan.co.uk and go to the Forum – or email your thoughts to Tourism Concern at info@tourismconcern.org.uk.

Smaller operators, not surprisingly, have led the way. In 2001, for example, the UK's Association of Independent Tour Operators (AITO), which represents many of the specialist companies in the tourism business, drew up a set of responsible tourism guidelines for its members. The guidelines govern general good practice and are now a precondition of membership. Since then AITO has introduced a three-star responsible tourism policy for members to work towards. To achieve this, operators have to show that they have implemented – and continue to improve on – their responsible tourism policy. To gain three stars, the company must also undertake a project that contributes to the economy, culture or environment of a destination. By 2006, 20 of its more than 150 members had achieved three stars.

In 2001, VSO launched its campaign, Becoming WorldWise, which reported on UK tour operators' attitudes towards fairer tourism. It found that companies (again the smaller ones led the way) no longer ignored 'fairer' tourism, and did not see that an ethical approach was in conflict with 'the bottom line'. Companies had become interested in building good relationships with hosts, but they were uncertain how to promote best practice in destinations. Indeed, action was piecemeal. VSO concluded that 'an overarching ethical policy addressing a broad range of social-economic issues was rare...there is still a long way to go before the social, economic and cultural problems raised by tourism are fully addressed'.

FELEX, UCOTA

Bushara swimdock on Lake Bunyoni, Uganda, built by the Uganda Community Tourism Association (which has many years experience providing sustainable tourism)

Beach bungalows at Ranweli Holiday Village, Sri Lanka

British Airways – despite, or perhaps because of, its contribution to increased greenhouse emissions – is one of few large companies to adopt international guidelines for sustainability. It also pioneered sustainable tourism through its Tourism for Tomorrow Awards, given to all sectors of the industry for outstanding environmental performance. The criteria for the awards have been extended to include social issues as well as economic benefits to local communities.

One short-lived initiative by British Airways Holidays, in partnership with the International Hotels Environment Initiative, tried to provide consumer guidance by focusing on the environmental good practice of 100 hotels in the Caribbean. Following an audit of the hotels' management of waste, water and energy, community relations and purchasing policy, 16 of them were awarded an environmental logo. The idea was to set a benchmark, to indicate good standards of practice. However, this interesting programme was discontinued. While the hotels were keen on it, it was hard to measure whether consumers took notice of it in their booking decisions.

The Thomson Travel group has also initiated and supported programmes towards sustainable tourism. It has, for example, established a code of conduct around the sexual exploitation of children, while it has also helped hotels in Malta improve their environmental management. Pockets of forward thinking – often behind the scenes – by a range of tour operators show a commitment to partnerships, training and 'local capacity building' – buzzwords that can help develop change for host countries.

The other side of the coin, however, shows that change is slow in coming. In its report, 'Tourism – Putting Ethics into Practice', Tearfund discovered that only half the companies that responded had any kind of policy regarding responsible tourism, and just one third gave information to tourists on responsible behaviour.

Hidden help

In any case, it is hard for tourists to know that any of this is happening; the boardrooms seem to be playing the ethical game close to their chests. None of the big companies flag their social responsibility policies; it takes many clicks to find their responsible tourism policies on their websites. As Tearfund said in the conclusion to its report: while it had had no difficulty in finding examples of good practice, this 'good practice is often hidden'. As a result, it prevents tourists from making an informed decision about their holiday organizers. It also 'prevents others from sharing this good practice and increasing the benefits they can bring to local communities and to clients'.

When VSO asked 50 UK operators of all sizes working in Kenya, Tanzania, the Gambia, India and Thailand, what travel advice they provided for their tourists, the result showed a mixed picture. The large operators – with the exception of BA and Kuoni – offered inadequate or poor advice to their customers. Indeed, some small operators also performed badly. Overall, VSO concluded that tourists don't get 'the guidance we need to get the most out of our holiday without undermining local customs and culture'. In short, we go on holiday ill-prepared.

Look at an average holiday brochure and what does it tell you? It uses its space to promote the delights of its holidays, which is fair enough; if it has a mission statement, it is hidden away. That's the norm. It's left to the specialist operators to be upfront about their responsible tourism policies. Exodus, for example, has a responsible tourism policy on its home page. Its mission statement says: 'We recognize that the cultures, environments and economies we visit are fragile, requiring a sustained commitment from us to ensure that we have a lasting positive effect. Our tourism can be a real help to local communities providing income, positive cultural exchanges and the financial incentive to protect the natural environment.'

THE ETHICAL TOURIST GOES TO SRI LANKA

William Shwetzer, a retired US Marine and physician, visited hill stations in Sri Lanka with Insider Tours.

'My goal was to not visit the usual tourist spots, but rather to meet with the "real" Sri Lankan people. Insider Tours did a wonderful job in getting me to the people, seeing the "out-of-the-way places" and experience things that most tourists don't get to.

'Also, I expressed a desire to use my medical skills to help the poor. That was the most impressive aspect of the tour I was able to accomplish. They arranged everything to the smallest detail, with a superior guide/driver. His knowledge in so many areas is unbelievable. Never did he lack in some titbit of information that made the trip even that much better.

'The trip was custom-made for my goals. I was able to hike, surf, raft to my heart's content. I treated so many people and feel very glad I was able to provide a service to these wonderful people of Sri Lanka. Food was superior and hospitality even higher. I am planning to return to Sri Lanka to continue my medical services.'

But even a mission statement as committed as that of Exodus is not necessarily an objective assessment of what the holiday delivers. It does not measure what actually happens on a holiday. Ethical claims by tour operators, especially those operating in the area of ecotourism, can turn out to be 'greenwash'. They embrace the concept – recognizing that customers are beginning to demand it – but masked by slick marketing there is little real evidence of good practice. As the Tearfund report sternly concluded: 'Simply writing a responsible tourism policy is no longer enough. Clients are becoming increasingly discerning and can see through companies that simply pay lip service to responsibility, but do little to change the way they operate. Companies will need to show practical examples of where they have made a difference.'

Checking their credentials

Some people argue that certification schemes – separating the sheep from the goats by setting a standard – can go some way to expose and shoot down the greenwash cowboys. But what schemes are there to help consumers make a discerning decision?

There are, in fact, some 100 accreditation schemes – a patchwork put together by different groups and focusing on different aspects and different locations. Many of these operate within Europe. Most of the schemes are based around beaches or hotels and concentrate, rather like the British Airways Holidays Caribbean project, on environmental practices. The result for the customer is that it is difficult to assess what is on offer. More seriously, perhaps, is that the schemes are rarely independently evaluated.

In 2000, the influential website planeta.com carried out a review of ecotourism certification. Ron Mader, of planeta.com wrote that while good intentions lay behind the idea, 'most of the programmes contradict one of the main components of ecotourism – local control. If certification programmes are not developed with broad support from various stakeholders, these initiatives jeopardize the goals they intend to support.' Mader claimed that most schemes failed to consult the grass roots, which, in many cases, did not feel that certification was a key to their well-being. This point is supported by a report from the Pro-Poor Tourism Research group, which discovered that few of the standards schemes examined the issue of how tourism could be used to fight poverty. Most concentrated on environmental concerns such as water-saving exercises rather than the socio-economic issues that affect poor people.

Green Globe is an international certification scheme. Launched in 1992 by the World Travel and Tourism Council at the first Earth Summit in Rio de Janeiro, Green Globe has done some interesting work. However, its critics point out that anyone can become a member of Green Globe, and that by paying a fee and promising to 'aspire to environmental improvement', any member can use the logo. A slightly modified logo is adopted by certified members.

Zanzibar traders

One of the best-known national accreditation schemes is the Certification in Sustainable Tourism of Costa Rica, a country that has made pioneering strides to promote sustainability. Costa Rica's tourism gurus have claimed that tourists are 'demanding a more active, more interactive tourism, with greater respect for the socio-cultural and ecological interests of the local communities, with higher standards of service, and with the ability to protect and regenerate the natural environment as well as to learn about local customs'. Their certification programme, in part, responds to these needs. It covers 55 properties with 'grades' from one to five; out of these, only two hotels have attained a level five. Looking at the list of hotels, however, it seems that many smaller businesses are not included; either they are not participating or the rigorous and labour-intensive questionnaire alienates the small, community-orientated properties.

This growth of schemes, while a useful boost for the reputation of the industry, is not, however, always a helpful tool for the consumer. Sometimes such a ragbag of schemes confuses rather than aids the consumer – and some people argue that, at worst, they contribute to a lack of consumer demand for certified holidays, or, at best, create apathy.

A hill tribe village, Cambodia

Community challenge

We are left, then, to struggle along searching for alternatives to the mass rip-offs of host countries by the tourist industry. And where do we find them? Increasingly, we are finding them in the partnerships established between radical tour operators and the 'service providers' themselves. As Ron Mader of planeta.com has written: 'Communities are taking the lead… Now the monies are flowing to grass roots efforts, and community-based tourism operations are increasing around the globe. New synergies have arisen that connect localities with regional and international tourism partners.'

The hundreds of thousands of porters in places such as Nepal, Kenya and Peru whose lives were blighted by harsh working conditions have come together with other groups – UK tour operators, local workers' organizations and NGOs – to promote change, under the initiative of Tourism Concern (see box opposite). Guidelines have been drawn up to ensure that porters are treated properly – for example, establishing a maximum weight to carry (20kg for the Machu Picchu porters in Peru), providing shelters and setting up educational programmes. In Peru, the Machu Picchu Porters' Syndicate led a strike in September 2001 demanding that regulation on porters' wages should be added to the existing regulations and that tour operators should pay porters a minimum of US$30 (roughly £17) for the four-day trek to Machu Picchu. While some indigenous porters working around Machu Picchu still suffer 'humiliation upon humiliation', others have created alternative trekking routes and tourism campsites. In Tanzania, a project pioneered by the UK operator Exodus, provides English language classes for porters, in the low season, to help them make progress in tourism.

Mothers meet after a traditional wedding ceremony in Haydom near Mbulu, Tanzania – cultural tourism breaks down cultural barriers and creates friendships

P2P SAFARIS, TANZANIA

Tourists notice such changes, according to Adventure Alternative director Gavin Bate. Having a policy on porters' rights provided a 'strong incentive for clients to book with us…' he said. 'When those same clients come to Africa or Nepal and see firsthand how treating people/employees right has a direct effect on the level of enjoyment, the professionalism, the stand and the success of their expedition or holiday, it makes them feel part of a family.'

TREKKING WRONGS: PORTERS' RIGHTS

Tourism Concern's campaign for fair working conditions for mountain porters raises awareness of the horrific conditions that trekking porters all over the world endure – and we are working to put a stop to these abuses.

Porters often face sub-zero conditions with no protective footwear, clothing or tents:

> *The wages we receive don't match the physical effort we put in . . . [and] the tour operators don't offer us equipment like sleeping bags and waterproofs...We have to sleep outside. We are contracted as 'beasts of burden'. . . and treated as if we weren't human.* Peruvian porters' syndicate

Kul Bahadur Rai is a Nepalese porter who was hit by altitude sickness while carrying a heavy load for tourists. An unsympathetic trek leader made him go on, then left him to descend alone. Kul Bahadur slipped into a coma, and woke in hospital to find that his frostbitten feet had to be partially amputated.

Porters earn as little as £2/US$3.50 a day.

How you can make a difference

Tourism Concern believes it's time for tour operators to accept responsibility for improving the harsh conditions in which porters work. As Agha Iqrar Haroon in Pakistan says: 'Tour operators can play a great role in protecting porters' rights. They shouldn't try and keep costs down at the expense of basic human rights.'

Tourism Concern has drawn up guidelines for tour operators on porters' working conditions. But we need your support, to put pressure on tour operators to adopt guidelines – and to make sure they're walking the walk, not just talking the talk.

- If you're thinking of going trekking, ask questions of tour operators:
  - Let them know that it's important to you that your trip doesn't exploit porters.
  - Ask them what policies they have on porters' working conditions – wages; loads; equipment; and what happens if porters have accidents or fall ill.
  If you would like to check which tour operators do have policies on porters, please contact Tourism Concern.
- While you're there, keep your eyes open:
  - What are the porters wearing? Do they have adequate protective clothing?
  - How big are the loads that the porters are carrying?
  - What are the porters eating and where are they sleeping at night?
- When you come back, act on what you saw.
  - If you saw things that worried you about the way porters were treated – speak up.
  - Tell your tour operator – and tell Tourism Concern.
  - And just as important – if the porters were treated fairly, let your tour operator know this was an important factor in an enjoyable trip.
- If you know someone who's going trekking, open their eyes to what's going on. Pass on this information, and get them involved.

If you want to stop human rights abuses in tourism across the board. . .

Join **Tourism Concern**. We fight exploitation in tourism and campaign to ensure tourism always benefits local communities in the places we visit.

If you'd like to find out more about our porters' campaign or our wider work, visit www.tourismconcern.org.uk, e-mail us at info@tourismconcern.org.uk or telephone +44(0)20 7133 3330

THE ETHICAL TOURIST GOES TO SOUTHERN INDIA

Marjorie Waite and Neal Weiss went to Kerala, southern India. Here is their tribute to tour operator Insider Tours.

'You do a terrific job of combining fascinating travel with the privilege for us of participating in forest and tribal village preservation efforts.

'I had thought I'd be able to say to you "the highpoint was. . .," but there were so many: the plantations of Tamil Nadu from the bullock cart (at the picnic stop by the dam we saw a goatherd across the river spearing and fighting with a huge cobra), the graciousness of Biju and others at Bamboo Grove ecolodge, the animals and birds we saw in the forest (elephants, monkeys, hornbill, wild boar, bison, and more), the bamboo raft on Lake Periyar in the Periyar tiger reserve, the friendliness of the people of the Mannan village, the overnight in Kochi at the lovely Old Courtyard, complete with classical musicians playing during dinner.'

The tourism literature is now full of material describing and analysing the workings of community projects that promote ethical or fair trade, and looking at how different institutions and management structures help or hinder such development. Local ownership and control, often in partnership with western tour operators, is a growing pattern. Examples, such as are found in this book, are expanding as never before as local people build on the connections between what their environment and culture can offer and what the more aware tourist is looking for.

The citations for responsibletravel.com's annual awards for 2004 illustrate some of these points. Calabash Trust and Tours, which offers township tours in Port Elizabeth, South Africa, was one of its winners – the citation describing it as a 'shining example' of how tourism can benefit

WILDERNESS SAFARIS

Charles Rhun, a community guide at Damaraland Camp in Torra Wildlife Conservancy, Namibia shares his local knowledge

the poor. Tourists can go on 'the real city tour' or the 'shebeen tour' where they can play pool, meet the locals and dance. Or there is, on the other side of the world, the Casaurina Beach hotel, on Barbados' south coast, which won its best hotel award for employing disabled people, supporting the poor and having a rigorous environmental policy.

Both these initiatives are about connections with people – creating benefits for local communities and changing their relationships with each other. Costa Rica, a pioneer of 'ecotourism', has had experience of both the best and the worst of the tourist experience. Here are some examples of radical change and optimism that have sprung from engagement with tourism in three Costa Rican communities:

- **Liliana Martinez Gonzalez, from the Isla de Chira** found that tourism created a political change among the women of her community. 'When the people saw what we had done, they started to call [our new lodge] the "ecotourism project of the women of Chira". They referred to us as "the women of Chira, the women who work". The men began to look at us differently. They began to change the way they treated us, not treating us badly anymore. We soon began to realize that we were women and that we had many rights, especially the right to work freely, not pressured by others. We had rights to do what we needed to do for our lives. When we realized all these rights, it felt like a huge liberation.'
- **Patricia Chavez, from El Copal** discovered an exchange of benefits with ecotourism. 'Before [we began the ecotourism project] we never knew the importance of the forest or tourism. We'd say, what's the forest for? Now we see that we can have tourists here and that they get excited about the natural beauty we have. We're thrilled to have something to offer to foreigners and even to Ticos (Costa Ricans). Now we meet more people and learn from them, and they learn from us, too.'
- **Vinczenz Schmack from La Laguna del Largarto lodge** near the Nicaraguan border, which he founded in 1992. He believes that the hotel has brought a new sense of self-confidence to the people. 'At the beginning, they were very sceptical and thought that no tourist will come to this godforsaken place, but when they saw the success, the village people now come to us for advice on all kinds of new projects they want to implement to create new employment. They are very proud that Boca Tapada is now on all the maps and in most of the international tourist guides.' Schmack also believes that through tourism there is now an awareness that preserving the rainforest for future generations can be more profitable than cutting it down.

These examples show how tourism can work to sustain and maintain. Out of this come positive results: children go to school, women get empowered, communities survive, old people retain respect, environments are cherished. And consumers from the rich north get holidays that earlier generations of tourists could never have dreamed of.

Getting it right

Yet consumers are not going to book an ethical holiday just for the sake of paying the producers fairly or contributing to a village library fund or supporting goat-rearing projects. Research suggests that ethical consumers want high standards and value for money just like any other consumer: they are, in fact, a bit fussier than the average holidaymaker. They don't just want a delightful hideaway using solar heating and recycling of waste, they want that same hideaway to provide high-grade local food (without Thousand Island dressings) and great local music (rather than wall-to-wall muzak) and an opportunity to get in touch with everyday life. They want everything to be just perfect; a hard act.

A new, cool image of ethical tourism, which is far removed from concepts of worthiness and old-fashioned, hippy do-gooding, needs to be inclusive. Ethical tourism also needs to address entrenched assumptions in customer relations as well as in its relationships with host communities. It's not, for example, just white people who go on holiday. 'Non-white faces in travel brochures are rare except as smiling foreign waiters and exotic entertainers,' said Michael Lomotey, who is black British. 'Perhaps it's assumed that black people all travel to visit friends and relatives and have no interest in travelling for leisure like everyone else – a crazy business assumption. Or is it unspoken racism within the tourism industry?'

So tourism is a tricky business and getting all the relationships to work is complicated. Often, communities anxious to benefit from tourism, develop lodges or reserves, treks or facilities but do not quite know what tourists want or need; they also have no expertise in selling their 'products' or services. Most significantly, they do not always have access to sophisticated marketing or public relations mechanisms.

Roger Diski, of Rainbow Tours, who has pioneered community tourism in southern Africa, visited a scheme set up by the local ANC Women's League in Transkei. There, Xhosa families provided tourists with an opportunity to visit – and even sleep in – their thatched, turquoise rondavals. But most tourists bypassed this experience – they never got to hear about it because the women could not afford a brochure. Slicker operations, closer to the main tourist centres and often developed without grass roots inputs, may be more commercially successful but cannot replace the buzz that you get from even a small taste of 'authenticity'. Given half a chance, punters will recognize the difference.

Indeed, that is one key advantage of ethical tourism over other fairly traded products and services – the consumer can see and taste the difference. 'A cup of fairly traded coffee or tea will not taste significantly different from other teas and coffees,' concluded Harold Goodwin and Justin Francis in a paper on ethical tourism and consumer trends. 'Responsible tourism holidays which bring particularly high-quality engagement with local communities and their environments can provide a superior product, the life-enhancing experience which a growing sector of the market craves.'

Going ethical is about having a better holiday – essentially about avoiding guilt trips. We, the tourist, can be part of the solution and not part of the problem. So keep on taking our holidays to their homes. The welcome, the smile, might just be genuine.

A difference of taste, high quality and unique accommodation run in a fairly traded way; TWIN's Kahawa Shamba

Make sure your next holiday isn't at someone else's expense.
Support Tourism Concern by buying a T-shirt.
Available from tourismconcern.org.uk for £15 each, plus p&p.

KONSTANTIN ISAEV, FIRN TRAVEL COMPANY

▲Lake Baikal in Russia is the world's deepest lake

ANNETTE, TAMARIND TREE

◄Discovering seahorses off Dominica

▼Making *bammy*, a traditional Arawak bread, the old fashioned way, in Jamaica

DIANA MCINTYRE-PIKE, COUNTRYSTYLE COMMUNITY TOURISM

▲ Learning jute-weaving, Bangladesh

◀ Camping at Udawalawa, Sri Lanka

▼ Many a favourite travel experience comes through food

ROGER DISKI, RAINBOW TOURS

▲Kombo, a staff member at a
community-run hotel in Mozambique

▼Dancing at Gudigwa lodge, Botswana, a community-based
enterprise of the Bukakhwe Cultural Conservation Trust

RAINBOW TOURS

▲Sunset in Essaouira – Morocco has much to offer, from the Atlas Mountains to Atlantic coast, and can be an exotic destination for those who wish to avoid flying

▶Hermit crab (*Dardanus megistos*) found on a Blue Ventures programme (see page 214)

▼A local guide takes a tourist on an ethno-botany tour in Kenya

⬆Walking the Sahara in Morocco

▲Shepherds in Wollo, Ethiopia

◄Getting to grips with the local wildlife in Rwanda

ACTUAR

CERRO ESCONDIDOZ, ACTUAR

Community-based tourism has many different travel experiences including insights into amazing culture, fantastic scenery and the chance to see wildlife at its most spectacular, as these South American scenes show (◄▲Costa Rica, ▼Peru)

Borneo has spectacular limestone and granite mountains (◄The White Mountain; ▼The Pinnacles in Mulu National Park), head-hunter trails, and vast natural rock chambers such as Wind Cave▲

KEY

ACCOM	accommodation only
AGRI	agritourism or working on local farms
BUDGET	basic accommodation
CENTRE	visitor centre or museum
DAY	full-day or part-day tours
DIS	disabled visitor-friendly
HOST	staying with a local family
LUX	upmarket accommodation
ORG	organization supporting community tourism initiatives and offering information about them
RAINFOREST	rainforest or cloud forest tours or lodges
SAFARI	wildlife tours, lodges
SCHOOL	classes or workshops in language, music, horse riding etc.
TOUR	tours, usually guided
TREK	multi-day hikes/trekking
VOL	volunteer work placements
WEBSITE	website with useful information

+ This symbol after any of the above indicates that some additional activities are included (eg HOST+ will offer local activities as well as staying with a family).

PAGES 56–97

PAGES 98–145

PAGES 146–178

PAGES 180–191

PAGES 192–203

PAGES 204–216

AFRICA

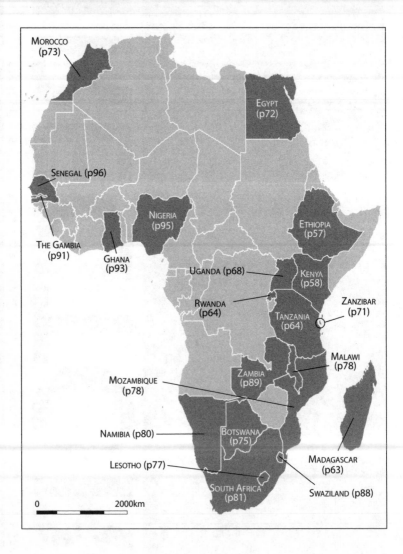

MOROCCO
(p73)

EGYPT
(p72)

SENEGAL (p96)

NIGERIA
(p95)

ETHIOPIA
(p57)

THE GAMBIA
(p91)

GHANA
(p93)

UGANDA (p68)

KENYA
(p58)

RWANDA
(p64)

ZANZIBAR
(p71)

TANZANIA
(p64)

MALAWI
(p78)

MOZAMBIQUE
(p78)

ZAMBIA
(p89)

NAMIBIA (p80)

BOTSWANA
(p75)

MADAGASCAR
(p63)

LESOTHO (p77)

SOUTH AFRICA
(p81)

SWAZILAND (p88)

0   2000km

ETHIOPIA
International dialling code +251

'Thirteen months of sunshine' say the travel posters. This refers to the fact that Ethiopia has never reformed its calendar – not the only strange thing about this country where the overworked word 'unique' is not out of place. Until 1974 Ethiopia was ruled by emperors, said to be descended from the Queen of Sheba's visit to the bed of King Solomon. The Ethiopian church is older than most in Europe, and the national alphabet is equally ancient. As if this was not enough, the last emperor, Haile Selassie, is the Ras Tafari worshipped by Rastafarians.

In spite of this glamour, Ethiopia's image has been badly tarnished by a series of famines, notably the 'biblical' one that led to the first Live Aid concert. These problems, caused by overpopulation and deforestation, only affect the north and east: governments have been trying to persuade, and sometimes force, people to move to the well-watered south. For those interested in history and art, the country is eminently worth a visit – the rock-hewn churches at Lalibela, the painted ceilings of monasteries, the stone colums at Axum, the 'theme park' of castles at Gondar, the ancient city of Harar. There is plenty of good scenery too – Lake Tana and the Blue Nile Falls, lakes in the south, desert in the east and several national parks. The food, music and dance are equally unlike anywhere else in Africa. The people are welcoming but also proud, and you can get mildly hassled by kids wanting pen friends, footballs and the like.

TREK/ACCOM
TOURISM IN ETHIOPIA FOR SUSTAINABLE FUTURE ALTERNATIVES (TESFA)

This trekking network of accommodation and facilities enables local farmers to host visitors. There are two sites, each housing a maximum of eight people in simple eco-friendly houses, with one more site planned. The local NGO, Tourism in Ethiopia for Sustainable Future Alternatives (TESFA), enables the communities to be able to offer a trekking package including accommodation, food, drinks, guides and pack animals. It's an opportunity for visitors to experience the local way of life. Its first sites are near Lalibela

Contact: Mark Chapman
Tel: 11 114 0583/123 3840
Cellular: 91 141 6452
Email: chapman@ethionet.et
Web: www.community-tourism-ethiopia.com
Address: C/O Save the Children UK, PO Box 7165, Addis Ababa, Ethiopia

in the Ethiopian highlands. The accommodation is clean and simple and the evening meals are focused on western palates. Of the charge of approximately £20/US$35 per night, 60 per cent stays with the community.

KENYA
International dialling code +254

700km

NAIROBI

Safari is really just the Kiswahili word for a journey, but in English it has become synonymous with game viewing – and Kenya is where it all started. The colonial carve-up left the British with the drier northern part of East Africa, including the railway line from the coast to Lake Victoria and Uganda. From the hot coastal plain the scenery changes to the high plateau, through the rift valley and into the green western provinces on the shore of Lake Victoria. The whole of East Africa was, and still is, incredibly rich in wild life. Maasai Mara, Tsavo, Amboseli and the Aberdares are among Kenya's well-known national parks. Even without the attractions of the safari, Kenya's coast would be a world-class tourist destination, with golden palm-fringed beaches, coral reefs and the historic city of Mombasa and the idyllic island town of Lamu, Kenya's answer to Zanzibar. Visitors arrive in Nairobi, the busy capital city with its glossy tower blocks, leafy residential areas, crowded back streets and muddy slums. Despite its reputation of being 'Nairobbery' it is a stimulating city and crime has reduced under the present government. Kenya produces good handicrafts such as Maasai bead work and wood carvings, which can be purchased from the producers themselves.

SAFARI+
AFRICAN PRO-POOR TOURISM DEVELOPMENT CENTRE (APTDC)

The operations of the APTDC are guided by the mantra 'give the local community a fish and you feed them for today, teach them to fish and you feed them forever'. Rooted in the local community, APTDC adheres to the principles underpinning fairly traded tourism. Its not-for-profit safaris and ecotours aim to take tourists to places where they can 'enjoy, admire and study [the] cultural and natural heritage of Kenya while empowering…marginalized communities'. Visitors can mingle with local people and better understand their lives. Eighty per cent of the cost (about £140/US$250 per day all-inclusive) goes to local communities. There is a clear code of conduct and environmental concerns are paramount.

Contact: Allan Mugwe
Tel: 2 318 522/2 310 276
Cellular: 722 566 725
Fax: 2 310 276
Email: info@propoortourism-kenya.org
Web: www.propoortourism-kenya.org
Address: African Pro-Poor Tourism Development Centre, 5th Floor, Windsor House, University Way /Muindi Mbingu St. PO Box 4293, 00200 Nairobi, Kenya

SAFARI
BASECAMP EXPLORER

The Basecamp Explorer Group's five companies are creating a global network of unusual meeting places where 'profound interaction take place between people, cultures, wildlife and the natural environment'. The impetus comes from a belief in responsible sustainable growth through the establishment of ecotourism destinations where there's a fair distribution of benefits to employees, owners and the community. You can choose from a wide variety of safaris, including a walking safari with the Maasai in the Maasai Mara.

Contact: Dr Lars Lindkvist
Tel: 722 321 409
Email: lars@basecampexplorer.com

TOUR
CAMPI YA KANZI

This is self-confessed luxury in the wilderness. Up to 14 guests are housed in seven thatched guesthouses. The operation is eco-friendly and green where possible. The Maasai own the land and the operators hope that the Camp demonstrates to the Maasai living there that their land can be a source of sustainable income for the community. There are guided game walks and drives and the opportunity to interact with the Maasai landlords. The Italian operators reason that responsible tourism can preserve both the Maasai wildlife heritage and their traditional way of life.

Contact: Dr Luca Belpietro
Tel : (0) 45 622 516/+88 2165 1103 557
Email: lucasaf@africaonline.co.ke
Web: www.campiyakanzi.com

TOUR/VOL
CAMPS INTERNATIONAL

Based on the Kenyan coast, Camps International is open to school groups, gap year students and also adults seeking a responsible travel experience. This UK company is deeply involved with local communities and committed to a five year development plan including marine workshops, constructing school classrooms, supplying drinking water. Camps are co-located with indigenous communities and wildlife. Plans are afoot to expand to four more African countries based on the Camp Kenya template and a new responsible holiday programme targeting a wider audience. This green operation offers its guests a very special time whilst representing responsible tourism. Of the income from the various categories of visitor, approximately £350/US$625 per person is invested in the community; in 2005 this amounted to more than £70,000/US$125,000. Participants are met in Mombasa.

Tel: +44 (0) 1425 485391/
    +254 (0) 40 320 2946/7/8
Fax: +44 (0) 1425 485398
Email: info@campsinternational.com
Web: www.campsinternational.com
UK address: Unit 1, Kingfisher Park,
    Headlands Business Park, Salisbury Rd,
    Blashford, Ringwood, Hampshire
    BH24 3NX, UK
Kenya address: PO Box 2, Ukunda, Kwale, Kenya

ACCOM
DIAMOND BEACH VILLAGE

This family-owned lodge is on Manda Island off the Kenyan coast and is reached by plane and boat via Nairobi or Mombasa. There are beach huts for varying numbers of people and meals are taken at the associated restaurant overlooking the Indian Ocean. The lifestyle respects the environment totally, using only local methods and materials to create an alternative style holiday. Guests and local people mingle easily. The behaviour expected by local people is explained. All food is sourced locally – and you can even begin to learn Swahili. Prices are around £26/US$46 per person for B&B.

Contact: Rachael Feiler
Tel: 0245 (0) 2791 5001
UK Tel: +44 (0) 77926 56740
Email: info@diamondbeachvillage.com
Web: www.diamondbeachvillage.com
Address: PO BOX 348, Lamu Island, Kenya

SAFARI+
EBENEZER CAMPSITE

Founded in 2000, this is a simple Maasai-owned and run site about 110km from Narok Town and near the Talek Gate of the Maasai Mara Reserve. All the profits go to help the local community and to fund local development projects. On offer are visits to the Maasai Mara, walking safaris, night game drives and an insight into Maasai life and culture. The rooms are well equipped, self-contained and have hot shower facilities. With food the cost is £40/US$70 per person per night and the entrance fee is £20/US$35. Transport costs are negotiable.

Contact: Cecilia Teeka
Tel: 50 22092
Cellular: 722 827 104
Fax: 50 22092
Email: davidkereto@hotmail.com
Address: PO Box 435, 20500 Narok, Kenya

TOUR/HOST
GSE ECOTOURS

GSE Ecotours is a tour operator providing community-based ecotourism tours to rural villages in Kenya. They offer a responsible tourism alternative to mass packaged holidays with a travel ethos of cooperation with local communities to improve their economy and protect their local environment. The host community provides accommodation for visitors in their homes or homesteads. In return visitors are required to respect and absorb their culture as they provide economic and social benefits to these communities.

Contact: Karen Fields
Tel: +44 (0) 870 766 9891/+254 (0) 722
516 454/+254 (0) 733 854 673
Fax: +44 (0) 870 766 9892
Email: enquiries@gse-ecotours.com
Web: www.gse-ecotours.com
Address: 50 Platts Rd, Enfield, Middlesex
EN3 5NA, UK

ORG
KECOBAT

This Network was established as recently as September 2005. Its raison d'etre is to act as a sort of 'union' for a range of community-based tourism enterprises, which means it could well become a useful one-stop for anyone seeking information on a community-based holiday in Kenya.

Contact: Ole Taiko Lemayian
Tel: 722 617998
Email: ltaiko@hotmail.com
Address: PO Box 42745, 00100 Nairobi, Kenya

SAFARI+
KOIYAKI GUIDING SCHOOL AND WILDERNESS CAMP

This project is Maasai owned and located on the northern edge of the Maasai Mara. The camp is being developed so that its income can sustain the guiding school. The area is an extension of the Maasai Mara ecosystem and visitors experience a rich environment with many large mammals. Still quite new, the project is wholly community owned and will be managed by selected graduates from the Koiyaki Guiding School. It is exceptional for local Maasai to receive such training. Visitors will be taken for walks in this unique landscape and receive deep exposure to the Maasai pastoralist culture and the hunter-gatherer Il Dorobo culture. The first visitors are scheduled for June 2006.

Contact: Looseiya Limited
Tel: +44 (0) 1747 831 005 (Via Tusk Trust)
Email: rekeroexpeditions@swiftkenya.com
Web: www.koiyaki.com
Address: PO Box 56923, Nairobi, Kenya

SAFARI/LUX
LEWA HOUSE

Lewa House is operated by the Lewa Wildlife Conservancy and offers a similar experience to the Safaris Camp but with exclusivity and comfort. If you book the house it will be all yours and fully staffed. Not unnaturally it costs more – £470/US$840 for up to 12 guests. The 12 beds are divided between six chalets. All your needs are taken care of by 27 local people.

Contact: Clare Moller
Tel: (0) 72 233 5877
Email: c.moller@lewa.org
Web: www.lewa.org
Address: PO Box 10607, 0100 Nairobi, Kenya

SAFARI/LUX
LEWA SAFARIS CAMP

The Lewa Safaris Camp is owned and operated by the Lewa Wildlife Conservancy. All profits are reinvested in their social, environmental, educational and health projects. There is an outstanding range of wildlife and visitors are more or less guaranteed the Big Five ecosystems. Associated

Contact: Anne-Marie Muchura
Tel: (0) 72 390 3672
Email: Anne-marie@lewa.org
Web: www.lewa.org
Address: PO Box 10607, 0100 Nairobi, Kenya

with Lewa are Il Ngwesi and Tassia Community Lodges. The luxurious tented camp sleeps 26 in 12 tents. Visitors learn about the five ecosystems, the community life of the area and are given the chance to join in the everyday activities of a working conservancy. Access is by road and by plane – two a day from Nairobi landing at the private airstrip. The cost is £160/US$285 per person per night fully inclusive.

SAFARI+
MAASAI CONSERVATION & DEVELOPMENT ORGANISATION (MCDO)

MCDO is a charity based on the southwestern border of the Maasai Mara National Reserve. Visitors stay at a campsite in an area of pristine wilderness, with spectacular wildlife including 253 species of bird. They offer walking safaris with

Contact: Resiato Martyn
Tel: 723 422 500
Email: olomanaa95@btinternet.com
Address: 15029, Karen 00509, Nairobi, Kenya

Maasai guides through varied trails. These can be long or short, depending on the visitor's requirements, and include walks on the sand river. They also organize birdwatching, photographic and cultural tours.

SAFARI
OL PEJETA CONSERVANCY LAIKIPIA

This is a 75,000 acre wildlife conservancy, 2.5 hours drive from Nairobi on good roads. There are two hotels offering 92 beds. Profits are invested either into the business or into the extensive local community assistance programme, with a current annual commitment of £170,000/US$300,000 programmed to become £280,000/US$500,000. The main features are the chimp sanctuary, which offers a refuge to orphaned/abused chimps coming from the bush-meat trade, the largest black rhino sanctuary in East Africa as well as the Big Five along with other animal and bird life. Chimp access is curtailed in their interest. One of the three trustees is the Lewa Conservancy. Prices vary with the seasons.

Contact: Serena Hotels
(www.serenahotels.com)
Tel: 62 32408/62 32436/62 32437
Fax: 62 31823
Email: pr@olpejetaconservancy.org
Web: www.olpejetaconservancy.org
Address: PO Box 167, Nanyuki, Kenya

SAFARI+
TRINITY TOURS & SAFARIS

Trinity Tours is a Nairobi-based enterprise, which began in 2005 and is linked with the Ebenezer Campsite. The company has a Christian ministry and aims to organize safaris geared to take care of the spiritual and physical enrichment of the tourists. This is 'not tourism for tourism's sake but tourism with a purpose'. Visitors share the homes and culture of local people and are advised as to the behaviour and conduct expected of them. Check the website for full details of different safaris and their prices, and you can join their mailing list to keep up with their activities if you wish.

Contact: John Gakang'a Kimani
Tel: 722 949 600
Email: johngk@trinitysafaris.com,
info@trinitysafaris.com
Denmark Contact: Erik Nikolajsen
(europe@trinitysafaris.com)
US Contact: Kathyrene Mulandi
(kathyrenem@trinitysafaris.com)
Web: www.trinitysafaris.com
Address: PO Box 5533-00200,
City Square, Nairobi, Kenya

DAY/TOUR
TWIN BUFFALOS SAFARIS

This small family-run tour and travel agency is Nairobi based. It aims to cover all the angles – to be in effect a one-stop shop for organizing travel arrangements especially for business travellers. It uses experienced safari guides and aims to introduce visitors to the wonders of Africa. The agency is different in that it offers urban safaris such as a secure slum safari walk, tours to local charitable projects and a women's jewellery making enterprise. All this ties in with its current support of the Daylove Children's Rehabilitation Centre, which aims to rescue street children in Nairobi. Some profits also go to other charitable organizations. Prices vary according to the package bought but project volunteers pay only £28/US$50 per night.

Contact: Mrs Margaret Ruiyi
Tel: 0202 48976/0202 50578
Fax: 0202 50593
Email: info@twinsafaris.com
UK Contact: David Njane
(David@twinsafaris.com)
Web: www.twinsafaris.com
Address: Bruce House, 10th Floor,
PO Box 48609, 00100 Nairobi, Kenya

MADAGASCAR
International dialling code +261

'La grande île' is an exceptional place: African, but with the feel of Southeast Asia. The people of the highlands of the interior are believed to have immigrated from Asia and their customs are very distinct from those of the coastal peoples. The island is very scenic, though sadly much of the forest cover has been destroyed and this risks the loss of some of the unique species of native animals (such as the lemur), birds and plants. The capital city, Antananarivo, is very attractive with its colourful marketplace and steep steps up the hillsides. What remains of the royal palaces is also worth visiting. There are also coastal resorts, but tourism (mostly French) is relatively underdeveloped and this makes it a good place to visit.

VOL
AZAFADY

This UK-registered charity working in partnership with an NGO in Madagascar recruits volunteers from around the world. They work with the 65 local Malagasy staff on integrated conservation and development projects intended to improve health, reduce environmental degradation and better the livelihood prospects for the poorest rural people. Such volunteers, besides helping directly, can also help to spread the word about the needs and the beauty of Madagascar.

Contact: Mal Mitchell
Tel: +44 (0) 20 8960 6629
Email: mal@azafady.org
Web: www.madagascar.co.uk

VOL
BLUE VENTURES

The raison d'etre of this UK registered charity is to support community-centred marine conservation initiatives in the developing world. The main focus of activity is a community-run marine protected area in the village of Andavadoaka, southwestern Madagascar. The commitment is to identify environmental issues vital to the community and address them with appropriate conservation, education and research plans. Research volunteers (13 max at present) can specialize because of the breadth of the Blue Ventures programme. It costs £1780/US$3170 for a six-week expedition, which reduces to £1380/US$2460 without the optional diving training.

Contact: Tom Savage
Tel: +44 (0) 208 341 9819
Fax: +44 (0) 208 341 4821
Email: tom@blueventures.org
Web: www.blueventures.org
Address: 52 Avenue Road, London, N6 5DR, UK

RWANDA

International dialling code +250

It is Rwanda's misfortune to be famous for a terrible event, the genocide of 1994. But that is no reason not to visit this beautiful little country, the land of mille collines, a thousand hills. (They call their villages collines even on the rare occasions when they are on the plains.) The country is green and fertile, with vistas of ridge upon ridge of hills and, as you ride north from the capital, Kigali, on a clear day, the thrilling view of the Virunga, the line of extinct volcanoes. This is the area most visitors come to see because this is still the home of the rare mountain gorillas. Visitors should also visit the excellent national museum at Butare in the south of the country and the various memorials for the genocide. Of course, people are still scarred by what happened in 1994 and bitterness and division exist beneath the surface. However, the visitor will find a very efficient country with regular minibus services, not too much bureaucracy and no visas for British visitors – and a very nice German coffee shop in Kigali!

HOST
AMAHORO TOURS

The Amahoro Tours Association (ATA) is located about one hour's drive from Kigali in Ruhengeri, northern Rwanda. On offer is responsible ecotourism with a bias towards community-based visits. ATA give the visitor a total immersion experience as you stay in family homes and partake fully in Rwandan daily life. Very small numbers of visitors are involved to ensure the intimacy and authenticity of the experience and also to guard against visitors impacting negatively on the local people and their way of life.

Contact: Greg Bakunzi
Tel: 08868 7448
Fax: 546877
Email: info@amahoro-tours.com
Web: www.amahoro-tours.com
Address: Market Street, Ruhengeri, PO Box 87, Ruhengeri, Rwanda

TANZANIA

International dialling code +255

The mainland of Tanzania was originally German East Africa though, unlike in Namibia, the only German remains are a few historic buildings. It is a huge country, famous for the wildlife in the Serengeti National Park, the Ngorongoro Crater, Lake Manyara and elsewhere. The main city, Dar es Salaam, is hot and laid back.

Away from the city the coastal area is fascinating, less developed than that of Kenya and therefore relatively unspoilt, with the historic town of Bagamoyo, ancient Muslim cemeteries, good fishing, nice beaches, palm groves…and the islands of Kilwa and Mafia where you can really get away from it all. In the interior you can sail down Lake Tanganyika or visit the hilly area near the border with Malawi or, the main attraction for which you do not have to be a mountaineer, climb Mount Kilimanjaro. It is easy to travel by bus from Nairobi and air services arrive at Arusha (Kilimanjaro airport) as well as Dar. Tanzania has a reputation for peace and stability, having got off to a good start under the popular president, Julius Nyerere. His policies of 'African socialism' came up against corruption and mismanagement and have, as elsewhere, been replaced by a more liberal model, which has left the poor poorer and the rich richer, but this is still a country at ease with itself where visitors feel free and welcome.

ACCOM+
CHOLE MJINI

Chole Mjini Hotel is a small (seven room) privately owned, tree house hotel on Chole Island in the Mafia Island Marine Park. Diving, snorkelling and historical tours of the area are available. The bird life is spectacular. It was founded in the belief that tourism could be a positive force and further rural development, economic diversification and support conservation initiatives. There is a commitment to responsible tourism that really benefits the

Contact: Jean De Villiers
Tel: 744 814081
Email: 2chole@bushmail.net
Web: www.cholemjini.com
Address: PO Box 20, Mafia Island, Tanzania

community. Guest levies and fund-raising have resulted in a health centre, kindergarten and a learning centre. It is easily reached by air from Dar es Salaam. Peak period season rates are £270/US$480 for 1–5 nights inclusive of everything including the levies.

TOUR
DUMA EXPLORER

Duma Explorer is a socially responsible adventure travel company offering comprehensive packages to the northern circuit safaris, Zanzibar and Bagamoyo beaches, as well as Kilmanajaro and Meru treks. It reinvests back into the local economy and its employees and also helps fund local education projects in Arusha. The company offers visits suiting all budgets

Contact: Mana Tominaga
Tel: (1) 310 402 3187/(27) 250 0115/
 744 288 467
Email: info@dumaexplorer.com
Web: www.dumaexplorer.com
Address: PO Box 56, Usa-River, Tanzani

with a maximum of five people per trip in accommodation ranging from budget camping to luxury tented camps. Clients are met at Tanzania's International Airport and transferred.

ACCOM+
KAHAWA SHAMBA COMMUNITY
KILIMANJARO NATIVE COOPERATIVE UNION (KNCU 1984)

This is a joint venture between the Union and coffee producers on the slopes of Kilimanjaro, and each owns 50 per cent of this new venture. The accommodation and cultural centre are on a coffee farm. Eight visitors can be housed in four traditional chagga huts – although these have en suite bathrooms with hot showers and western style toilets. There are many opportunities to interact with local communities and there is good walking in the area. The cost is £40/US$70 per person per night, with families receiv-

Contact: Emilson Malisa
Tel: 27 2750 464/27 2752 785
Fax: 27 2754 204
Email: kncutourism@kicheko.com,
 kncu@kicheko.com
UK Tel: Guy Marks at Tribes Travel:
 +44 (0) 1728 685 971
Cellular: 748 517995
Address: PO Box 3032, Moshi, Tanzania

ing 28 per cent of the fees, and 50 per cent of the whole income being set aside for Community Development. The main focus is on alleviating poverty among the coffee producers. The project is 47km from Kilimanjaro International Airport.

ORG/DAY/HOST/VOL
KILIMANJARO PORTERS' ASSISTANCE PROJECT (KPAP)

KPAP offer some day trips and homestays in the villages of Machame and Old Moshi. Visitors can volunteer with a local women's group drying food with a solar drier, learn the process of batik production, spend time with the local woodcarvers and tour and hike in the village area, gaining a glimpse into the

Contact: Karen Valenti
Tel: 0744 817 615
Email: info@kiliporters.org
Web: www.kiliporters.org
Address: PO Box 1275, Moshi, Tanzania

lives of the porters. KPAP is a Tanzanian NGO working on behalf of porters climbing Mount Kilimanjaro. They provide free clothing for any porter or tour company in need and conduct free classes to empower the porters in subjects like English, first aid, HIV/AIDS awareness and money management. All the proceeds from these visits benefit the porters' union, women's and artists' groups. KPAP also have an important role in educating the public as to porters' working conditions and proper treatment of porters.

SAFARI+
MULTI-ENVIRONMENTAL SOCIETY (MESO)

The MESO Project runs eco-cultural trips, together with safaris, in Karafu and the Tanzanian Rift Valley area. The trips begin mostly in Arusha where the visitor can experience a fantastic range of flora and fauna and also see a range of historical and contemporary cultural artefacts as well as get an insight into everyday tribal life. The main driver is a desire to combat community poverty and in parallel to conserve the social and cultural environment. A community involvement policy aims to maintain wildlife habitat, minimize wildlife/human conflict, foster sustainable and legal use of natural resources and improve the socio-economic health of the participating local communities.

Contact: Mr Rostico Bayo or Mr Petro Ahham
Tel: 27250 5859
Fax: 27250 5859
Cellular: 74446 7472
Email: mesotz@hotmail.com,
meso@meso-tz.org
Web: www.meso-tz.org
Address: PO Box 1304, Arusha, Tanzania

SAFARI+/HOST/TOUR
PEOPLE TO PEOPLE SAFARIS

This small family business wants to supplement the usual Tanzanian wildlife and scenery tourism with experiences of African cultures and to let people get an insight into the life, history and traditions of the area and how people have shared the land with the wild. Payment for the cultural visits to villages is made direct to the villages; wildlife tours are carried out in national parks by 4WD vehicle. Clients stay in selected lodges and guesthouses with occasional options for homestays and camping. A full day village tour costs US$35 (£20) for 2/4 people, which breaks down transparently as: US$8 for local guide, US$10 to the village and homes visited, US$7 for meals and US$10 for company expenses and profit.

Contact: Gloria Mlola
Tel: 744 664 569
Email: p2psafaris@z4a.com,
tanzaniacultures@yahoo.com
UK Tel: +44 (0) 208 2091974,
UK Email: colin@kijijivision.org
Web: www.p2psafaris.z4a.com,
www.peopletopeople.co.tz
Address: PO Box 11840, Arusha, Tanzania
UK address: Colin Hastings, 83 Hampstead Way, London, NW11 7LG, UK
Norway tel: 5142 6404
Norway email: ams@amsreiser.com
Norway address: Arvid Maeland, AMS Reiser Hauge, 4340 Bryne, Norway
Norway tel: 5142 6404

TOUR
SIMPLY TANZANIA

This London-based company works in partnership with the Tanzanian company Comfort Tours and Car Hire. It stresses that any local development involving community tourism or responsible tourism needs two parties – client receivers and client senders. On offer is a wide range of holidays from safaris to study tours; clients are encouraged to experience local cultures, behave appropriately and to pay locally for any add-ons, so helping the local economy. If it spoke in mission statement jargon it would say that it existed to help the visitor to 'see the real Tanzania'.

Contact: Tony Janes/Sophia Ng'wango
Tel: +44 (0) 20898 60615/+255 22218 3136
Fax: +44(0) 20898 60615/+255 22218 3136
Email: info@simplytanzania.co.uk,
ctch@cats-net.com
Web: www.simplytanzania.co.uk
Address: 54 Cotesbach Road, London E5 9QJ, UK
Tanzania address: Comfort Tours, PO Box 31737, Dar es Salaam, Tanzania

TOUR/TREK
TANZANIA JOURNEYS

Tanzania Journeys is an ethical and innovative tour operator. They believe everyone working for them should benefit from fair wages and good working conditions. They offer Kilimanjaro and other mountain climbs with consideration for the porters' welfare, and game drive safaris combined with walks, boats and bikes. They also organize activity holidays such as trekking, biking, running, team sports and yoga. Cultural and historical tours may include discovering film, music, sculpture and architecture. Tanzania Journeys' community development perspective bears on all trips they organize, and they act responsibly, always considering the social, economical and environmental impacts of their tours.

Contact: Mike Kilawila
Tel: 27 2750 549
Fax: 27 2754 016
Email: info@tanzaniajourneys.com
Web: www.tanzaniajourneys.com
Address: PO Box 1724, Moshi, Tanzania

UGANDA
International dialling code +256

500km
KAMPALA

Straddling the equator and flanked by Mount Elgon in the west and the Ruwenzori mountain range in the east, Uganda is hailed as one of Africa's success stories and, with the exception of the arid northwest, is one of the most fertile places in Africa. Comprising the four kingdoms of Baganda, Bunyoro, Ankole and Toro and with over 30 indigenous languages spoken, Ugandans, whose common language is English, are an accommodating and friendly people. Uganda contains diverse flora and fauna: from the unique plant life of the fabled Mountains of the Moon and the big game of the Queen Elizabeth National Park to the mountain gorillas and chimpanzees of the impenetrable forests of Bwindi and Kibale.

Well known for the atrocities of the Idi Amin and Milton Obote regimes during which hundreds of thousands of Ugandans were killed, as well as the 1972 expulsion of 35,000 Ugandan Asians, Uganda has enjoyed almost two decades of stability and growing prosperity since Yoweri Museveni came to power in 1986. Yet for all the optimism, the country is not without its problems. Although the nation has a lot to thank Museveni for, many are frustrated by his insistence on an effective one party state and his constitutional amendment allowing him to run for a third successive term. Meanwhile, the Lord's Resistance Army is wreaking havoc on the Sudanese border, and the country is embroiled in the civil war in neighbouring Democratic Republic of Congo. Like many African countries Uganda has been blighted by the ravages of AIDS, which, it is estimated, has left close to one million children orphaned.

As a destination Uganda certainly has a lot to offer the visitor; if neither the beauty of this lush landscape nor the vast array of wildlife have bowled you over the hospitality and generosity of its people certainly will.

ACCOM+
ACTION FOR TOURISM DEVELOPMENT (AFTOD)

AFTOD, which is a Uganda-wide organization, operates a campsite and offers trips to cultural heritage sites and to animal sanctuaries. Action for Tourism Development is the umbrella title for a group aiming to train both students and local people on environmental protection and conservation. Cultural tourism plans are in train. It works with

Contact: Paul Bisaso
Tel: 71 499 349/71 677 847
Email: aftod@yahoo.com
Web: www.aftod.8m.com
Address: Action for Tourism Development, PO Box 33844, Kampala, Uganda

local people so that they can best benefit from tourism and conservation. Local people benefit to the tune of 10 per cent of the costs, which range from £56/US$100 to £112/US$200 a day.

ACCOM
THE LAKE BUNYONYI DEVELOPMENT PROJECT

Bushara Island Camp is owned by the Lake Bunyoni Development Company, which is a non-profit enterprise. It is great for birdwatching and marine-based activity – and just relaxing. It's about 6.5 hours from Entebbe Airport by road and then, briefly, motorboat. All the money earned is used on development projects for those living around the lake: four orphan

Contact: Bampabwire Edith
Tel: (0) 4862 6110/(0) 7746 4585
Email: busharaisland@africaonline.co.ug
Web: www.acts.ca/lbdc
Address: Bushara Isalnd Camp, PO Box 794, Kabale, Uganda

centres are supported, schools sponsored, widows introduced to new skills such as tie-dieing and local people taught hospitality skills. Experiments in land management and agroforestry have filtered through and become local practice. The most you can pay is £22.50/US$40 a night for a cottage. A tent costs £12/US$22 a night for a double. Recommended by UCOTA.

AGRI
NEAT SAFARIS

NEAT or Nyamburubani Eco-Agro-Tourism is the initiative of a farming family proselytizing organic approaches to farming. They feel that agri-ecotourism has the potential to unite peoples, pass on skills, and by increasing a farm's income help towards sustain-

Contact: Ms Naome Maliro Kisembo
Tel: 006 071 729914/006 078 586329
Email: neatsafaris@yahoo.co.uk
Address: PO Box 231, Kasese, Uganda

ability. On offer is an introduction to the life of the people living on the slopes and plains of the Rwenzoris. Up to 20 guests stay in Bandas, dormitories, or camp. The food is seasonal organic produce and guests can experience the dance and music of the area. The charges are £17/US$30 full board per person per Banda (£25/US$45 for two persons). If you camp, the meals are also very well priced. Thirty per cent of this income is given to a Training and Development Centre.

HOST
REAL AFRICA EXCURSIONS

Real Africa Excursions offer the visitor a vacation giving insight into local community life and culture and to benefit both parties: visitors and local people. All the products used and the services offered are sourced locally. Visitors are encouraged to buy at local shops and markets. The target audience is those who want more than a conventional package.

You may not see the Big Five, but you will leave having breathed the air of the real Africa and improved things for people. How? Simply because you will have had six days of work and six days leisure and adventure – living, eating, drinking, singing and laughing in local homes.

Contact: Mr Denis Kigongo
Tel: +44 (0) 16268 70249
Cellular: +44 (0) 77763 11266
Email: info@real-africa.co.uk
Web: www.real-africa.co.uk
Address: Top Flat, 4 Mill Lane, Teignmouth, Devon, TQ14 9BJ, UK
Uganda address: PO Box 25395 Kampala, Uganda

ACCOM+
RUBONI COMMUNITY CENTRE

This locally owned project is a campsite with a restaurant; indoor accommodation is also provided. There is capacity for 20 campers and six indoor beds as well as a restaurant. The campsite hosts traditional dances as well as organizing nature and village walks. Recommended by Uganda Community Tourism Association (UCOTA).

Contact: Kamalha Felex
Tel: 4150 1866/7550 3445
Email: peaktourisminfo@yahoo.com
Address: PO Box 320, Kasese, Uganda

ORG/ACCOM+
RWENZORI MOUNTAINEERING AND COMMUNITY TRAIL TOURS TOURISM

Whether you chose to stay in a hotel or a camp, you will be able to meet the people and see mountains, lakes, rivers and a range of primates to make your friends green with envy. Pick from a smorgasbord of trail or cultural activities – and even have a hot shower at the end. The owner, the Bakonzo Culture Association, is a registered NGO that started in 2003. All the profits go into community concerns. But please do book and don't just turn up, because they want to arrange your programme properly for you.

Contact: Mr John Munakenya-Kijumba
Tel: 006 075 639781
Email: bakonzoculture@yahoo.com
Address: PO Box 538, Bwera-Kasese, Uganda

ORG
THE UGANDA COMMUNITY TOURISM ASSOCIATION (UCOTA)

UCOTA has worked over several years to empower local communities in sustainable development through small-scale tourism and handicraft enterprises. Local people are involved in the planning, decision-making and implementation of all their accommodation, guiding services, restaurants and craft shops. Income funds clinics, schools, water sources and literacy programmes. UCOTA tourism sites are located close to the protected areas and tourist highlights. They offer a cultural experience as well as the natural beauty of Uganda: village walks, music and dance performances, discussions with traditional healers, but also birdwatching tours and trekking in the mountains.

Tel: (0) 41-501866
Email: ucota@africaonline.co.ug
Web: www.ucota.or.ug
Address: PO Box 27159, Plot 157, Kabalagala, Kampala-Uganda

ZANZIBAR
International dialling code +255

Mosques, narrow streets and the smell of cloves...what could be more exotic than Zanzibar? It is an autonomous province of the United Republic of Tanzania and consists of two main islands, Zanzibar (Unguja) and Pemba; it became important through the Arab slave trade. It is a lovely, relaxing place for a holiday with plenty of beaches, the beautiful 'stone town' with its historic buildings, good facilities, boat trips, fishing, luscious fruits...Pemba can be visited by boat; in fact, you can reach Zanzibar by boat from Dar es Salaam as an alternative to flying. There is some political tension between the arabized townspeople and the mainly rural population, especially on Pemba, but this is unlikely to disturb the welcome given to visitors.

ACCOM+
CHUMBE ISLAND CORAL PARK (CHICOP)

This stunning all-inclusive enterprise is built entirely of local materials. The eco-bungalows, all overlooking the sea, are designed to provide both privacy and a sense of freedom of living in the open. Chumbe was born from the desire to create a conservation area funded from the proceeds of ecotourism – out of the then uninhabited Chumbe Island.

Contact: Generose Ngulimi
Tel & Fax: (0) 24 2231 040
Fax UK: + 44 (0) 870 1341284
Email: chumbe@zitec.org,
   info@chumbeisland.com
Web: www.chumbeisland.com
Address: PO Box 3203, Zanzibar, Tanzania

The Chumbe Project works to build environmental awareness in Zanzibar and its education programme sponsors school visits, teacher training workshops and the development of teaching aids. Few children have a chance to visit coral reefs and this is a unique opportunity for girls to learn to swim or snorkel. This is the best kind of all-inclusive holiday: only the alcohol is extra!

NORTH AFRICA

EGYPT
International dialling code +20

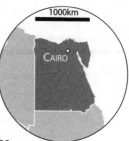

1000km

CAIRO

What can we tell you that you do not already know? Egypt, however, is not just the land of pyramids, tombs and mummies. From magnificent corals to stunning desert landscape, a lot of Egypt waits to be discovered by the majority of tourists.

The huge draws of the Pyramids of Giza and the downtown museum with its treasures of Tutankhamun are the main attractions in Cairo. Those that head further south to Luxor aim for the Theban Necropolis and the Valley of the Kings. But venture off the beaten track to places like the memorial temple of Sety I on the Nile at Luxor, to see one of the best preserved sites in Egypt. If you get the chance, head for Aswan and sail on a traditional Nile felucca from Luxor – a wonderful way to see the country. The tourist boom continues but most visitors are on organized tours, leaving many places free for the traveller. Visit sites out of main hours and you'll have the place to yourself. And don't forget the natural environment: the contrasts between the Red Sea, deserts, the irrigated agricultural lands and the Nile are awesome. But what makes any trip to Egypt special is the hospitality of the Egyptian people. Wherever you are, take time for tea and a chat and you will be rewarded with friends for life.

ACCOM
BASATA

A groundbreaking venture for Egypt, this unique reed-built environmentally friendly resort on the Red Sea coast, north of Nuweiba, challenges the colossal development of the all-inclusive hotels that have concretized most of this coastline. Sherif El-Ghamrawy works closely with the local Bedouin and has created a Montessori school with them in the desert.

Contact: Sherif El-Ghamrawy
Tel: 69 3500 480
Fax: 69 3500 481
Email: basata@basata.com
Web: www.basata.com
Address: Nuweiba-Taba Road, Sinai, Egypt

TOUR
WIND, SAND & STARS

Wind, Sand & Stars is a British company working closely with the Bedouin to develop journeys through the Sinai and also to the Western Desert in order to add elements of discovery and adventure to their tours. Their work is equally shared amongst the local

Bedouin tribes in order to contribute towards a sustainable lifestyle for their families. On offer too are special interest tours and other customized itineraries. They have started several projects including irrigation schemes, dams and dentistry clinics.

Tel: +44 (0) 20 7359 7551
Fax: +44 (0) 20 7359 4936
Email: office@windsandstars.co.uk
Web: www.windsandstars.co.uk
Address: 6 Tyndale Terrace, London, N1 2AT, UK

MOROCCO
International dialling code +212

Morocco has to be one of the world's most exciting tourist experiences. The greatest attractions are: first, the four great imperial cities – Fes, Meknes, Marrakesh and Rabat – and secondly, the chance to experience the Sahara Desert in relative comfort. Add to this the two dramatic mountain ranges of the Atlas and the Rif; numerous delightful smaller towns such as Tetuan, Tangier, Chefchaouen, Safi and Essaouira; the Atlantic coast resorts around Agadir, colonized by the package tour industry; and the cosmopolitan city of Casablanca with its stupendous new Grande Mosquée. Moroccan craftsmanship is legendary, exemplified in the traditional architecture, textiles, jewellery and pottery. Shopping for these things in the souk is also part of the fun, provided you can cope with the high-pressure sales talk. Having a meal in the Djemaa el Fna, the big open air square in Marrakesh, is also unforgettable – and likely to be delicious. Apart from its incredible variety, Morocco is very easy to visit by land and ferry or by air and it can cater for all tastes and budgets.

ORG/BUDGET+
ASSOCIATION AKHIAM

A warm welcome is promised by AKHIAM, an association working on sustainable development projects in the high valleys of the Atlas Mountains. A ten-day trip is on offer at the Auberge Ibrahim, during which the visitor will be introduced to local lifestyles, go on walking and mule-riding excursions, and above all join in daily village life. The week ends with a Berber evening of food and traditional music. Opportunity to discuss the projects with villagers is given. Of especial concern are issues of education, water supply, health and the fight against soil erosion. Although comfort is not guaranteed, prices are £7/US$12 at the auberge for food, accommodation and shower.

Contact: Marghine Lhou
Tel: 7125 1339
Fax: 3768 1340
France Tel: +33 62668 8665 (Marghine Lhou)
Email: weimilchil@yahoo.fr,
    assoakhiam@yahoo.fr
Web: www.akhiam.5u.com
Address: Ksar Agoudal Imilchil, Errachidia, Morocco

ACCOM+
KASBAH DU TOUBKAL

The Kasbah prefers to call itself a Berber Hospitality Centre rather than a hotel. Located in the mountainous Toubkal National Park it was transformed by traditional methods from the home of a feudal Caid into 'an unprecedented haven'. Owned by Discover Ltd UK and operated by Moroccan staff, the Kasbah strives to maximize the economic trickle down by buying locally and using local mule transport for goods. Five per cent of the profits go to the Village Association. The B&B prices for this Berber/European partnership range from €30 (£20/US$36) for a shared Berber salon, through to €170–400 (£115–275/US$200–480) for real luxury. The Kasbah is only 15 minutes drive from Marrakech followed by a ten-minute walk or mule ride. They also organize tours and trekking.

Contact: Kerrie Wrigley
Tel: 4448 5611
Fax: 4448 5636
France Tel: +33 46645 8395
France Fax: +33 46645 8473
Email: kasbah@discover.ltd.uk
Web: www.kasbahdutoubkal.com
Address: Kasbah du Toubkal, BP 31,
   Imlil, Asni, Par Marrakech, Morocco

A more recent development is the Toubkal Lodge, a 'sister' place to stay, some four hours by foot from the Kasbah (including a traverse of a pass at 2500m altitude). The Lodge provides an option for the adventurous or energetic to stay somewhere else in the area.

TOUR
NATURALLY MOROCCO

Aiming to provide reasonably priced, clean and comfortable accommodation giving a taste of Moroccan culture, Naturally Morocco strives to provide this service with the lowest practicable cost to the environment and to local culture. On offer is a week's holiday at their delightful house in Taroudannt with opportunities to get immersed in an interesting variety of cultural activities. They're dedicated to making a long-term contribution to sustainability and conservation education and have been involved in a number of projects promoting sustainable forms of agriculture and tourism and the conservation of wildlife in Morocco.

Tel: +44 (0) 845 345 7195
Fax: +44 (0) 709 237 9725
Email: webenq@naturallymorocco.co.uk
Web: www.naturallymorocco.co.uk

SOUTHERN AFRICA

ORG
RETOSA

The Regional Tourism Organization of Southern Africa, RETOSA, is an exciting concept in regional tourism cooperation intended to develop the combined tourism interests of its 14 member states well into the next century. Representing the full spread of stakeholder interests in the region – public and private sectors, and community – they help to increase consumer awareness and motivation by identifying many southern African initiatives.

Tel: +27 11 315 2420/1
Fax: +27 11 315 2422
Email: retosa@iafrica.com
Web: www.retosa.org
Address: Lone Creek, Unit 40, Cnr MacMac Road & Howick Close, Waterfall Park, Midrand, P.O. Box 7381, Halfway House, 1685, Republic of South Africa

BOTSWANA
International dialling code +267

One of Africa's success stories, Botswana was a haven of peace even while South Africa was still a land of apartheid. It is today one of the most democratic and prosperous African countries, although badly affected by AIDS. Most of its huge area consists of the Kalahari Desert, worth a visit in itself, but it is the north of the country that attracts tourists. The Chobe National Park on the border with Zambia and Namibia's Caprivi Strip (and handy for a side trip to the Victoria Falls) is one of Africa's greatest game parks and home to more elephants than you can ever imagine. Further west is the amazing Okavango Delta, where a major river splits into a vast swamp and soaks away into the desert, providing refuge for a variety of antelope and a paradise for birdwatchers. The populated areas in the east and south of the country are also worth a visit. The large traditional villages such as Serowe and Mochudi, the size of small towns, are the base from which people take their cattle out to distant 'cattle posts' on the edge of the desert during the (slightly) rainy season. Gaborone, the capital, is modern and expanding fast. It is the home of that famous fictional character, Mma Precious Ramotswe of the Ladies' No.1 Detective Agency.

ORG
BOCOBONET

Bocobonet identifies itself as the voice of community-based organizations (CBOs) working on natural resource management. It represents their common interests as well as offering support in terms of organizational strengthening, institutional development, skill development, technical and financial assistance and promotion.

Tel: 3185 081
Fax: 3185 081
Email: bocobonet@mega.bw, information@cbnrm.bw
Web: www.cbnrm.bw/pages_ sub_dir/BOCOBONET.html
Address: Private Bag BO 166, Gaborone, Botswana

ACCOM/SAFARI+/LUX
DUBA PLAINS CAMP

The camp can accommodate 12 visitors at any one time and they receive an exceptional big game experience.

Web: www.wilderness-safaris.com

Guests have an opportunity to learn directly from locals about the environment and dip into local culture. This camp is wholly owned by the company, which leases the land from the community, in the form of the Okavango Community Trust. The cost is a fully inclusive £280/US$500 per person per night and the contribution to the community in the form of rent is approximately 460 pulas (£48/US$85 per year). Access to the camp is by light aircraft.

TOUR+
KAIE TOURS

This one-man company offers tours to villages in southern Botswana and into the Kalahari with Bushmen. There are plans to expand by offering village social history programmes. Both itineraries offer the opportunity to interact with either local people or Bushmen and in each case to get some insight into their lifestyle. The Kalahari trips continue but the relocation of the

Contact: Christopher Toye
Tel: 397 3388
Email: toye@it.bw
Web: www.kaietours.com
Address: PO Box 26053, Game City, Gaborone, Botswana

Bushmen makes things a little fraught. It is very valuable for local people's sense of self-worth to realise that they have things to teach visitors such as exhibiting a way of life in perfect harmony with the environment. The company pays its guides well above the Botswana minimum wage. Visitors are picked up from the capital Gaborone.

ACCOM/SAFARI
SANTAWANI LODGE AND KAZIIKINI CAMP

The villagers at Sunkuyo offer visitors great game viewing at reasonable prices. There is both a Lodge, offering clean comfort and good food in a friendly atmosphere, or traditional 'rondawel' hut style accommodation and camping facilities. Located on the southern border of the Moremi Game Reserve the villagers wholly own the

Contact: Evelyn Weskob/Dux Mareja
Tel: 6800 664
Fax: 6800 665
Email: santawani@dynabyte.bw, info@santawani.com
Web: www.santawani.com
Address: PO Box 21797, Maun, Botswana

management trust that runs the Lodge and Camp. All the income goes to the Trust, which uses it to help individuals and local good causes. Everyone working with the guests is an owner and so fully committed to the enterprise's success. Access is by 4WD.

LESOTHO
International dialling code +266

'The Kingdom in the Sky' is the much reduced realm of the Basotho who held out in this mountain fortress against the attacks of the Boers in the 19th century and the area was then preserved as a British protectorate until its independence in 1966.

Most of the country is a high plateau, linked to the Drakensberg in KwaZulu-Natal but most of the population lives in the lowlands in the west of the country. It is a great country for horse trekking – traditionally every Mosotho had a horse. The scenery is great and there are some rock paintings too. Maseru, the capital, is a laid-back place with reasonable restaurants and plenty of good handicraft products available such as tapestries, angora wool and the famous basotho straw hats. Tourism is a vital trade, as the country has little cultivable land and few other resources. It exports water to South Africa from the huge Oxbow project. Traditionally manpower was exported to the mines, which had harmful social consequences but did bring in some income. This is now much reduced and the final straws have been some years of bad rainfall plus the change in US tariffs, which has led to the closure of several textile factories.

ACCOM/TREK
MALEALEA LODGE AND PONY TREK CENTRE

Malealea Lodge and the community are inter-reliant. Visitors are given guidelines as to behaviour, are encouraged to mix with local people and to interest themselves in development projects. Wherever possible services are procured locally. Great efforts are being made in the areas of water conservation, waste management and energy conservation. Visitors comprise a willing market for local handicrafts and so on. Pony

Contact: Di Jones
Tel: +27 (0) 51 436 6766
Cellular: 082 552 4215
Email: malealea@mweb.co.za
Web: www.malealea.co.ls
Address: PO Box 27974, Danhof, Bloemfontein, 9310 Lesotho

trekking and hiking allow visitors to get right away and sample village life in remote mountain areas. The Lodge has a Development Trust that contributes to the local community through education, infrastructure, health, environment, and economic self-sufficiency.

MALAWI
International dialling code +265

500km

LILONGWE

'The warm heart of Africa' and 'the land of the lake' are the standard tourist slogans, and they fit the bill. This is a very lovable little country which follows the southern end of the Great Rift Valley, most of which consists of Lake Malawi.

The scenery is never dull and sometimes stunning, ranging from the wooded shores of the lake to the cool Nyika Plateau, Zomba Mountain and Mount Mulanje, approached through green tea gardens. There are pleasant lakeside resorts such as Salima and Monkey Bay and historic mission stations at Livingstonia and on Likoma Island in the lake. The main towns are the commercial capital, Blantyre, the new capital at Lilongwe and the rather charming old capital, now the university town of Zomba. Communications and the climate are good and the people are very friendly.

BUDGET+
LUWAWA FOREST LODGE

This lodge and outdoors adventure centre was founded in 1998. A maximum of 30 persons have a choice of camping for £2.25/US$4, a bunkhouse for £4.50/US$8, or en-suite chalets for £17/US$30 per person. The setting is indigenous woodland and a range of outdoor activities and sports is offered. They have developed the Community Craft Cooperative, made up of the nine villages surrounding the Lodge and the forest reserve. The Lodge donates to the village school development projects and to the traditional dancers who perform for guests. A cultural village visit is offered. The Lodge is three hours drive from Lilongwe and 10km off the main highway.

Contact: Rose Luhanga
Tel: 9915 442/9328 917
Email: wardlow@malawi.net,
   enquiries@malawi.com
Web: www.luwawalodgemalawi.com,
   www.plusdata.uklinux.net
Address: Luwawa Forest Lodge,
   Private Bag 43, Mzimba, Malawi

MOZAMBIQUE
International dialling code +258

1000km

MAPUTO

Mozambique is unusual: a welcoming country where tourism is rare. Wracked by civil war until 1992, recovery was set back by the El Niño flooding of 2000. Mozambique has suffered, but such difficulties are in the past, and it's now emerging as a tempting jewel on the east coast of Africa. Bordering both South Africa and Tanzania, Mozambique's coast stretches 2500km, hence centuries of trade with Arabia and India, but it was the Portuguese who left the greatest legacy. Portuguese is the official language, and many towns have a Mediterranean flavour, from the bustling capital of Maputo to the faded glory of Ilha do Moçambique – a UNESCO World Heritage site that marks the oldest European settlement in East Africa.

Most of Mozambique's coral reefs and marine life are pristine and largely unexplored. The southern islands of Bazaruto and Benguerra, with top diving sites and exclusive beach lodges, are emerging as world-class attractions while the northern Qurimbas Archipelago, like much of the country's interior, remains unexplored but offers huge potential for discovery.

ACCOM+
GULUDO BEACH LODGE

On the coast and in a national park in the north of the country, where bush meets beach, the camp offers numerous land and sea activities and has nine locally built, custom-designed tents. Guludo offers to provide the ultimate holiday experience while helping to reduce poverty by maximizing benefits locally and promoting cultural and biological diversity. It's a fair-trade resort where guests can choose to work on community or conservation projects. Guludo was set up to train and employ locals with the ultimate aim of local management. The owners believe tourism can be a vehicle for sustainable development, paying five per cent of the fees to the local Regeneration Fund and a portion of the profits.

Contact: Dominique Pooley
Tel: +44 (0) 1323 766 655
Fax: +44 (0) 1323 766 655
Email: contact@bespokeexperience.com
Web: www.guludo.com

ACCOM/LUX
MANDA WILDERNESS PROJECT (MWP) NKWICHI LODGE

Nkwichi is a luxury eco-lodge set on the shore of Lake Niassa. It offers a high standard of accommodation, ideal for romantic getaways and family holidays. Guests can relax on the white sands, swim in the transparent waters, or lie in a hammock in the shade. If they are feeling active they can take guided walks in the forest, overnight treks and canoe trips, as well as visit local communities and learn about their ways of life. By visiting this lodge, your money will directly benefit the local communities through salaries and development projects. MWP, the parent company, in partnership with communities who have bought into the project, builds structures such as schools and health posts, roads and maize mills.

Email: mdw01@bushmail.net, info@mandawilderness.org
Web: www.mandawilderness.org
Address: CP123 Lichinga, Provincia de Niassa, Mozambique

ORG
OF ROAD AND SEA

This is a project that is still at the implementation stage but the website offers an e-guide for the tourist and a vehicle for social, cultural and environmental awareness in Mozambique. The organizers are determined that theirs will be an ecologically friendly and sustainable project and also a source of empowerment for the local community.

Contact: Laura Carneiro or Steve Hodges
Tel: +44 779 3204 894
Email: diversdiverse@yahoo.com
Web: www.ofroadandsea.com

NAMIBIA
International dialling code +264

Namibia, with its vast areas of wilderness, has an extraordinary variety of unique landscapes and ecosystems, from the rich wildlife around the Etosha Pan and the Waterberg Plateau to the magnificent scenery of the Fish River Canyon, the sand dunes around Walvis Bay, the wild Kakaoveld in the northwest and the miles of stony desert in the South. For those interested in prehistory, some of Africa's most stunning rock art can be seen at Twyfelfontein and the Brandberg. The coastal towns of Swakopmund and Luderitz preserve the atmosphere of the Kaiser's Germany: until recently you could still find Bismarckstrasse and Bahnhofstrasse, and there are still many people of German descent. This explains why this is the only African country where you can find *kaffee und kuchen* in abundance and may be why Windhoek, the capital, has to be the cleanest city in Africa.

The majority of Namibia's small population is found in the little visited Ovamboland in the north. Smaller ethnic groups include the Damara-Nama, related to the *san* ('bushmen'), and the remains of the Herero, victims of genocide during German rule; also the biggest landowners, white Afrikaners. Independent only since 1990, Namibia has been stable and prosperous up to now – but struggles over land ownership, hopefully peaceful, can be expected in future.

SAFARI/LUX
DAMARALAND CAMP
Wilderness Safaris operate small, intimate and luxurious camps in pristine wilderness areas. Damaraland was **Web:** www.wilderness-safaris.com
opened after the local community (Torra Conservancy) was approached with a business plan and a proposal. A maximum of 20 people can experience desert adapted wildlife (for example, elephant, black rhinos) existing side by side with traditional pastoralists and forming a key part of the community economy. Trips go to the magnificent rock engravings at Twyfelfontein. Ten per cent of the revenue is paid to the Conservancy and, from 2006, 20 per cent of the ownership will revert to the community. It costs 2620 Namibian dollars (£240/US$425) per person per night and about 1 million Namibian dollars (£92,000/US$160,000) goes to the community annually. The camp can be reached by road.

SAFARI/LUX
DORO NAWAS CAMP
This intimate camp in a pristine wilderness area was established when the local community approached the **Web:** www.wilderness-safaris.com
company with a proposal for a joint venture. Reachable by road, it offers an opportunity to see wildlife (for example, elephant, springbok, giraffe) existing alongside traditional pastoral activities. Cultural aspects are omnipresent as the concession overlaps village and

farming activity. Trips to the rock engravings at Twyfelfontein can be arranged. The land is leased from the community, which owns 40 per cent of the Camp, as do Wilderness Safaris, and 20 per cent by a Namibian black empowerment company. It costs 695 Namibian dollars (£64/US$115) per person for B&B of which 40 per cent goes to the community.

SOUTH AFRICA
International dialling code +27

Once boycotted for its apartheid regime, South Africa has changed a lot. For many of its people, however, it has not changed enough. You will still find areas, both rural and urban, of startling poverty close to wealthy suburbs (formerly all white but now with a sprinkling of wealthy blacks), modern industries and productive farms. The government has to hold a balance between encouraging the (still capitalist) economy and providing for the poor – in spite of some impressive improvements the poor tend to lose out. There are many different reasons for wanting to travel in South Africa. Don't be put off by street crime. It exists – just watch out when you are in town. Among the many attractions are: the Cape area and the Garden Route, world famous destinations with all modern facilities and excellent wine; KwaZulu-Natal with its superb coast around Durban and the beautiful Drakensberg Mountains inland, perfect for pony trekking and looking for prehistoric rock art; and the famous Kruger National Park in the northeast. To understand the realities of life and recent history you can visit Soweto, the museum and Market Theatre in Johannesburg, the District 6 Museum and Robben Island at Cape Town.

TOUR+
BONANI OUR PRIDE TOURS

This micro-enterprise is a good example of the growing sector of township tours, offering visitors an opportunity to see, know and experience local lifestyles. Bonani was conceived in order to be able to share stories of the past and present with those interested in the heritage and history of South Africa. Personal contact with locals is encouraged in order to contribute towards peace and healing. Bonani means

Contact: Mandisa St.Clair
Tel: 21 5314 291
Fax: 21 5314 291
Email: ourpride@mweb.co.za
Web: www.bonanitours.co.za
Address: PO Box 330, Sea Point 8060, Cape Town, South Africa

'to see', but there are opportunities to enjoy all the senses with Township Music and Gospel Tours. They support two youth projects out of their income. Prices range from 270–510 rand (£25–47/US$44–83) to 4420 rand (£407/US$720) for local tours for the four-day Garden Route Tour. Come as a visitor, leave as a friend – this could be their motto.

SAFARI+

BUFFALO RIDGE SAFARI LODGE

Buffalo Lodge is the first wholly owned community-based safari lodge in South Africa. It is a tourism partnership between North-West Parks, the Balete Ba Lekgophung Community and the operator Nature Workshop. It is in the western section of the Madikwe Game Reserve. Nature Workshop has an operating contract for

Contact: Rhona Katiah
Tel: 011 537 4600
Fax: 011 447 0993
Email: reservations@buffaloridgesafari.com
Web: www.buffaloridgesafari.com
Address: PO Box 2993, Rivonia 2128, South Africa

15 years and the community has a 45-year lease for the lodge with traversing rights across the Reserve. Nature Workshop intends to hand over the management of the lodge at the end of the contractual period.

ACCOM+

BULUNGULA LODGE

Situated on a beautiful South African beach on the Wild Coast at Umtata, where dolphins and whales are common, guests can explore the surrounding forests or wander around the village and experience community living in this Xhosa speaking part of the country. An integral part of the village community,

Contact: Dave Martin
Tel: 47 577 8900
Fax: 86 653 1327
Email: dave@bulungula.com
Web: www.bulungula.com
Address: PO Box 345, Elliotdale, 5070, South Africa

the Lodge is run on solar energy with water conservation showers, compost toilets, and has planted 10,000 mangrove seeds to rehabilitate the surrounding mangrove forest. The Nqileni village owns 40 per cent of the Lodge. The many activities include horse riding, learning to prepare traditional food, fishing with the fishermen and walking with local people. Accommodation in lovely huts starts from 60 rand (£5.50/US$10) per person and camping at 30 rand (£2.75/US$5) per person.

DAY+

CALABASH TOURS (FTTSA accredited)

Certified by Fair Trade in Tourism South Africa (FTTSA), Calabash Tours offers Real City Tours covering both the historical heart of the city of Port Elizabeth, the vibrant black townships and the Xhosa culture. Visitors will also enjoy the Shebeen Tour as an opportunity to relax and meet local people,

Tel: 41 585 6162
Fax: 41 585 0985
Email: calabash@iafrica.com
Web: www.calabashlodge.co.za
Address: 8 Dollery Street, Central, Port Elizabeth, Eastern Cape, 6001 South Africa

understand social issues, play a game of pool and dance to African rhythms. Calabash Tours is a commercial venture with a strong social agenda. Working closely with the Calabash Trust, it ensures that local, and often disadvantaged, communities benefit from the visits through services provided either by community projects or black-owned township businesses. The Trust has many programmes in nearby townships benefiting children and young people.

TOUR/ACCOM
CAPE CAPERS TOURS/CAPE CARE ROUTE
A 'trail of two cities' tour

Cape Capers shows the visitor a different face of what is now known as township tours. The operation offers day tours of the usual kind such as the Winelands, Cape Peninsula and the Township Experience, but their core product is The Cape Care Route, the trail of two cities. Three routes, each covering five to seven projects or destinations introduce visitors to the myriad ways in which communities are coping with such pressing social and environmental problems as

Contact: Faizal Gangat
Tel: 21 448 3117
Cellular: 83 358 0193
Fax: 21 448 3117
Email: tourcape@mweb.co.za
Web: www.tourcapers.co.za
Address: PO Box 13213, Mowbray 7705, Cape Town, South Africa

HIV/AIDS, homelessness and skills development. The full day tour has a lunch stop in the townships and overnight stays in a township guesthouse can be arranged. If you want to experience the energy of the previously disadvantaged try Cape Capers for size.

DIS/VOL/TOUR
DAKTARI WILDLIFE ORPHANAGE

Daktari was established so that disabled people can be part of a team that works together for five weeks with sick and orphaned animals. Teams consist of one handicapped person and one non-handicapped person, and their task is to take care of one, or several,

Tel: (0)15 795 5219
Fax: (0)15 795 5219
Email: daktari.sa@mweb.co.za
Web: www.africanorphanage.com

animals for that period. This involves specialized feeding, supervision and providing the nursing necessary. Included are visits to animal rehabilitation centres, private game reserves and the Kruger National Park. 'There is no reason why this dream cannot be shared by the handicapped. We can enable people, from all walks of life, to have this amazing experience.' Accommodation is in four spacious 'rondavels', two of which are wheelchair friendly. Meals can be taken in the covered 'lapa' by the swimming pool with its view over the waterhole and the bush.

SAFARI/LUX
DJUMA GAME RESERVE (FTTSA accredited)

At Djuma, guests can have a safari drive and see the Big Five while staying at one of three luxury game lodges. As well as offering a breathtaking setting, Djuma has shown a consistent commitment to promoting community development and poverty allevi-

Tel: 13 735 5119
Fax: 13 735 5559
Email: djuma@djuma.co.za
Web: www.djuma.com
Address: PO Box 338, Hluvukani, 1363, South Africa

ation. It has developed programmes that champion local socio-economic development, has supported two local primary schools and a media training centre. It is working with the Djuma and Shangaan communities to realize their shared vision to conserve the land for future generations in a way that benefits the wider community. Hluvukani is the closest town to Djuma Game Reserve.

ORG
FAIR TRADE IN TOURISM IN SOUTH AFRICA (FTTSA accredited)

The South African listings include several accredited by Fair Trade Tourism in South Africa. FTTSA's involvement in tourism dates from its formal establishment in 2001. It is a non-profit certifying agency issuing a fair trade trademark to South African establishments. Social and environmental practices provide the main criteria for assessment. It also supports people and organizations wishing to start up fair trade tourism.

Contact: Jennifer Seif
Tel: 12 342 8307
Fax: 12 342 8289
Email: info@fairtourismsa.org.za
Web: www.fairtourismsa.org.za
Address: Fair Trade in Tourism South Africa (FTTSA), PO Box 11536, Hatfield, Pretoria, 0028 South Africa

ACCOM+
HILUVARI LAKESIDE LODGE (FTTSA accredited)

Shiluvari Lakeside Lodge on the banks of the Luvhuvhu River is well sited to explore the rich diversity of cultures and the beauty of the northern reaches of Limpopo Province. Its thatched chalets offer a sweeping view of the Albasini Dam and mountains. Shiluvari is passionate about growing tourism in the area; one of its significant achievements has been its success in establishing the Ribolla Tourism Association together with the area's numerous artists. The Lodge offers B&B or half board. The ownership structure of the Lodge is multiracial. Shiluvari's sister company is Kuvona Cultural Tours, which concentrates on cultural tourism in the area with two local support groups benefiting.

Contact: Betty Hlungwane
Tel: 15 556 3406
Fax: 15 556 3413
Email: shiluvar@llantic.net, clare@shiluvari.com
Web: www.shiluvari.com
Address: PO Box 560, Louis Trichardt 0920, Limpopo Province, South Africa

ACCOM
HOG HOLLOW COUNTRY LODGE (FTTSA accredited)

This four-star lodge is set on the edge of a private nature reserve with panoramic views of the surrounding indigenous forests, valleys and mountains. The location used to be an alien wattle plantation in the semi-wilds of a little known area of the Tsitikamma (Garden Route) known as the Crags. Staff are able to assist guests to plan day-trips encompassing everything from eco-adventure activities to a local community tour. Hog Hollow is committed to supporting its local economy through procurement and employment.

Tel: (0) 44 534 8879
Fax: (0) 44 534 8879
Email: info@hog-hollow.com
Web: www.hog-hollow.com
Address: PO Box 503, Plettenberg Bay, 6600, South Africa

ACCOM
IMVUBU (FTTSA accredited)

Imvubu offers an excellent escape from the rush of city life in the Rondevlei Nature Reserve. To experience all that Rondevlei has to offer, Imvubu provides a variety of guided tours including their popular walk into Rondevlei's medicine cabinet, where guests can learn the medicinal and cultural value of indigenous vegetation. Demonstrating a strong commitment to sustainable and responsible tourism, Imvubu operates with a strong community-based approach and also supports education programmes for local scholars and residents.

Tel: 21 706 0842
Fax: 21 706 9793
Email: info@imvubu.co.za
Web: www.imvubu.co.za
Address: Rondevlei Nature Reserve, 1 Fisherman's Walk, 7941, South Africa

ACCOM
JAN HARMSGAT COUNTRY HOUSE (FTTSA accredited)

Situated about two hours from Cape Town in the Western Cape, this guesthouse is on a working farm. There is real involvement with the community on both economic and cultural levels. Visitors are given the opportunity to indulge in an authentic country ambience and history. Linked with the enterprise is the Old Gaol coffee shop and

Contact: Lizl Kruger/Michelle Dolf
Tel: 23 6164 307/6163 311
Fax: 23 6163 201
Email: brinreb@iafrica.com
Web: www.jhghouse.com
Address: PO Box 161, Swellendam, Western Cape, 6740, South Africa

restaurant in the nearby town of Swellendam, transformed from the old jail. The mission at the outset was to get the local community involved in tourism through skills training and development. Women from disadvantaged communities were trained and given a stake in the cafe where delicacies like springbok carpaccio and local cheeses are served.

ACCOM
KLIPPE RIVIER COUNTRY HOUSE (FTTSA accredited)

One philosophy of Klippe Rivier is to support small enterprises and buy local whenever possible. Guests are encouraged to visit local art and craft businesses. Klippe Rivier Country House has installed a wastewater management system and utilizes low-volume toilet systems. Waste separation and alien vegeta-

Tel: 28 514 3341
Fax: 28 514 3337
Email: info@klipperivier.com
Web: www.klipperivier.com
Address: PO Box 483, Swellendam, Western Cape, 6740, South Africa

tion removal are practiced on its grounds. The establishment has also invested considerably in the preservation of the historic homestead and surrounding buildings. Klippe Rivier has developed fair working conditions.

ACCOM+
MASAKALA TRADITIONAL GUESTHOUSE (FTTSA accredited)

Situated in the rural village of Masakala (near Matatiele), bordering the Eastern Cape and KwaZulu-Natal, the Guesthouse offers panoramic views of the southern Drakensberg Mountains towards Lesotho. Masakala's activities include walking tours to rock art treasures, birdwatching and horse riding. Guests can visit local projects, meet local crafters or simply to enjoy the serenity. Mehloding Community

Contact: Nomonde Makaula
Tel: (0) 39 737 3289
Fax: (0) 39 737 3289
Email: masakala@telkomsa.net, mehloding@telkomsa.net
Web: www.mehloding.co.za
Address: PO Box 406, Matatiele, KwaZulu-Natal, 4730, South Africa

Tourism Trust, which owns the Guesthouse, represents more than 25 villages in the area. Masakala purchases locally, has an organic vegetable garden and practices soil and water conservation and recycling. Herders are trained to identify and preserve rock art and locals to harvest indigenous medicinal plants.

SAFARI/LUX
PAFURI CAMP

Another of the luxurious, small and intimate camps operated by Wilderness Safaris, Pafuri is wholly owned **Web:** www.wilderness-safaris.com

company on land leased from the local community. Over the first five years (from 2005) 40–50 per cent of the net profits will go to the community, members of which approached the company with a joint venture proposal. The accommodation offers 52 beds at a fully inclusive rate of 1295 rand (£120/US$210) per person per night. Pafuri is in a unique part of the Kruger National Park, reachable by road, and distinguished by its exceptional biodiversity and big game. Visitors have the assurance that comes from knowing that their presence in the Kruger is helping to support both the game and the environment.

DAY/TOUR/HOST
PHAPHAMA INITIATIVES
TALK Tourism

Phaphama Initiatives offers tours, homestays and immersion into South African culture through a community-based tourism initiative called TALK Tourism. Everything is flexibly structured in terms of group size, duration and itinerary; fees contribute directly to the community guide and host

Tel: (0) 11 487 1798
Fax: (0) 88 0 11 487 1950
Email: info@phaphama.org
Web: www.phaphama.org/index.php?sid=24&l=eng
Address: PO Box 94144, Yeoville 2143, Johannesburg, South Africa

family, as well as to the peace work of this non-profit organization. You can choose from Cape Town, Johannesburg, Soweto, KwaZulu-Natal. TALK Tourism arranges for small groups of tourists (ideally one to four people) wishing to experience rural African culture, to stay for up to a month with an extended family, usually in KwaZulu-Natal. Visitors are accompanied by trained TALK Tourism helpers on this trip. The focus can be to learn the language, enjoy the area's rich historical and natural attractions, or simply to experience family life. Visitors will be requested to attend a thorough briefing to prepare them for such a stay.

ACCOM
PHUMULANI LODGE (FTTSA accredited)

Phumulani Lodge is the outcome of the vision of the late Chief Mdluli for his people, based on his dream that tourism would one day ensure local employment and community development. The lodge is 100 per cent owned by the Mdluli Trust, which is deeply

Tel: 13 789 0020
Fax: 13 789 0025
Email: phumulanilodge@soft.co.za
Address: PO Box 2044, Hazyview, Mpumalanga, 1242, South Africa

committed to the social, economic and environmental well-being of its staff and community. Phumulani Lodge is not an ordinary four-star lodge. It is an experience created by the local host community, which provides personalized service and serenity in the heart of the bushveld.

HOST/TOUR
SOWETO NIGHTS, SAFARI DAYS

This is an outstanding opportunity for visitors to arrive in Johannesburg, experience community-based bed and breakfast hospitality in Soweto and also take tours of the Kruger National Park. The Soweto stays give visitors an insight into the new South Africa and also educate them about the historical, cultural and political conditions,

Contact: Stephen Mendel
Tel: +44 (0) 207 254 4957
Fax: +44 (0) 207 254 4957
Email: stephen.mendel@talk21.com
Web: www.sowetonights.co.uk
Address: PO Box 54622, London N16 8YX, UK

which gave birth to this South Africa. Eighty per cent of the fees go to the people providing the accommodation and the tours. For the safari element, the Kruger was chosen because tour income helps fund the preservation of both animals and the environment. The daily fee in Soweto is £85/US$150 per person (meals, accommodation and tours) and the three nights Kruger tour costs £385/US$685.

ACCOM+
STORMSRIVER ADVENTURES (FTTSA accredited)

Stormsriver Adventures is a community-based eco-adventure company situated in the heart of the rural Tsitsikamma in the Eastern Cape offering 16 varied activities. Training and development of local staff has been a cornerstone philosophy of the company and equal opportunity for all has led to the establishment

Tel: 42 281 1836
Fax: 42 281 1609
Email: adventure@gardenroute.co.za
Web: www.stormsriver.com
Address: PO Box 116, Stormsriver, Eastern Cape, 6308, South Africa

of a catering company where the staff holds 80 per cent of the equity. Stormsriver Aventures' involvement in community development is diverse and includes environmental education and food provision programmes for local schools. A committed environmental policy is rigidly applied, ensuring the protection of the surrounding sensitive environment.

SAFARI
UMLANI BUSHCAMP (FTTSA accredited)

Umlani Bushcamp accommodates up to 16 guests in traditional African reed and thatch huts. Umlani's philosophy of simplistic luxury and getting back to nature is enhanced by the romance of candlelight and oil lamps, which replace electricity. Open-air bush showers complete the experience. There are game drives,

Tel: 12 346 4028
Fax: 12 346 4203
Email: info@umlani.com
Web: www.umlani.com
Address: PO Box 11604, Maroelana, 0161, South Africa

guided bush walks and tracking game on foot with experienced Shangaan rangers and trackers in over 10,000 hectares of Big Five territory. The Camp has a staff HIV/AIDS programme, designed by a local expert, and has developed a youth leadership programme at Welverdiend Village, where the majority of staff are based. Umlani Bushcamp prioritises human development and uplift.

AFRICA SOUTHERN

SWAZILAND
International dialling code +268

400km

MBANANE

'Minibus crash – 15 princesses inside'. Swazi-land is an African Ruritania where the King chooses a new wife (he has plenty already) from among the maidens who parade bare-breasted each year at the Reed Dance. Apart from his sexual appetite, this young king has real political power and a cowed opposition. The country is tiny, the size of Wales, but very green and scenic and has well-developed roads, hotels, shopping, etc. The deep Ezulwini Valley is the touristic heart of the country, with a small game reserve and the 'cuddle puddle' hot springs. The valley links the two main towns, both pleasantly small, Mbabane up in the hills, the capital, and Manzini, down in the 'middle veld', which is close to the airport. Sadly, however, Swaziland now has a record level of AIDS infection and has suffered some years of poor rainfall. In the days of apartheid in South Africa, Swaziland's tourist trade was based on prostitution and the availability of pornographic and political literature that was banned across the border. This has changed and, with exports of sugar cane and pineapples earning less than they used to, legitimate tourism is a much needed factor in the economy.

DAY/ACCOM+
WOZA NAWE CAMPSITE & TRADITIONAL TOURS

This project is owned by Mxolisi Myxo Mdluli who set it up with the aim of benefiting the community of kaPhunga in Swaziland. Here the idea is to experience community life on the Community Farm of Kaphunga, about 65km from the nearest town, in the hills of Swaziland. He offers hostel accommodation and traditional style lodging in the country. If you really want to get to know Swazi people, to help with the family chores and maybe bring in the cows or plough, and also have a chance to help the local kids with their English in school this could be for you. Day tours costs 300 rand (£27.50/US$50) and overnight stays 420 rand (£40/US$70). Visitors receive clear instruction on how to dress and behave, and what to expect and not expect.

Contact: Myxo Mxolisi Mdluli
Tel: 6044 102/5056 018
Fax: 5656 018
Email: wozanawe@realnet.co.sz
Web: www.earthfoot.org/sz.htm
Address: PO Box 2455, Manzini, Swaziland

ZAMBIA

International dialling code +260

Set on an undulating plateau at the base of Africa's backbone, Zambia is one of the continent's largest and most sparsely populated countries but also one of its most diverse. Its strangely shaped borders contain over 70 different ethnic groups and vast expanses of wilderness filled with a rich and varied wildlife.

Although the world's fourth largest supplier of copper (accounting for 75 per cent of its foreign currency) Zambia is a desperately poor country being both at the mercy of the international copper market and crippled by its national debt. Any hope of a recovery has sadly been hindered by the World Bank and IMF, who made the receipt of aid, on which the country is dependent, conditional on the liberalization of its markets. The results are catastrophic with the decimation of many of the country's state run enterprises, high unemployment and increased prices for basic commodities. In a country where two thirds of the population lives on less than US$1 a day and 85 per cent are subsistence farmers, for every dollar it receives in aid it must pay three times that on debt repayments. In an effort to revitalize the stagnant economy, tourism is seen as an alternative source of revenue, and in this respect the country's vast tracts of uninhabited wilderness and the hospitality of its people are its greatest asset. In recent years a number of the country's 19 national parks have been revitalized but even the more visited parks receive relatively few visitors and it is this that Zambia can offer, which its neighbours cannot. Compared to its southerly neighbours, the effort required to travel here independently is greater but then so too are the rewards.

SAFARI/LUX
KAWAZA VILLAGE

Robin Pope Safaris is the most established and successful safari operator in the South Luangwa National Park, Zambia. Their three camps, Nkwali, Nsefu and the famous Tena Tena offer personalized safaris combining genuine African bush with simple yet stylish luxury. Each camp is individual in atmosphere and location.

Robin's Safaris are renowned for being one of the all time safari experiences. For 15 years they have supported a school in the Nsefu Village area, which is now seen as a model of how tourism can contribute to a community. Guests who visit the school and are keen to learn more about local lifestyles can stay at Kawaza Village overnight or for a day. The Kawaza project is now self-running, overseen by a committee, and the income supports the village and also helps to run the school.

Contact: Chris McIntyre
Email: info@expertafrica.com
Web: www.kawazavillage.co.uk, www.expertafrica.com
Or contact Robin Pope Safaris direct:
Tel: 6 246 090/91/92
Fax: 6 246 094
Web: www.robinpopesafaris.net

ACCOM+
NAKAPALAYO TOURISM PROJECT

Community based, owned and managed, Nakapalayo village is well located between Kasanka National Park and the spectacular Bangweulu. It was founded by the community and offers 'an authentic experience in a traditional village'. A quarter of its income goes to community development and conservation projects. Accommodation is in comfortable mud-brick huts

Contact: Kim Farmer
Tel: +873 76206 7957
Fax: +873 76206 7959
Email: KAS14@bushmail.net
Web: www.kasanka.com
Address: PO Box 850073, Serenje, Zambia

but visitors can choose to camp. A local guide accompanies visitors throughout their stay to introduce them to local life and culture, to do's and don'ts and to translate. The huts take 12 people and the campsite eight. An overnight stay with meals, village tour and entertainment costs £17/US$30 per person. Profits go to fund the local school and pay the teacher.

VOL
YOUTH ASSOCIATION OF ZAMBIA (YAZ)

This is not where you go if you want to sip wine under a million stars and dream of the Big Five tomorrow. This is a work and study camp organization that gives volunteers the chance to visit tourist sites during excursions. You will be working mainly on environmen-

Contact: Evans Mambwe Musonda
Tel: 9775 9444
Email: yazinfor@yahoo.com,
    musonda5@yahoo.com
Address: PO Box 31852, Lusaka, Zambia

tal outreach programmes and offering your skills to support their take-up; you will be having an inter-cultural experience beyond measure. It offers volunteers an orientation workshop on arrival (which you pay for) and this ensures you receive 'a less shock if any' during your stay. Volunteers have the opportunity to be given a wide choice of camps in Zambia, which can be extended worldwide as YAZ is a member of many work camp networks worldwide.

WEST AFRICA

THE GAMBIA
International dialling code +220

Gambia is an accident of history. The British got here first but the French moved inland and created the colony of Senegal, which surrounds the tiny Gambia, a narrow strip on both sides of the Gambia River. Having few resources other than groundnuts, the country has developed tourism as its main industry. The coastal strip has become a major package holiday destination with cheap charter flights but not much benefit to the majority of the population. Being such a small country, it is possible to combine a beach holiday with interesting visits to the nearby Tanbi mangrove swamp, the Makasutu Culture Forest and the small capital city, Banjul. Further up-country you can visit historic Janjanbureh Island; or Juffureh, the village which purports to be the original home of Kunta Kinte, the hero of Alex Haley's novel and TV saga, Roots. The Gambia has a good climate, warm but not unbearably hot in winter.

ORG
ASSOCIATION OF SMALL-SCALE ENTERPRISES IN TOURISM (ASSET)

ASSET is a unique trade association with some 2500 members working in a wide variety of tourism jobs, including guiding, fruit juicing, bar, guest house and hotel owners, taxi drivers and handicraft vendors. As such it does not provide services directly but enables its members to improve their services and products to tourists. It also works with the tour operators and ground operators using the services and products of ASSET members so that even mainstream holidays can better include what's on offer from them. ASSET means that people formerly marginalized by the mainstream industry can now be a positive part of its development. It has won a major international award for its work to ensure that tourism alleviates poverty.

Contact: Daouda Njie
Tel: 4497 675
Email: info@asset-gambia.com
Web: www.asset-gambia.com
Address: ASSET Resource Centre, Fajara, The Gambia

ORG
KART

Situated at the southernmost border of the coast this village was cut off by a very bad road until the recent construction of the Coastal Road. Now, it is not a case of if tourism comes, but when. The village of Kartong is committing itself to developing tourism in a responsible way. Unspoilt beaches, cooling breezes and a sense of a community that is embracing the future on its terms, Kartong is developing good examples of sustainable tourism.

Contact: Geri Mitchell
Tel: 4495887/4497841
Email: geri@gamspirit.com
Web: www.gamspirit.com
Address: PO Box 4590, Bakau, The Gambia

The Village Development Committee has declared that all tourism enterprises in Kartong should be members of KART (Kartong Association for Responsible Tourism). KART has established an Information Centre and Honey Café in the village opposite the Mosque. Call in and discover the latest that the village has to offer.

DAY/ACCOM/LUX
MAKASUTU AND MANDINA RIVER LODGE

This extraordinary venture, the vision of two British men, consists of day trips to the 1000 acre reserve or staying in their exotic, eco-floating accommodation on a tributary of the River Gambia, the Mandina Bolong. The day trip offers a

Contact: Lawrence or James
Tel: 48 3335/900279
Email: info@asset-gambia.com
Web: www.asset-gambia.com
Address: PO Box 2309, Serrekunda, The Gambia

walk through the primal forest, lunch and dancing, drumming and craft making. The accommodation has won international awards. All of this is with the ethos of working with local people and the environment so that benefits are shared by all.

ACCOM
SAFARI GARDEN HOTEL

A delightful, friendly small hotel operating in a very green fashion, is working on becoming even more sustainable and environmentally sound. Unusually for The Gambia , food is sourced locally where possible. What is on offer is a quiet relaxing holiday experience where guests get a chance to

Contact: Geri Mitchell
Tel: 4495 887
Email: geri@gamspirit.com
Web: www.gamspirit.com

meet the interesting people who pass through and always use the hotel. A double room with breakfast costs (February 2005) £30/US$55 a night. Although in an urban residential area and so not located in a 'community', the hotel has a close relationship with the village of Kartong some 40km distant. No direct contribution is made to the community but the hotel and guests support projects in Kartong.

ACCOM/SCHOOL
SANDALE ECO-RETREAT & LEARNING CENTRE

Set in probably the most beautiful beach in The Gambia, the retreat has up market accommodation built in a manner that is an example of sustainable building in itself. The Learning Centre will be completed by the end of 2006 and will run courses on a wide range of sustainability issues. There will be

Contact: Geri Mitchell
Tel: 4495887/4497841
Email: geri@gamspirit.com
Web: www.gamspirit.com
Address: PO Box 4590, Bakau, The Gambia

moderately priced guest rooms attached. The intention is to change the normal dynamic of tourism and put Gambians in the role of teachers and mentors rather than performers and servants. On the other hand it will put the visitor in the role of participant rather than voyeur.

DAY/ACCOM+
TUMANI TENDA ECOTOURISM CAMP

You can visit Tumani Tenda, south of Banjul, for the day or stay overnight. This Jola village has built its indigenous accommodation near the riverside from which you can take a canoe trip to the

Contact: Sulaymen Soksa
Tel: 90 3662/462057/988167
Email: tumanitenda@hotmail.com
Web: www.asset-gambia.com/members/eco/tumanitenda

mangroves where the women collect oysters, see their farm, take walks into the forest, eat delicious meals and enjoy being a part of the community in their daily lives. They wholly own the camp.

GHANA

International dialling code +233

Ghana is an exciting and varied place that offers many different and wonderful experiences. The absence of a long-term, well established tourism industry means this country with its bustling cities, unique cultures and fascinating people retains its own very distinct flavour. Festivals and cultural celebrations are as different in what they celebrate as the number of different languages spoken in the country – over a hundred. Ghana also has an infamous legacy in the trade of stolen people, manifest in the many well-preserved slaving forts dotted along its sandy coastline. The African diaspora are drawn towards Ghana, including many African Americans. A strong cultural etiquette exists, which is worth checking out before arrival. Music is all-pervasive; high life music and hip-life, Ghana youth's original blend of indigenous music and US style hip-hop, originated in Ghana.

The country has scores of fantastic beaches, rainforest, savannah and the dry dusty deserts of the north, making it a utopia for lovers of nature – it's a birdwatcher's paradise. Kakum, Mole and Ankasa National Parks are just a few of the places set up to preserve wildlife.

If there is one memorable point that defines Ghana it is the use of folk sayings that manifest themselves most visibly on the ubiquitous tro-tro's – the minibuses that make up the bulk of Ghana's transport system. Take a trip on 'I Shall Return' or visit 'It Will Grow Back' hairdressers and eat, if you still have an appetite, at 'Stomach Takes No Holiday' chop bar.

DAY/TOUR/ACCOM/HOST/VOL
ADDAI & DWUMAH TOUR

This is a company with offices throughout Ghana, rooted in the communities within which it operates. On offer is a range of activities: attractions, tours, safaris, internships, homestays, voluntary work, also drumming and dancing lessons. A particular feature is the history of the slave trade. All visitors are met at the airport and taken to their hotels or host families and from there to their tours or community-based work. The maximum number for any one tour group is 28 to avoid negative environmental impacts, with a countrywide limit of 100 people. An all-inclusive tour of seven days (six nights) costs £705/US$1260 including a contribution towards community support.

Contact: Nicholas Boamah
Tel: 24 3316 443/24 226 2950/24 226 2951
Email: infom@ghanatour.org,
    customer-service@ghanatour.org
Web: www.ghanatour.org, www.tours.ghanatour.org
Address: PO Box 187, Offinso-Ashanti, Ghana

ORG/DAY/ACCOM
GHANA TOURIST BOARD

The Tourist Board is an umbrella organization covering a wide range of community-based projects and tours. Local communities, have been introduced to best practice to protect wildlife and conserve the environment and are also taught about ecotourism. There is a range of sites and projects to visit that illuminate the harmonious coexistence of local communities with their environment. Included are the Paga Crocodile Ponds, Tongo Hills and Tengzug Shirnes, the Widnaba Elephant trails and the Sirigu Women and Art works. Revenues go directly to the community that maintains the attraction. The four key sites offer accommodation, refreshment and traditional entertainment.

Contact: Ms Mary M. Agangmikre
Tel: 7223 416
Fax: 7223 578
Email: imagefocus2000@yahoo.co.uk
Web: www.ghanatourism.gov.gh
Address: PO Box 305, Bolgatanga,
    Upper East Region, Ghana

TOUR
GHANADVENTURE

Ghanadventure is a new venture run by Village Exchange International and Village Exchange Ghana and opens up a range of opportunities to bike, hike, birdwatch, visit caves, villages and shrines in the Volta region. On offer is a ten-day tour for approximately £675/US$1200. The profits will be entirely reinvested in supporting Village Exchange Ghana projects.

Contact: Yannick Milev
Tel: 9125 164
Cellular: 24466 7302
Email: ymilev@ghanadventure.com
Web: www.ghanadventure.com
Address: PO Box 756, Ho, Volta Region, Ghana

HOST+
HOHOE DISTRICT'S COMMUNITY-BASED ECOTOURISM

This is a unique opportunity to directly participate in the daily lives of the people of the Hohoe district of Ghana. Visitors stay in private Ghanaian homes and take part in everyday activities from preparing local dishes to shopping in the market to working on the land. Guests have many choices of activities included guided nature walks, birdwatching, participating in palm wine and palm oil production, boat construction and fishing. In the evening you are invited to take part in dancing and drumming. The income from visitors is held in trust by the communities themselves and used for projects such as water pumps and school fees.

Contact: Kofi Thompson
Tel: 27 7453 109
Fax: 21 256 712
Email: peakofithompson@yahoo.co.uk
Web: www.akwantupa.org
Address: PO Box KIA 9732, Accra, Ghana

TOUR/ACCOM/SCHOOL
KASAPA CENTRE

The centre is about 40km from Accra and visitors are met at the airport. Two holiday programmes are on offer: holidays with excursions, and workshops for traditional drumming and dancing. Guests do not face a levy to support local projects but as a rule are so enthused by their experience that they give voluntarily; to date more than £20,000/US$35,000 has been donated. The entire operation is eco-friendly. The centre is a small village on the coast with six guest chalets, each with two double rooms. Stays are for two, three or four weeks and the cost varies with length and programme selected but a range of £440–550/US$780–980 for two weeks is a fair indicator. The Centre pays the community for the lease of the land.

Contact: Hoelscher Walther-Weltreisen
Tel: +49 228 661 239
Email: walther-weltreisen@t-online.de
Web: www.kasapa.de

TOUR/ACCOM/HOST
KWAHU TOURISM PROJECT
Community Tours & Concerns

This is a small-scale enterprise but hoping to grow. Visitors stay with host families in the community if they wish and so get the chance to make one-to-one relationships and to learn about the local culture and society. Weekend tours of the project area in the Kwahu Region off the Afadjato-Mampong mountain range are also provided. Traditional leaders suggest places and things to see and select the people to guide and provide services. Trips cost £17/US$30 per person and accommodation £11/US$20.

Contact: Nash Sam
Tel: 244 753 755
Email: kwasisam@yahoo.com,
fieldingmj@gmail.com
Web: www.geocities.com/apexmediagh
Address: PO Box KN 2485, Kaneshie-
Accra, Ghana
UK Address: Mathew Fielding, C/O 214
Norton Leys, Rugby, Warwickshire CV22 5RY, UK

NIGERIA
International dialling code +234

Nigeria and Nigerians get a bad press but if you can put up with a bit of noise, dirt and hassle it is a fascinating place. With its population of over 120 million and oil wealth it should be Africa's superpower but it has never really got its act together. It is more like three countries: the southwest peopled by the Yoruba with their traditional towns such as Ibadan and Ife, plus the megalopolis of Lagos, the country's commercial capital; the southeast where the hardworking Igbos are the majority; and the immense Islamic north where Kano is the best example among a number of traditional cities. Nigeria is top of the African league for art, historical heritage and literature: visit the shrines at Oshogbo, the brilliant museums at Jos, Lagos and Ibadan and read

Chinua Achebe and Wole Soyinka. It is also proud of its cuisine, though you need to like pepper! The cities, the culture and the people are the main attractions and you can expect a warm welcome, partly because few tourists make the trip. There are some interesting rural sights such as Wikki Warm Springs and the Cross River National Park. You can also find excellent handicrafts, especially the leather work and jewellery from the north.

ORG
AFRICAN LEGACY

'African Legacy owns nothing but is privileged to share the goldmine of knowledge "owned" by local Nigerians'. It operates whenever time and funds allow. It is non-profit making and seeks to kick-start the backpacker element needed for the long-term viability of Nigeria's potential future tourist industry. The main project is the 'discovery' and publication of all Nigeria's incredible visible archaeology and…rich cultural landscapes'. This is for visitors who would like to be introduced to Nigeria's culture, live with its welcoming people and help trace and document the evidence of its glorious cultural and archaeological heritage, often in remote areas.

Contact: Dr Patrick Darling
Tel: +44 1202 554735
Email: explore@africanlegacy.info
Web: www.csweb.bournemouth.uk.ac/africanlegacy
Address: 46A Ophir Road, Bournemouth, BH8 8LT, UK

SENEGAL
International dialling code +221

There's a certain glamour to Senegal – baobab trees, tall women in magnificent dresses and topknots, handsome colonial architecture, vibrant music and nightlife. Dakar may be too noisy for some but it is easy to escape. You can take a ferry to the island of Gorée, an atmospheric reminder of the slave trade but a beautiful spot, especially at sunset. Or you can head north to the faded splendour of St Louis, the original French colonial capital. Going south along the coast in a taxi brousse you get to the Saloum Delta with abundant birds and turtles. Further south after crossing in and out of the Gambia, you reach Casamance with its excellent beaches, lush and well watered compared to the semi-desert of most of Senegal. In the interior are the large Niokolo Koba National Park and the remote, hilly Pays Bassari.

Senegal was the first French colony in Africa and it has become the most democratic of the former French countries. It has a rich intellectual and cultural tradition – Senegal's first president was Léopold Sédar Senghor, the poet of négritude. The country's best known writer and film-maker is Ousmane Sembene, and Baaba Maal, Youssou N'Dour and Ismael Lô are among the many famous names in Senegalese music.

TOUR/HOST/VOL
SENEVOLU

Senevolu is dedicated to promoting community tourism and welcomes volunteers and travellers who wish to discover the cultural differences Senegal has to offer, while being part of the community. Senevolu offers unique community tourism programmes that are designed for everyone (groups and individuals) holidaymakers and volunteers, who will enjoy experiencing the Senegalese culture and teranga (Wolof for hospitality) while staying in a host family or a hostel. Programmes are available all year long. Homestays are offered for £350/US$625 for three weeks, and the volunteer programme is £295/US$525 for four weeks. Everyone first undergoes a five-day course near the capital to learn the basics of Senegalese culture.

Contact: Maguèye Sy
Tel: 559 6735
Fax: 892 4464
Email: senevolu@mypage.org
Web: www.senevolu.mypage.org
Address: PO Box 26, 557 P.A. Dakar, Sénégal

AFRICA WEST

^{THE}AMERICAS

0   4000km

USA (p123)

CUBA (p99)

HAWAII (p122)   MEXICO   BELIZE
                      (p118)   (p106)   HONDURAS (p117)

                      GUATEMALA   VENEZUELA
                      (p113)   (p144)

NICARAGUA (p120)

COSTA RICA (p107)   COLOMBIA (p132)

          ECUADOR
          (p134)   PERU
                          (p139)   BRAZIL (p128)

                              DOMINICAN REPUBLIC
                              (p102)

HAITI (p103)   BOLIVIA
                                                      (p125)

JAMAICA
(p104)

          DOMINICA (p100)

0   1000km

CARIBBEAN

CUBA
International dialling code +53

Cuba is a country on everyone's 'to do list', teetering on the edge of change, as the world holds its breath waiting for Fidel Castro and his 50-year regime to pass into the realms of history. Cuba is the largest of the Caribbean islands, and has the broadest racial mix. It lies only 90 miles off the Florida Coast, yet despite its enduring, crippling relationship with the US, boasts one of the world's best health and education systems. Havana, its capital city, is characterized by its classic American cars and old colonial buildings, many now being given a new lease of life in an innovative restoration programme. Poverty, prostitution and corruption are communist Cuba's inheritance, and as part of an attempt to challenge its isolation and to bring in foreign currency, there has been massive development of the tourism industry. The capital, with its faded grandeur and intoxicating mix of heady Afro-Caribbean music and dance, is the first stop for most tourists, yet there are many opportunities for interesting experiences elsewhere in this vibrant and colourful country. Beach resorts sweep the length and breadth of the country and picturesque towns and colonial cities abound. Cuba vibrates with an energy and charisma not anticipated of a communist state. With characters like Che Guevara and Fidel Castro dominating the historic landscape of Cuba and the revolution still seeming to be current, it's not surprising to find this a country of passionate, intelligent and resilient people, with a fiery culture to match.

TOUR/HOST
CALEDONIA LANGUAGES

Established in Cuba since 1998, Caledonia specializes in Spanish language, cultural tourism, dance, music and percussion trips. Spanish/Salsa holidays are available for two weeks in March, July, October and Christmas each year, with a trekking option. Spanish summer school in July/August 2006 in Santiago de Cuba with daily Spanish classes and supplementary dance/percussion lessons. Tailor-made trips include trekking, diving and special interest cultural tours. Accommodation in local homestays or hotels.

Tel: +44 (0) 131 621 7721
Fax: +44 (0) 131 555 6262
Email: courses@caledonialanguages.co.uk
Web: www.caledonialanguages.co.uk
Address: The Clockhouse, Bonnington Mill, 72 Newhaven Road, Edinburgh EH6 5QG, Scotland, UK

ACCOM
SANTA ISABEL

Santa Isabel, former house of the Count of Santovenia, is today a fancy hotel. In the centre of Old Havana, this five-star hotel combines the modern with a colonial style. Santa Isabel is part of the new and exciting restoration of Old Havana, which is a very important move, not just for tourists but for the residents of this splendid city.

Tel: 7 860 8201
Fax: 7 860 8391
Email: comercial@habaguanexhsisabel.co.cu
Address: Calle Baratillo, No.9 e/Obispo y
Narciso López, La Habana Vieja, Cuba

DOMINICA
International dialling code +1767

400km

ROSEAU

Dominica is the Nature Island of the Caribbean: dazzling greenery, towering mountain ranges, extensive rainforest (including a UNESCO World Heritage site) intersected by rushing rivers, waterfalls, volcanoes, bubbling hot pools and the second largest Boiling Lake in the world ('I survived the Boiling Lake hike' is a website in itself). So forget the stereotypes of a Caribbean beach holiday.

A former British colony sandwiched between Guadeloupe and Martinique and independent since 1978, Dominica also has a strong Afro-French culture – the Creole language, dance, music (home of zouk) and food (where else does the airport cafe stretch to fresh mandarin juice?). The Caribs (or Kalinagos), the indigenous peoples of the Caribbean, who, only on Dominica, survived the arrival of the Europeans, live on the northeast coast: fishermen and farmers, they are also great basket-makers. Roseau, the capital, has some charming French colonial architecture, an excellent museum and a Saturday morning market to die for. Villages are dreamy places, on breezy hillsides or tucked into hidden coves. Tourism is based around locally owned guesthouses – small scale, unpretentious, with an emphasis on environmental well-being. Photographers, artists, botanists, gardeners, hikers and divers (it has some of the best diving in the world) go mad in Dominica, seduced by its wildness and natural exuberance. And watch out for the island in *Pirates of the Caribbean* (parts 2 and 3), it provides a spectacular backdrop to Johnny Depp's antics.

ACCOM
PAPILLOTE WILDERNESS RETREAT

A small, secluded inn offering a tranquil respite perched at the head of the Roseau River Valley. Gardens, mountains, waterfalls and pristine rainforest wilderness surround the comfortable rooms, with trails criss-crossed by hot and cold streams and natural hot mineral bathing pools. The restaurant serves produce bought from local farmers, and freshly caught fish. Papillote's non-profit botanical garden is a unique aspect of the property. Garden tours are available. Papillote has been running since 1970, employing and training young staff from the local village of Trafalgar and is closely integrated into village life, sponsoring sports and cultural events. The property is protected as a wildlife reserve, does not use chemicals, recycles tins and bottles and composts vegetable matter.

Contact: Anne Jno Baptiste or Evalyn Denis
Tel: 448 2287
Fax: 448 2285
Email: Papillote@cwdom.dm
Web: www.papillote.dm
Address: PO Box 2287, Roseau, Commonwealth of Dominica

ACCOM/DIS
THE TAMARIND TREE

This west-coast hotel and restaurant, on a hill overlooking the sea and 1km from the village of Salisbury, is family-run and aims to introduce guests to the country – its customs, people, attractions and environment. Activities on offer include diving and guided hiking. The business is a Green Globe 21 accommodation provider and strives to be as green as possible. All rooms are wheelchair accessible. The food is bought locally. They collaborate with other local businesses on a non-commissioned basis and guests are encouraged to patronize local shops.

Contact: Annette Peyer Loerner
Tel: 449 73 95
Fax: 449 73 95
Email: hotel@tamarindtreedominica.com
Web: www.tamarindtreedominica.com
Address: PO Box 754, Roseau, Commonwealth of Dominica

ACCOM+
THREE RIVERS ECO LODGE

Surrounded by pristine rivers and with a backdrop of the rain forest and the Morne Trois Pitons national work (a UNESCO World Heritage site), this Lodge comprises cottages and campsite, restaurant and bar, and a UN-funded sustainable living education centre. The latter teaches local people organic farming techniques and the use and manufacture of forms of renewable energy. The operation aims to be as environmentally responsible as possible and won the Caribbean Hotel Association's Green Hotel of the Year Award (2005). All the funds from the community life package go to local people: visitors can participate in community activities such as helping at the school, making traditional craft, or learning traditional Creole dance.

Contact: Jem Winston
Tel: 446 1886
Fax: 1 270 517 4588
Email: info@3riversdominica.com
Web: www.3riversdominica.com
Address: PO Box 1292, Rosalie, Commonwealth of Dominica

THE AMERICAS CARIBBEAN

DOMINICAN REPUBLIC
International dialling code +1809

1000km

SANTO
DOMINGO

Tourism, based primarily around all-inclusive resort holidays, has grown strongly in the Spanish-speaking Dominican Republic (often called the DR) since the 1980s, and is playing a significant part in its economic development. Visitors to this substantial island – which it shares with its neighbour Haiti – are attracted to strings of idyllic Caribbean beaches: clear blue sea, white sandy shores, palm-tree fringes and opportunities for water sports (including surfing, windsurfing and diving) and whale-watching excursions.

Venturing beyond the resorts independently, whilst requiring a bigger budget, is more than worth the effort. To escape the tropical heat of the coast, you can head up to the alpine interior of the Central Highlands, where there are excellent possibilities for hiking from attractive market-garden towns through sugar and fruit plantations to forested national parks and high mountain peaks (Pico Duarte is the highest in the Caribbean).

If your trip coincides with one of the carnivals or festivals held throughout the year, it will be especially memorable. Non-stop dancing, blasting music (particularly Merengue), dazzling costumes and gallons of rum make for a real air of communal extravagance. During quieter periods, you can savour the DR's rich artistic tradition. From ancient Taino rock paintings and brightly hued farmhouses, which stretch across the countryside, to the great colonial city of Santo Domingo (the first in the new world) you are definitely guaranteed a colourful stay.

VOL
DREAM PROJECT

The Dominican Republic Education and Mentoring Project is a non-profit organization, which provides the structure necessary to support philanthropic tourism. It tries to educate tourists in the realities of responsible tourism practices. Volunteers can work with underprivileged children in rural areas and small communities and are provided with accommodation, food and training. DREAM offers volunteers the opportunity to work in DREAM-sponsored schools.

Contact: Patricia Thorndike Suriel
Tel: 571 0497
Fax: 571 9551
Email: info@dominicandream.org
Web: www.dominicandream.org
Address: Plaza el Patio,
Calle Principal, Cabarete,
República Dominicana

TOUR+
IGUANA MAMA TOURS

Based in Cabarete, on the north coast, a town famous for windsurfing, Iguana Mama Tours market themselves as 'the leaders in outstanding adventures in the Dominican Republic' – mountain biking, hiking, river sports and ecological adventures. This is a different way of getting to know the country, moving around in small groups with expert guides in an environmentally sustainable way and respecting local communities. Ten per cent of the annual income goes to local causes.

Contact: Junior Perez
Tel: 571 0908
Fax: 571 0734
Email: info@iguanamama.com
Web: www.iguanamama.com
Address: Calle Principal 74, Cabarete, República Dominicana

HAITI
International dialling code +509

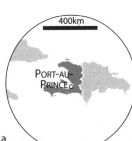

Voodoo and violence are probably the two things most people would associate with Haiti. In many ways, this sums up the conundrum for any prospective tourist: the country's vibrant culture makes it a fascinating place to visit, but only when it is safe to do so. Haiti has a unique but chaotic political history – the world's oldest black-led republic, and the only one established on the back of a successful rebellion by slaves (95 per cent of today's population is of African descent), it has endured colonization by both Spain and France, occupation by the US, and then decades of brutal dictatorship, unstable governance and civil unrest. This persists to the present day – the general security situation is poor, and the personal security of foreign nationals is also at risk (at the time of writing, official advice was for essential travel only).

Plagued with this turbulent past, and a series of natural disasters (made worse by serious deforestation), Haiti is, perhaps unsurprisingly, one of the poorest countries in the world. Voodoo holds an important cohesive role in society, as well as being of fundamental religious and spiritual significance. There is also a rich tradition of dance, music and folk art, delicious Caribbean-French fusion cooking and a very warm welcome. Its traditions are closer to Africa than other Caribbean countries. Its art is internationally acclaimed and its colonial architecture is a gem (for example, the Hotel Oloffson in Port-au-Prince, the setting for Graham Greene's *The Comedians*). Haiti, as a whole, is like Greene's prose – beautiful, tortured and mysterious.

HOST
BEYOND BORDERS

A Christian, US non-profit organization, which works with a Haitian organization, Limye Lavi (Light for Life) to offer small groups an opportunity to stay for a week with a host family and to experience how Haitians live. The experience is called 'transformational travel' and participants learn that hospitality does not depend on electricity or running water.

Contact: Jonathan Haggard
Tel: +1 610 277 5045
Fax: +1 610 277 5045 (call first)
Email: mail@beyondborders.net
Web: www.beyondborders.net
Address: PO Box 2132, Norristown, PA 19404, USA

JAMAICA
International dialling code +1876

Bigger, brasher, more intoxicating than other Caribbean islands, Jamaica lives on its wits and the talents of its people. It's gorgeous, too, and offers a contrast of landscapes – from idyllic beaches to the curious limestone Cockpit country and the glorious Blue Mountains (a great hike to the summit, best climbed at night to meet the dawn). 'Jamaica: we're more than a beach, we're a country' was an apt advertising slogan of the 1970s and one that's still relevant.

Kingston, the capital, has a sadly dangerous reputation (Jamaica has much poverty and infamous ghettos) but it doesn't have to be like that. The Bob Marley museum is in Kingston as is the National Gallery of Art (a fabulous collection that tells the story of the island's art history). Music is at the heart of the culture – Jamaica, of course, is the home of reggae, the great music form with a worldwide reputation, and its sounds are everywhere.

Jamaica has a long tourism tradition but latterly all-inclusives have come to dominate. The north coast, around Montego Bay, and Negril, originally cultivated by hippies, are the main tourist drags. Jamaica, however, is much more than the sum of its resorts. Apart from the cities of Kingston and Montego Bay, Jamaica has wonderful examples of Georgian architecture, such as at Falmouth, great plantation houses and the former homes of expatriates such as Noel Coward and Ian Fleming, who lived a sybaritic bohemian lifestyle. Jamaicans, too, take their pleasures seriously and open their lives and culture to tourists with great generosity.

ACCOM+
COCKPIT COUNTRY ADVENTURE TOURS

Cockpit Country is noted for its biodiversity and is an important Jamaican wilderness area. The company, based in Albert Town, Trelawny, offers a range of rural experiences including hiking and birdwatching, and guests stay with local bed and breakfast hosts. Goods and services are sourced locally. This gives local people a commitment to the company. Any profits are invested in community concerns. This is a low impact operation aiming to give visitors an environmental and social package that will genuinely educate them about the area and its culture. It's family friendly too.

Contact: Donavan Haughton/Hyacinth Record
Tel: 610 0818
Fax: 610 1676
Email: stea@cwjamaica.com
Web: www.stea.net
Address: #3 Grants Office Complex, Albert Town PO, Trelawny, Jamaica

ACCOM+
COUNTRYSTYLE COMMUNITY TOURISM

The two packages available are the 'Community Experience' vacation package and the 'Jamaica Home Experience' package; what you do depends on your special interests. This is your chance to become a Jamaican for a week and join in everything. Countrystyle is based in Mandeville, home town of Diana McIntyre-Pike, the charismatic pioneer of community tourism in Jamaica. It is a network of island-wide hotels, restaurants, visitor centres and so on. It is partnered with the Sustainable Communities Foundation through Tourism (SCF), which is a community tourism NGO with chapters all over the Caribbean and the USA. There is a real commitment to peace through tourism and its interactions.

Contact: Diana McIntyre-Pike/Barry Bonitto
Tel: 962 7758/538 4325/488 7207
Fax: 962 1461/962 0700
Email: Countrystyle@mail.infochan.com, countrystyletourism@yahoo.com
Web: www.countrystylecommunitytourism.com, www.uniquejamaica.com
Address: Countrystyle International Ltd, 62 Ward Avenue, PO Box 60, Mandeville, Manchester, Jamaica

ACCOM
HOTEL MOCKING BIRD HILL

Since its opening in 1993, this eco-friendly ten-roomed boutique hotel, run by two women, has operated on environmentally sensitive principles. The secluded hotel overlooks Port Antonio, the coast and the Blue Mountains. Activities include hiking, birdwatching, diving and so on. It contributes to the local economy – with operators, guides, attractions, restaurants – and works to conserve the environment. Its extensive mission statement says: 'We believe in ethical business practices and see our enterprise as a force for social change.'

Contact: Barbara Walker
Tel: 993 7267
Fax: 993 7133
Email: mockbrd@cwjamaica.com
Web: www.hotelmockingbirdhill.com
Address: PO Box 254, Port Antonio, Jamaica

ACCOM
ZION COUNTRY BEACH CABINS

Ten beachside cabins – throw a line and catch a fish – in Muirton, Portland, east Jamaica. The operation is rooted in the local people and suppliers. Low-budget and laid-back: if you believe in give-and-take, are eco-minded, then just lean back into the vibe and enjoy.

Contact: Free-I Fredericus Enneking
Tel: 993 0435
Email: info@zioncountry.com
Web: www.zioncountry.com
Address: Muirton Pen P.A (Long Road), Portland, Jamaica

THE AMERICAS CARIBBEAN

CENTRAL AMERICA

BELIZE
International dialling code +501

500km

BELMOPAN

Belize is a bit different from its Central America neighbours – it has had a relatively uneventful political past as a British colony, and is now independent. The official language is English but significant minorities have Spanish, Mayan and other dialects as their native tongues. It is also the only country in the region without a volcano or, coincidentally, a Pacific coastline. In fact, it will definitely strike the visitor as having a more 'Caribbean' feel, with much of its tourist activity centred around the many small islands, or 'cayes', dotted offshore towards its barrier reef, the longest in the western hemisphere. The cayes provide an excellent base from which to explore the habitats of marine life, both above and below water. However, there are jungle trekking adventures to be had inland as well, where you may well stumble onto one of the many ruined ancient Mayan archaeological sites that remain overgrown and

largely unexplored. Whether snorkelling after manatees and rays, or stalking jaguars in the forest, Belize is a real tropical paradise for nature lovers. The climate stays hot and humid throughout the year, but there is a brief dry season from February to May.

RAINFOREST
SAN IGNACIO RESORT HOTEL

About 1.5 hours drive west of Belize International Airport, San Ignacio (with 24 rooms) offers 'The only jungle in town' with its medicinal trails that focus on traditional uses of indigenous plants and trees. There is a unique protection/conservation programme for the green iguana, which was started in 1987. The room tariff ranges between £22.50/US$40 and £62/US$110, while the tours to the Medicinal Trails and the Iguana Project cost £5.50/US$10. The hotel opened in 1976, and is owned by four Belizean sisters (all the management are women). Although it's quite a modern, glitzy hotel, it is committed to conservation and education (school parties visit for free), contributes to the elderly of the community and supports women in sport.

Contact: Sandra Morris
Tel: 924 2034/824 2125
Fax: 824 2134
Email: mariam@sanignaciobelize.com, reservations@sanignaciobelize.com
Web: www.sanignaciobelize.com
Address: PO Box 33, San Ignacio Town, Belize

ACCOM+
TOLEDO ECOTOURISM ASSOCIATION (TEA)

Toledo is a small area, in the south of Belize, but with many different cultures. The project consists of eight village guesthouses, wholly owned by local people, in ten villages. Two more guesthouses are being developed. The money earned by the TEA helps fund health, education and community projects (for example, an ecopark) and to buy aids, such as wheelchairs, for the disabled. It also increases educational and employment opportunities for women. Visitors stay in the host communities and eat traditionally with families. The real thrust of the enterprise is to ensure that visitors see, participate and feel how the Mayan and Garifuna communities live. Various tours are available. Of TEA income, 20 per cent is returned to the host village for health and education. Constant efforts are made to raise awareness of environmental concerns.

Contact: Pablo Ack
Tel: 722 2096
Email: ttea@btl.net, pabloack@hotmail.com
Web: www.ecoclub.com/toledo
Address: PO box 157, Punta Gorda Town, Toledo District, Belize

COSTA RICA
International dialling code +506

Costa Rica is sometimes called the Switzerland of Central America – it has the region's longest history of political stability, its soundest economy and highest standard of living. During the past decades, it has also become somewhat of a Mecca for ecotourists – a well-

400km

SAN JOSÉ

deserved reputation. The country can boast more than a quarter of its territory as protected national park and forest reserve, and is justly proud of its enlightened environmental policy. Most of these conservation areas are easily accessible and provide some of the continent's best chances of encountering a bewildering array of exotic (and occasionally endangered) plant and animal species. For added variety, you can make trips to active volcanoes and hot springs, and then, of course, there isn't just one 'rich coast' to see (here decidedly ends the Swiss comparison). Both Costa Rica's Caribbean and Pacific shores are lined with beautiful beaches (turtle-nesting included).

Costa Rica is rich in local cultures, and you can feel the change as you move around – from the sabanero 'cowboy' culture of the northwest to the Afro-Caribbean feel of the east coast. Overwhelmingly, though, you will be impressed by the warmth and friendliness of the Costa Ricans, or 'ticos'.

ORG/AGRI
ACTUAR

ACTUAR is the acronym for the Costa Rican Community-based Rural Tourism Association and comprises more than 20 community-based enterprises. Their mission is to promote the environmental, social, cultural and economic sustainability of community-based rural tourism initiatives. Such tourism breaks down the barriers between the visitor and the essence of rural life; with your campesino hosts you meet local traditions and way of life.

Contact: Kyra Cruz
Tel: 228 5695
Fax: 228 5695
Email: actuar@racsa.co.cr
Web: www.actuarcostarica.com
Address: PO Box 719 –1260, Costa Rica

ACCOM+
ASOCIACION DE DESARROLLO SAN JOSE RURAL (ADESSARU) (member of ACTUAR)

The Rural San Jose Development Association, less than one hour's drive from San Jose, owns and runs a community-based rural tourism lodge, which has an environmental education centre. There is a sustainable development plan for the area that includes sustainable tourism initiatives. They can accommodate 30 visitors in their eight rooms with private bathrooms. This is an opportunity for guests to learn about green lifestyles and to see one in action.

Contact: Kyra Cruz:
Tel: 228 5695
Fax: 228 5695
Email: actuar@racsa.co.cr
Web: www.nacientespalmichal.com,
   www.actuarcostarica.com
Address: PO Box 719 –1260, Costa Rica

ORG/TOUR/DAY
ATEC - TALAMENCA·DISCOVERY

Founded in 1990 by local residents and based in Puerto Viejo de Talamanca, ATEC (Talamancan Association of Ecotourism and Conservation) is an educational/enabling agency aiming to foster cultural self-awareness and pride, to educate tourists about traditional lifestyles and values, and to foster ecologically appropriate local tourism. ATEC staff arrange hikes and tours, which are all locally guided. These include a range of trips to farms, jungle, indigenous people, boat trips and turtle watch. The costs are £11/US$20 to £40/US$70.

Contact: Alaine Berg
Tel: 750 0398
Fax: 750 0191
Email: atecmail@racsa.co.cr
Web: www.greencoast.com/atec.htm
Address: ATEC c/o Mel Baker, Apdo 05-7304,
Puerto Viejo de Talamanca, Limón, Costa Rica

RAINFOREST
BOSQUE ALEGRE (Feral Life Centre and Refuge)

This project is located in northern Costa Rica, three hours by road from San Jose. Visitors stay in a ranch in the rainforest overlooking a volcanic lagoon. Bosque Alegre organizes excursions to observe flora and fauna in the rainforest, including a visit to a butterfly farm and a solar

Contact: Lidieth Madrigal
Tel: 476 0194/382 8683
Email: lagunahule@yahoo.com
Web: www.redturs.org

dryer for medicinal plants. Other attractions include rivers, waterfalls, volcanic lagoons and the Poas volcano. Travellers will have the opportunity to fish, navigate by boat and camp in the rainforest. Within the host community, visitors have the chance to share the life of the local population in their daily activities of food production and conservation.

RAINFOREST +
CASA CALATEAS (member of ACTUAR)

This community-based rural tourism lodge, a four-hour drive from San Jose in the mountains, offers horse riding and walking trails in the forest to see campesino life. It's especially good for bird lovers. It is a member of ACTUAR (see above) and the Talamanca community-based ecotourism network. It is owned by a community farmers' association dedicated to the protection of the area's biodiversity and the environment.

Contact: Kyra Cruz
Tel: 228 5695
Fax: 228 5695
Email: actuar@racsa.co.cr
Web: www.actuarcostarica.com
Address: PO Box 719 –1260, Costa Rica

RAINFOREST +
CASACODE (member of ACTUAR)

Casacode's campesinos are happy to tell stories and create theatre about Talamanca for their guests. The protected area of Casacode hosts a great variety of amphibians and reptiles, as well as aquatic, nocturnal and day-time birds. Owned by St Michael's Conservation and Development Association, this rural tourism lodge is a member of ACTUAR. It was established in 1989 by small landholders to preserve the region's declining natural resources. The tourism income supports community development.

Contact: Kyra Cruz
Tel: 228 5695
Fax: 228 5695
Email: actuar@racsa.co.cr
Web: www.actuarcostarica.com
Address: PO Box 719 –1260, Costa Rica

RAINFOREST +
CERRO ESCONDIDO LODGE (member of ACTUAR)

This lodge, in the middle of a private wildlife reserve, is owned by the Ecologist Association of Paquera; it offers guests horse riding and walking tours with opportunities to swim in

THE AMERICAS CENTRAL

natural pools and visit a waterfall. Four cabins, with balconies and private bathrooms, can accommodate 16 people. The lodge is in the Karen Mogensen Reserve on the Nicoya Peninsula. All the income from the lodge goes into conservation and environmental education programmes.

Contact: Kyra Cruz
Tel: 228 5695
Fax: 228 5695
Email: actuar@racsa.co.cr
Web: www.actuarcostarica.com
Address: PO Box 719 –1260, Costa Rica

RAINFOREST
DANTICA LODGE & GALLERY

Near San Jose and in a primary cloud forest reserve, yet only 4km from the Panamerican Highway, this project, which opened in spring 2005, consists of a hotel and restaurant and art gallery. The latter specializes in Latin American artisan, indigenous art, design and jewellery. As far as possible the operation is run on green lines. The lodge is fully equipped

Contact: Joost Wilms
Tel: 352 2761
Email: info@dantica.com
Web: www.dantica.com
Address: PO Box 7-8055,
San Marcos de Tarrazu, San Jose, Costa Rica

and there is access to private primary forest with birdwatching trails (offering a chance to glimpse the Resplendent Quetzal – for some, the main reason for visiting the cloud forest or even Costa Rica). The accommodation charge is £67/US$120 a night for two inclusive of taxes and breakfast. Gallery prices go as high as £840/US$1500, of which half goes to the local communities producing the work sold.

ACCOM+
EL COPAL (member of ACTUAR)

A community-based rural tourism lodge, El Copal can accommodate up to 20 people in five rooms with bunk beds and shared bathrooms. This is where biodiversity and agri-ecotourism coexist. El Copal was established with the twin aims of conservation and generating alternative income for the farmers involved in the initiative. The area offers outstanding birdwatching, with 380 species identified, from toucans and trogons to pelicans and boobies.

Contact: Kyra Cruz
Tel: 228 5695
Fax: 228 5695
Email: actuar@racsa.co.cr
Web: www.actuarcostarica.com
Address: PO Box 719 –1260, Costa Rica

DAY
EL ENCANTO DE LA PIEDRA BLANCA (member of ACTUAR)

The Charm of the White Mountain is owned by the Association for the Conservation and Development of Escazu Mountains. An unusual experience, this is a rural tour on the urban fringe, near San Jose. There are half- and full-day tours centred on the Escazu mountains. Since 1985 the community of San Antonio has been resisting attempts by the nearby city to acquire its mountains for residential housing.

Contact: Kyra Cruz
Tel: 228 5695
Fax: 228 5695
Email: actuar@racsa.co.cr
Web: www.actuarcostarica.com
Address: PO Box 719 –1260, Costa Rica

ACCOM+/DAY/VOL
EL YUE AGRO-ECO FARM & LODGE (member of ACTUAR)

El Yue is a women's, community-based rural tourism initiative. A distinctive feature is its garden of medicinal plants. El Yue is another example of local people wanting to improve their position by diversifying, but without endangering their environment. You can stay there and take a two-day tour.

Contact: Kyra Cruz
Tel: 228 5695
Fax: 228 5695
Email: actuar@racsa.co.cr
Web: www.actuarcostarica.com
Address: PO Box 719 –1260, Costa Rica

HOST+/AGRI
FINCA SONADOR - LONGO MAI

The land of Finca Sonador, 160km from San Jose, is owned by a chain of European cooperatives. This award winning initiative believes that tourism should remain a valuable economic diversification rather than the be-all and end-all of existence. Visitors stay with local families and spend time with them.

Contact: Roland Spendlingwimmer
Tel: 771 4239
Fax: 771 4239
Email: rolspendling@gmx.net
Web: www.sonador.info/FincaSonador-LongoMai
Address: 292-8000, San Isidro P.Z., Costa Rica

Interestingly they have their own phrase, 'project tourism', which means that guests can choose from a menu of activities, including language classses; Spanish dancing; hikes in the forest; or learning about local agriculture. The Finca began life as a refugee project in 1978. Its daily rate is £4/US$7 per day, all of which goes to the host family.

ACCOM+
ISLA DE CHIRA LODGE (member of ACTUAR)

A community-based rural tourism lodge in the Gulf of Nicoya owned by the Association of the Women of Chira Island. It was established in 2000 with the aim of generating alternative income sources for the island's fisherwomen and to foster the conservation and sustainable use of the island's natural resources. Tours of the island – the mangroves are an important

Contact: Kyra Cruz
Tel: 228 5695
Fax: 228 5695
Email: actuar@racsa.co.cr
Web: www.actuarcostarica.com
Address: PO Box 719 –1260, Costa Rica

resource – are also on offer and the comfortable lodges (cabin with two rooms each with a double and two single beds) also have private bathrooms. There's delicious local food.

ACCOM+/AGRI/VOL
JOVENES AGRO ECOLOGISTA DE LA ZONA NORTE (JAZON)

JAZON works with the young people of small farming families in the north region of Costa Rica, offering accommodation with full board and tours. Located in a rural, mountainous national park, the idea of the project is to provide the tourist with an innovative experience of the local culture. The tour provides an insight on agricultural production, and

Contact: Christian Vea Solis
Tel: 460 5106/302 3765/354 6047
Fax: 460 5106
Email: christian@costaricaruraltours.com,
   info@costaricaruraltours.com
Web: www.costaricaruraltours.com

also offers horse riding, trekking and boat tours. The objective of the project is to generate alternatives for young people, thereby stopping migration from the region. There is also a voluntary programme ('Vacations with Farmer Families') – see their website for details.

RAINFOREST+
KEKOLDI INDIGENOUS RESERVE (member of ACTUAR)

This community-based rural tourism lodge is owned by the Asociacion Indigena Kekoldi Wak Ka Koneke (Kekoldi's Keepers) in the Talamanca mountains. It offers a special glimpse of the Bribri and Cabecar culture. Tourism helps the community acquire more land for conservation and reforestation. Local guides introduce visitors to the flora and fauna, handicrafts and so on.

Contact: Kyra Cruz
Tel: 228 5695
Fax: 228 5695
Email: actuar@racsa.co.cr
Web: www.actuarcostarica.com
Address: PO Box 719 –1260, Costa Rica

RAINFOREST+
LA LAGUNA DEL LAGARTO LODGE

This is a family-owned Lodge, 150km from San Jose near the Nicaraguan border. It is surrounded by 500 hectares of tropical virgin forest where you can explore the ecosystem with guides. The lodge, which has 20 double rooms (hot water and ceiling fans), offers traditional meals cooked with products from the community farm, canoeing, hiking, horseback riding and trips on the river.

The lodge supports the local community in many ways. Their ambition is to be a leading ecolodge in Costa Rica.

Contact: Kurt Schmack
Tel: 2898 163
Fax: 2895 295
Email: lagarto@racsa.co.cr
Web: www.lagarto-lodge-costa-rica.com
Address: 995-1007 San José, Costa Rica

RAINFOREST+
LOS CAMPESINOS (member of ACTUAR)

This is a rural tourism lodge offering tours (forest, waterfall and organic farms), horse riding and hiking. It is owned by the Asociacion Productores de Vainilla (Vanilla Producers Association) and can accommodate six people in two cabins with balconies and private bathrooms. There's also a canopy walkway. Originally the Association set out to try to protect their environment but a hurricane and the poor quality of the soil pushed the community to work together to generate alternative income – through tourism.

Contact: Kyra Cruz
Tel: 228 5695
Fax: 228 5695
Email: actuar@racsa.co.cr
Web: www.actuarcostarica.com
Address: PO Box 719 –1260, Costa Rica

ACCOM+/AGRI
MONTANA VERDE (member of ACTUAR)

This enterprise, owned by the Asociacion Montana Verde (Green Mountain Association), is a community-based rural tourism lodge and is a member of ACTUAR. It gives visitors the chance to meet people who live in harmony with their surroundings and, if you wish, to join them in their projects including organic gardening, research and reforestation.

Contact: Kyra Cruz
Tel: 228 5695
Fax: 228 5695
Email: actuar@racsa.co.cr
Web: www.actuarcostarica.com
Address: PO Box 719 –1260, Costa Rica

RAINFOREST+
STIBRAWPA CASA DE LAS MUJERES (member of ACTUAR)

On the border between Costa Rica and Panama, you reach Yorkin with a dug out canoe, just one hour from Bambu. In 1985 the local women came together to set up Stibrawpa (an association of craftswomen) in order to diversify their means of production and to preserve their culture alongside the creation of alternative income sources. With additional income from tourism, the Bribri people of Yorkin can take their children to school. The women are proud to share their Bribri culture. In the small town a maximum of 20 people can stay in Bribri-style lodgings with shared bathrooms.

Contact: Kyra Cruz
Tel: 228 5695
Fax: 228 5695
Email: actuar@racsa.co.cr
Web: www.actuarcostarica.com
Address: PO Box 719 –1260, Costa Rica

RAINFOREST+/VOL
TESORO VERDE (member of ACTUAR)

This is a community-based rural tourism lodge on the Osa Peninsula. It is associated with an environmental school. A few decades ago local people had the dream of increasing their self-sufficiency and yet remaining in harmony with their surroundings – their own reserve and the Corcovado National Park. On offer is accommodation and a three- or four-day tour package.

Contact: Kyra Cruz
Tel: 228 5695
Fax: 228 5695
Email: actuar@racsa.co.cr
Web: www.actuarcostarica.com
Address: PO Box 719 –1260, Costa Rica

GUATEMALA
International dialling code +502

Guatemala has become a popular and inexpensive place to learn Spanish, and many visitors choose to take in a few weeks' homestay study during their travels. Small but geographically diverse, Guatemala's cool mountainous highlands graduate into the tropical jungle lowland north of the Pacific coastline. This spectacular scenery envelops active volcanoes and ancient Mayan ruins, lush rainforest with abundant wildlife and the stunning Lake Atitlán to explore. Guatemala is also rich culturally, with an indigenous population of over 40 per cent, much higher than elsewhere in the region. You can encounter this in numerous native dialects, the fusion of Mayan and Catholic religious practices, and traditional dress and handicrafts, perhaps displayed at a colourful town market or fiesta. Guatemala also has year-round good weather, hence its nickname 'the Land of Eternal Spring', although the dry season is November–April. Almost a decade of civil peace has made it a must-see destination for many travellers, but unfortunately it has become less safe to visit recently.

Tourists should take a cautious and vigilant approach to travel, as foreigners can be targets for armed robberies and muggings, even in much-visited areas. Travelling at night is inadvisable, and do take great care if travelling unaccompanied or by public bus. Also, always remember to ask permission before photographing local people, as this has caused problems in the past. But bring extra film along too, as you will really want to capture this beautiful country.

RAINFOREST+
ASSOCIATION AK'TENAMIT

This is an NGO that runs two ecotourism projects 30 minutes by motorboat from Livingston, in the heart of the Guatemalan rainforest close to the Caribbean, and inside the Rio Dulce national park. Staying in comfortable guesthouses in a Mayan village, visitors can enjoy guided tours in the rainforest, traditional dance and music, handicrafts made by local Mayan women and

Contact: Guillermo Perez
Tel: 254 1560/254 3346/908 3392
Fax: 254 1560/254 3346
Email: gperez@aktenamit.org/ ecoturismo@aktenamit.org
Web: www.aktenamit.org
Address: 11 Avenida "A" 9-39 zona 2, Guatemala

traditional pre-Columbian religious ceremonies. Or try self-guided trails through the jungle, discovering caves, lagoons, waterfalls, rivers and a rich diversity of flora and fauna.

ACCOM+
AVENTURA MAYA K'ICHE

Aventura Maya K'Iche is an umbrella organization covering a range of Mayan community groups, from musicians to host families, in San Miguel Totonicapan in the western highlands. They 'present visitors with a different experience based on sharing with the host community and

Contact: Carlos Molina
Tel: 7766 1575
Cellular: 5998 8648
Fax: 7766 1575
Email: aventuramayakiche@yahoo.com, kiche78@hotmail.com
Web: www.larutamayaonline.com/aventura
Address: 7a. avenida 1-26 zona 1 Totonicapán, Guatemala

its ancestral traditions'. The community is especially noted for handicrafts, music and dance. Tourists stay in a guesthouse or with local families on a bed and breakfast basis, and are spread around the community to ensure that the economic benefits are widespread. Real efforts are made to raise the profile of local women in the tourism context.

TOUR
CAYAYA BIRDING

This is a specialist birdwatching operator. Tours can start from any main centre, and can also include culture, nature and archaeological guiding. For lodging, transport, food and guiding they cooperate with indigenous communities, conservationist NGOs

Contact: Claudis Avendano
Tel: 5308 5160/5906 6479
Fax: 2433 0544
Email: info@cayaya-birding.com
Web: www.cayaya-birding.com
Address: Knut Eisermann, PO Box 98 Periferico, Guatemala

and other enterprises. A guiding principle is that local people will value the environment more and conserve it if they see it as something that attracts visitors and is therefore economically valuable. Local people receive ten per cent tips for the services provided.

RAINFOREST+/AGRI
COMUNIDAD 'NUEVA ALIANZA'

This collective of 40 families owns a fair trade organic coffee and macadamia nut plantation. In 2005 it opened an eco-lodge which accommodates 25 people and is managed and run by the community's women's collective. On offer are tours of the plantation with an opportunity to learn about the work of the growers and about the medicinal and edible herbs and plants of the tropical forest. Every person has an equal stake in the entire operation and all profits are equally shared. As well as the drive to be fully organic they are also involved in sustainable energy projects including a UN-funded mini-hydroelectric plant. Transport is arranged from Cuatro Caminos.

Contact: Javier Jiménez Recinos
Tel: 5979 8241/5819 2282 (English speaker)
Email: info@alianza.org
Web: www.comunidadnuevaalianza.org
Address: El Palmar, Quetzaltenango, Guatemala

ACCOM+
ECO HOTEL UXLABIL - ATITLAN

Lake Atitlan offers you an expanse of crystal clear water and three volcanoes. If you want to get away from it all, stay in an environmentally friendly hotel, meet local people and experience their weaving and painting on a one-to-one basis, eat both local and international cooking, and stay within reach of a jacuzzi – this is for you.

Contact: Elizabeth Echeverría
Tel: 2366 9555
Fax: 2366 9555 ext 116
Email: atitlan@uxlabil.com
Web: www.uxlabil.com
Address: 11 calle y 15 Avenida Final,
12-53 zona 10 Oakland, Edificio Uxlabil,
CP. 01010, Guatemala

RAINFOREST+
ECOMAYA

This is a project in the Maya Biosphere Reserve in El Peten, the northernmost province of Guatemala. The closest town is Flores City. Ecomaya offers trekking and horseback expeditions in the jungle. Transportation can also be by 4WD or motorboat. There is camping in the jungle accompanied by local guides. Among the many tourist attractions in the area is the archaeological site of El Mirador, the largest city in the Mayan world, containing the El Tigre pyramid. The reserve is also rich in animal and bird life, including crocodiles, bats and the endangered scarlet macaw. Ecomaya is an active partner in local community initiatives.

Tel: 926 3202
Fax: 926 3202
Email: ecomaya@guate.net
Web: www.ecomaya.com
Address: Calle Centroamerica, Ciudada Flores,
Peten, 17001, Guatemala

ACCOM
HOTEL DOS LUNAS

A comfortable hotel located less than a kilometre south of La Aurora International Airport in Guatemala City, in a safe residential area. The hotel is recommended by several travel guides and has various amenities including free internet access, tourist information, a travel agency and a free airport shuttle. It's very much concerned with the conservation of natural and cultural resources. Its owner, Lorena Artola, coordinated the research and

Tel: 334 5264
Fax: 334 5264
Email: doslunas@itelgua.com
Web: www.xelapages.com/doslunas

edited Mosaic of Guatemala, the first magazine about ecotourism in Guatemala. In 2001, she was a co-founder of a non-profit organization called Red de Turismo Sostenible de Guatemala. Its aim is to promote and market alternative tourism products of small and micro enterprises.

ACCOM
LA CASA DE DON DAVID

This hotel, restaurant and tour business is to be found in the village of El Remate, on a main road about 15 minutes before Tikal National Park. It is privately owned and run and its main thrust comes from a strong belief in sustainability although, interestingly, they see the need

Contact: Yohana Rodas
Tel: 7928 8469
Email: info@lacasadedondavid.com
Web: www.lacasadedondavid.com
Address: 14 El Remate, Flores Peten, Guatemala

coming for controlled sustainable tourism with an emphasis on local education. They have 15 rooms, with a total of 39 beds. The charges range from £18–31/US$32–56 for a double with breakfast. There is easy bus access from Flores Airport 28km away.

ORG/ACCOM/DAY
PACAYA VOLCANO NATIONAL PARK

The Pacaya is an active volcano with constant gas emissions. Visitors can climb up to the crater via a cold lava path and then climb down to the Calderas lagoon set in a volcanic crater, as well as visit various lava caves, watching the gas emissions. The area also offers many activities including horse riding tours,

Contact: Rosario H. Munoz
Tel: 416 5829/471 268
Fax: 471 8351
Email: rosariohm@terra.com, rhaydee@terra.com, vpacaya@terra.com
Address: 4a Avenida 0-91, Canton Las Flores, San Vicente Pacaya, Escuintla, Guatemala

mountain trekking and cockleboat and bike tours around the lagoon. Accommodation is available in the area, and visitors can participate in religious and cultural events, or learn about life in the community by taking part in coffee sowing and harvesting. This enterprise was established to support community initiatives.

ACCOM/DAY
THE PORTAL TO THE MAYAN WORLD

This community-based tourism corridor in the municipality of Chisec in the foothills of the Guatemalan highlands is an ideal tourist destination since it combines natural, cultural and archaeo-

Tel: 979 7517
Email: puertaalmundomaya@yahoo.com
Web: www.puertaalmundomaya.com
Address: Municipality of Chisec, Alta Verapaz, Guatemala

logical attractions. In Sepalau an interpretive trail leads the visitor to the Sepalau lagoons, crystalline lakes surrounded by karst hills, covered by rainforest full of wildlife. In Bombil Pek, expert guides use specialized mountain-climbing equipment to lead visitors to see pre-Mayan drawings in a mystical cave. Candelaria contains Central America's longest potholing lap, where a subterranean river winds through enormous caverns lit by natural windows. Along the Passion River is the archaeological site of Cancuen, where archaeologists are excavating one of the largest palaces in the Mayan world.

HONDURAS
International dialling code +504

As the legend goes, Columbus named Honduras when finding shelter from sea-storms in its calming waters. These days, its Caribbean coastline is one of the main tourist draws, as visitors gravitate to enjoy the laid back atmosphere of its fishing villages and coconut islands. The Bay Islands, in particular, are great for reef diving, and are among the world's cheapest places to learn this from scratch (using reputable operators only). Away from the coast, Honduras is practically all mountainous, making for great hiking country, featuring old mining settlements, cloud forest reserves and the fantastic Mayan ruin of Copán, famed for its exquisite carvings. If you really want to get away from it all, the barely inhabited swampy jungle region of the Mosquito Coast region is a true wilderness.

On your travels, you will meet landscapes of coffee and banana planta-tions, crops vital to the Honduran economy. The country cannot escape its legacy as the first 'banana republic', with its more recent economic and polit-ical history dominated by foreign fruit interests, to its general detriment. The devastation wreaked by Hurricane Mitch in 1998 is also a painful memory.

Attacks on tourists do sometimes occur, and public buses are prone to hold-ups and accidents. However, if you do take care there is no reason not to follow in Columbus' footsteps: go, explore and find your own calm waters in this beautiful country.

DAY
CALENTURA & GUALMORETO FOUNDATION

The Foundation's main purpose is to conserve the national rainforest park and the wildlife refuge in cooperation with the indigenous peoples of the area. There are three programmes: health and environmental education, agroforestry and natural resources management. What is on offer is the natural beauty of the area accessed through the agency of a company called Ecotours. The Foundation has had financial difficulties but once it is back on a sounder financial footing will be more actively involved with accommodation and tours.

Contact: Hector Avila
Tel: 434 3294
Fax: 434 4294
Email: Fucagua@yahoo.com
Address: Barrio Buenos aires una cuadra de la Cruz del Calvario, Trujillo, Colon, Honduras

DAY
IGUANA RESEARCH & BREEDING STATION

Located in the municipality of Utila, the project is dedicated to the conservation of the Utila iguana. It's only ten minutes walk from Utila fire station and can also be reached by car and bicycle. Small groups of visitors can tour the centre for a fee of £1.25/US$2.20 and gain an introduction to the local ecosystems. Tours of the island's natural site can be arranged. All the income goes to the conservation project. Maybe this is not a holiday per se but it would make a fascinating visit if you were in the area.

Contact: Dr Lutz Dirksen
Cellular: 373 3778
Email: station@utila-iguana.de
Web: www.utila-iguana.de
Address: Barrio Jerico, Utila, Islas de la Bahia, Honduras

ORG
RED DE DESAROLLO SOSTENIBLE (RDS-HN)

Born of an alliance between academia, NGOs and the RDS-HN, the operational premise here is the use of a dedicated website to promote initiatives towards Honduran sustainable tourism. It is hoped that the site will become an information gateway for anyone studying the subject or wishing to exchange information on it. To this virtual community they hope to add radio programmes and documentary videos.

Contact: Raquel Isaula
Tel: 235 4141
Fax: 235 5721
Email: raquel@rds.org.hn
Web: www.rds.org.hn, www.migracion-remesas.org.hn

ORG/ACCOM/DAY
RIO PLATANO BIOSPHERE RESERVE (RPBR)

The Reserve offers a range of experiences: a sandy coast with its sea turtle protection project, lowland tropical forests and a watery world of inland lagoons and rivers where all travel is by boat or on foot. The whole project is a partnership between indigenous Miskito, Pech and Garifuna peoples and national and international organizations. All the tourism-related activities and enterprises are eco-conscious and locally owned and operated. Since its inception the prevailing doctrine has been best summed up as a marriage of sustainable resource with community development goals. A guidebook is available.

Contact: Arden Anderson
Tel: +970 642 4454
Fax: +970 642 4425
Email: Arden_Anderson@co.blm.gov
Web: www.planeta.com/planeta/97/0597mosquitia.html
Address: Arden Anderson, BLM – Gunnison Field Office, 216 N. Colorado St, Gunnison, CO 81230, USA

MEXICO
International dialling code +52

This vast country can cater for every tourist taste under the sun. Whilst it can take some time to explore fully just the principal areas of attraction, you will be richly rewarded if you venture off the beaten track. This is made particularly easy by the country's extensive, sophisticated and reliable network of buses (there are different classes depending on the level of adventure you're after as well!). Wherever you do go, though, you will encounter the fascinating mix of three cultures that seems to define the place: its indigenous heritage – including spectacular ancient ruins and a wealth of native languages and traditions – the legacy of the Spanish colonial period, including beautifully preserved cities and a very strong sense of the Catholic, reflected in ornate church design, and the modern, bustling, industrialized Mexico, home to one of the world's megalopolises, and constantly dealing with its complex social and economic interrelationship with its rich northern neighbour. However, throughout its often turbulent political history, Mexico has maintained a strong tradition in art and crafts, music, literature and, more recently, film. The country's beauty lies truly in its diversity, not just culturally, but also geographically, biologically – where it is ranked top three in the world – and even climatically (though the wet season, where it does occur, is generally in summer). Whatever you are looking for, Mexico can guarantee to deliver it in spades.

BUDGET/SCHOOL
ALBERGUE- CAMPEMENTO KENNEDY - TATEJE

This hostel, near Contepec, offers dormitory-style living in three rooms each accommodating 12 people in bunk beds. There's lots of room to play (pack the frisbee!); it is aimed at young people with its several pre-university programmes of study including one on the principles of ecotourism. The JFK Institute opened this project.

Contact: Gerardo Osornio
Tel: 55 5389 4764
Fax: 55 5534 8532
Email: gosornio58@yahoo.com,
   galtamirano58@yahoo.com.mx
Address: López Mateos No. 4 Pueblo Nuevo
   Contepec, Mich. CP 61020, México

ACCOM+/SCHOOL
HOTEL MAR DE JADE

On the Pacific Ocean, about an hour and a half north of Puerto Vallarta, this project has grown from huts in 1983 to today's elegant (as self-described) accommodation for up to 80 guests. You can have the usual kind of beach/marine-based vacation but the real speciality of Mar de Jade is its

Contact: Laura del Valle
USA Tel: +1 800 257 0532
Email: info@mardejade.com
Web: www.mardejade.com

peace and quiet. It is a great place for yoga, meditation and retreats. It's also possible to stay three weeks and learn Spanish. The operation finances and runs a primary care community clinic and a child care programme – and more besides. It's not cheap (£110–140/US$200–250 per night with meals) but you see where the money is going.

NICARAGUA

International dialling code +505

500km

MANAGUA

Geographically the largest country in Central America, Nicaragua has featured far more in the foreign psyche as a bloody war zone than as a potential holiday hotspot. Although both the human and physical damage from its notorious 'civil' conflict in the 1970s/80s is still evident today, to think of the country only in this regard is a great injustice, both to Nicaragua and yourself. It is a less well-known tourist destination not because it has little to offer, but because its cultural and natural wealth has been largely ignored. Take another look, and you will be well rewarded.

Nicaragua's tourism infrastructure is far less developed than that of neighbouring Costa Rica, but this heightens the sense of adventure. A word of warning, though: road safety conditions are poor, so keep this in mind when planning each journey. And there are several worth making – across beautiful volcanic landscapes, to colonial cities steeped in history, to sandy beaches with stunning backdrops at sunset, and to the country's jewel, Lake Nicaragua. Amongst the world's largest freshwater lakes, its captivating islets and archipelagos, teeming with wildlife, are just waiting to be explored.

This is an excellent country for walking, particularly around volcanoes, but it is always best to go with a guide – mainly for reasons of safety, but also purely for the chat. Nicaraguans are great conversationalists, guaranteed to bring the country even more to life.

DAY/ACCOM
COMMUNITY TOURS

'Our people, culture and nature' – their own words are a fair summary. Five short tours – a few hours or a half-day – around the community of Ostional, on the south coast of the Nicaraguan Pacific, take in a look at local culture and agriculture, flora and fauna, and fishing. Plans are being finalized for stays with a family or in self-catering accommodation. Sounds good if you want to learn how Nicaraguan families live. Accommodation is also available.

Contact: Mariela Cerda
Tel: 8836 753
Fax: 5682 465
Email: communitytours@yahoo.es
Web: www.geocities.com/communitytours
Address: Apartado Postal 1762, Managua,
De la cabañita – c al norte, Nicaragua

RAINFOREST+/HOST
FINCA ESPERANZA VERDE

Located in the beautiful mountains of San Ramon, in the state of Matagalpa, this prizewinning finca can accommodate a maximum of 26 people but you can also stay with local families. Visitors are guided by locals on horseback or can hike in the rainforest. The supporting NGO network facilitates the sale of almost all the campesinos' organically farmed coffee to an eco-oriented roaster in the US, at well above the world price. The earnings have improved local education and utilities and ten per cent of ecotours' revenue also goes on local projects.

Contact: Yelba Valenzuela
Tel: +11 505 772-5003
USA tel: 919 489 1656
Fax: 919 493 5908
Email: herma@ibw.com.ni,
    info@durham-sanramon.org
Web: www.fincaesperanza-verde.org,
    www.durham-sanramon.org
Address: Apartado 28, Matagalpa, Nicaragua
USA address: 1320 Shepherd St., Durham,
    NC 27707, USA

DAY
LANDCRUISER TOURS

This two-person company (one incomer plus one local student of sustainable tourism), based in Granada, offers tours that stress the traditions and culture of Nicaragua with commentaries on history, politics and social issues. They are also developing Foreign Retirement Services, a combination of tours and presentations for Europeans and Anglo-

Contact: Lawrence Goodlive
Tel: 895 5244
Email: legoodlive@att.net
Web: www.landcruisertours.com
Address: 101 Callejon Central America,
    Granada, Nicaragua

Americans who are thinking of living in or retiring to Nicaragua. A daily tour costs about £27.50/US$49 per person with a maximum of six people per tour. Most of the income generated is reinvested in the community, which supports local companies and projects that aim to protect the environment.

ACCOM+
SELVA

This is an environmental NGO for the development of ecotourism to benefit local people and reforestation (done with the communities). It has built up a collective women's group, and campaigns through radio to support local rights. It can arrange accommodation for visitors in, for example, typical 'ranchos', near the Tezoatega ecological park for just £5.50/US$10 a night.

Contact: Maritza Carillo/Vidal Andino
Tel: 6289 162/8646 711/8849 156
Email: infocomap@apcomanejo.com,
    selvanic@hotmail.com
Address: Apartado postal 91 El Viejo,
    Departamento de Chinandega, Nicaragua

THE AMERICAS CENTRAL

NORTH AMERICA

HAWAI'I

400km

HONOLULU

Although Hawai'i is primarily a traditional sun, sea and sand vacation paradise, the high rise beach front hotel developments are concentrated in a few areas, in particular in Honolulu on Oahu island, and the west coast of Maui. Away from those concentrations are empty landscapes where visitors can go hiking in forests, among volcanic mountains and waterfalls. There are near-deserted beaches on The Big Island, where the rainy climate deters most '3-S' vacationers. As well as youth hostels and budget hotels, there are many private homes offering B&B, which generally have excellent facilities. Public transportation is almost non-existent apart from on Oahu, but bicycles can be rented easily and fairly inexpensively elsewhere. However, for all but the fittest cyclists, many of the steep mountainous coastal roads are inaccessible except by car. Fortunately, here as elsewhere in the US, car rental is relatively inexpensive. (NB: under-25s cannot hire cars anywhere in the USA.) Hawai'i is where East meets West, and many independent travellers visit Hawai'i to take courses in various New Age therapies and spiritualities, and to experience the native Kahuna culture. As elsewhere in the USA, this selling of native culture to visitors is controversial.

ACCOM
HANA MAUI BOTANICAL GARDENS

The project consists of a ten-acre botanical garden (self-guided with a map, £1.70/US$3 admission with free parking) on Maui, together with two studios near the Volcano National Park, which are let at £84/US$150 per night for two people reducing to £56/US$100 for two or more nights, or you can stay six and get the seventh free. The botanical stress is on the removal of non-native invasive species and the fostering of local ones.

Contact: JoLoyce Kaia
Tel: 808 248 7725
Fax: 808 248 7725
Email: JoLoyce@aol.com
Web: www.ecoclub.com/hanamaui
Address: PO Box 404, Hana, Maui, Hawai'i 96713, USA

ORG/ACCOM/DAY
THE NATIVE HAWAIIAN HOSPITALITY ASSOCIATION

The Native Hawaiian Hospitality Association (NaHHA) is a private, non-profit corporation founded in 1997 whose main purpose has been to restore an authentic spirit of aloha and Hawaiian culture to the planning, advertising and tourist attractions that are at the core of the visitor industry. NaHHA is committed to promoting Native approaches to tourism, including the creation of their own destiny in Hawai'i's dominant economic industry. NaHHA believes it is crucial to return a 'Hawaiian sense of place' to the many destination properties through which visitors experience our island home.

Tel: General Enquires: 808 441 1404
Programme Enquiries: 808 441 1348
Email: information@nahha.com
Web: www.nahha.com
Address: The Native Hawaiian Hospitality Association, 900 Fort Street Mall, Suite 1300, Honolulu, HI 96813, USA

ACCOM/DIS
VOLCANO GUEST HOUSE

This is a family-owned and operated enterprise of bed and breakfast housekeeping cottages and apartments located five minutes from the Hawai'i Volcanoes National Park. It is both child- and wheelchair-friendly. The prices range between £48/US$85 and £60/US$105 per night for two people. This is an extremely green operation.

Contact: Bonnie Goodell or Alan Miller
Tel: 866 886 5226
Fax: 808 985 7056
Email: innkeeper@volcanoguesthouse.com
Web: www.volcanoguesthouse.com
Address: PO Box 6, Volcano HI 96785-0006, USA

USA
International dialling code +1

The USA is one of the easiest countries to travel around independently. Travel and accommodation are relatively cheap, and it is not always necessary to book well in advance. There is no tourism high season as such – with such a vast area encompassing almost every kind of terrain and climate, it is always the ideal time to visit at least one region. In addition to visiting the great cities and National Parks, and obvious attractions such as Disneyland and Universal Studios, visitors can also take tours on Native American Reservations, organized by the residents themselves, with profits staying on the reservations. As well as seeing the spectacular landscapes, in particular Monument Valley on the Navajo Reservation and the mesa-top Hopi pueblos, visitors can participate in ceremonies such as Sweat Lodges and even Vision Quests. However, this is the subject of heated controversy among Native Americans, some of whom feel strongly that this is commodifying and degrading their culture. There are also gambling casinos (alcohol-free) on some reservations, which although very profitable are likewise controversial. Some reservations, such as the Apache Reservation in Arizona, have facilities for more traditional outdoor vacation activities such as horse riding and fishing.

TOUR
GO NATIVE AMERICA

Go Native offers 10- to 14-day trips into Native American traditional tribal homelands and reservations. All the guiding is done by Native Americans, whose role in the company is earmarked for expansion. The company aims to make fairly traded tourism into the standard for the Northern Plains, to raise visitor awareness of relevant issues, and to run a green operation. After your arrival in a designated US city everything is then down to the company. The price range is £840–1060/US$1500–1900.

Contact: Sarah Chapman
Tel: 01924 840111
Email:info@gonativeamerica.com
Web: www.gonativeamerica.com
USA address: 821 N 27th St, no. 120, Billings, MT 59101, USA
UK address: 2nd Floor, 145–157 St John Street, London EC1V 4PY, UK

ORG
INDIAN COUNTRY TOURISM

Indian Country Tourism is operated by Medicine Root, Inc. in Louisville, Colorado. Its purpose is to promote and support Native destinations by arranging and booking tours to locations listed on its web where you can search by state and/or tribe. From the displayed listing you can select places, native-owned businesses and tours that match your interest. For example, Indigenous Landscape Tours is headquartered in Manderson, South Dakota, near the middle of the Pine Ridge Indian Reservation. Manderson is just a few miles from historic Wounded Knee. The Badlands National Park is a short drive from Manderson. The host and guide is Richard Sherman, an ecologist; though a member of the Oglala Lakota Nation on the Pine Ridge Reservation, Richard is a direct descendent of Makes the Song, the grandfather of Crazy Horse.

Contact: Ben Sherman or Dana EchoHawk
Tel: +303 661 9819
Fax: +303 664 5139
Email: info@indiancountrytourism.com
Web: www.indiancountrytourism.com
Address: PO Box 788, Louisville, Colorado 80027, USA

THE AMERICAS NORTH

SOUTH AMERICA

ORG
REDTURS

REDTURS is a network of communities, institutions, technical skills and resources devoted to supporting the sustainable development of tourism, seeking compatibility between the objectives of economic efficiency, social equity and cultural identity. Its mission is to shape and strengthen networks of community-based tourism, at the national and regional level, throughout Latin America. Their website supplies tourists, tour operators, public and private institutions with comprehensive and updated information about such community destinations.

Email: info@redturs.org
Web: www.redturs.org

BOLIVIA

International dialling code +591

Bolivia is a landlocked country with dramatic extremes in climate, cultures and natural environments. Between declaring independence from Spain in 1825 and the civil revolution in 1952 Bolivia claims an astonishing record of more than one military coup per year. Che Gevara's attempt to establish a Bolivian workers' guerrilla group ended with his assassination there in 1967. A descendent European elite rule over a majority of politically disengaged indigenous Aymará and Quencha peoples in a country with 33 languages. Political stability has recently encouraged tourism although a limited infrastructure and challenging terrain mean much of it remains untapped by tourists. La Paz, the highest capital in the world, is a focal point with its Spanish architecture on the cold, dry, barren highland altiplano plateau, where herds of llamas, a local source of meat, can be seen. Other popular attractions include the annual carnival between February and March and Silver Mountain at Potosi. Lake Titicaca, the world highest navigable lake, is a popular spot from which trekkers, climbers and mountain bikers can explore the Andes with its ice-capped mountains reaching over 6000 metres.

Over half of the country's population are engaged in farming in the subtropical eastern valleys growing cash crops such as coffee and coca, which supports the decreasing yet substantial and illegal trade in cocaine. To the northeast is the vast Amazonian lowland wilderness with its bird life, rivers and amazing pink freshwater dolphin.

ACCOM+
AGUA BLANCA LODGE

If you are fit and well-prepared for altitude you will find a challenge trekking and mountaineering in this area, the protect area of Apolobamba, a 12-hour journey from La Paz. There is the Andean landscape, with archaeological sites and goldmines, to explore. Or, you could just revel in the flora and fauna. Whichever you opt for you will have the simple life (lodging and food) among the local population. This is a cocktail of the eco- with the ethno- with more than a dash of adventure. The lodge was created by community members who work together to provide services.

Contact: Juan Carlos Gomez
Tel: 2 413 432
Fax: 2 413 432
Email: apolobambapea@hotmail.com, apolobambapea@todito.com
Address: Area Natural de Manejo Integrado Nacional Apolobamba, Calle Mendez Arcos No. 848, La Paz, Bolivia

ACCOM+
AMBORO

Here is ecotourism mixed with local tradition and culture. Five different communities in the department of Santa Cruz are involved; they have been providing services for five years now and control the whole of this activity. Around every community you will find natural pools, waterfalls and natural water slides. Each community offers its own specialities. Three of the villages are only open to tourists in the dry season (Aug to Nov).

Contact: Susan Davis
Tel: 3 427871
Cellular: 7708 2798
Fax: 3 555 053
Email: sedavis@141.com
Address: COBIMI, Santa Cruz, Bolivia

RAINFOREST
CHALALAN ECOLODGE
Sustainable Development in Madidi National Park

The setting is in the heart of the rainforest in the Madidi National park with its amazing wildlife. The eco-lodge was an ecotourism initiative between Conservation International and the Quecha-Tecana villagers of San Jose de Uchupiamonas who have been responsible for the operation since 2001. The community benefits from 50 per cent of the profits. The lodge is fully sustainable and most provisions are sourced locally. The final stage of the journey is a spectacular six-hour canoe trip up the Rivers Beni and Tuichi to the lodge after a short flight (20 minutes) from La Paz to Rurrenabaque.

Contact: Eileen Gutierrez
Tel/Fax: 38 922 309/38 922 419
Email: reservas@chalalan.com
Web: www.chalalan.com
Address: Chalalán Ecolodge Information Centre, Rurrenabaque, Bolivia

ACCOM
LA ESTANCIA ECOLODGE

This is a modern-style eco-lodge on the Island of the Sun on Lake Titicaca. You can trek, kayak and enjoy the cultural mix around you: folklore bred out of Inca religion and Catholicism, pre-Columbian archaeology, wonderful churches, and, of course, the natural world. The Lodge is run by the Aymara Indian community of La Estancia.

Contact: Edgar Tamayo
Tel: 2 244 2727
Fax: 2 244 3060
Email: info@ecolodge-laketiticaca.com
Web: www.ecolodge-laketiticaca.com
Address: Capitan Ravelo St. 2101, La Paz, Bolivia

ACCOM+
MALLKU CUEVA/VILLA MAR

There is community-based accommodation in this
village in the immense plateau of the Salar de Uyuni.
Visitors can enjoy the beautiful green and red lagoons.
Both are home to many species of birds. The Reserva
Eduardo Avaroa (60km away) is home to many different
types of birds and animals such as llamas and alpacas.
There's fishing in the lagoons and excursions are organized to the Mallku Cave, a spiritual site for the locals; an
interpretation museum and handicrafts market is due
to open soon.

Contact: Juan Quezada
Tel: 2 6932 989
Fax: 2 6932 989
Email: jardinesdeuyuni@atinmail.com
Web: www.salaruyuni.com
Address: Potosi Av. Nr. 113, Bolivia

RAINFOREST
MAPAJO ECOLODGE

This is a lodge built in the traditional style of the area,
based in the bio-reserve and indigenous territory of
Lajas Pylon, department of Beni. Outdoor activities
include swimming and sunbathing, nocturnal treks in
the forest and journeys by boat and canoe, with permit-
ted camping in the forest. Guests can also visit
indigenous communities and participate in various
cultural activities. Apart from trekking through the forest, guests can also find beaches on
the shores of the Quinquibey River where they can observe the birds, mammals and
reptiles native to the tropical forest. MAPAJO Ecoturismo Indígena is fully owned and
operated by the indigenous communities of the Quiquibey River.

Tel: 3 892 317
Fax: 3 892 317
Email: mapajo_eco@yahoo.com
Web: www.mapajo.com
Address: C. Comercio Rurrenabaque,
    Beni, Bolivia

TOURS
MICHAEL BLENDINGER NATURE TOURS

The owner, Michael Blendinger, based in
Santa Cruz, feels a bit of an ecotourism
pioneer. A qualified ecologist he endeav-
ours to run a green operation and to
ensure that his 'flora and fauna' trips to
national parks are in harmony with the
environment. Local community-run
projects benefit.

Contact: Michael Blendinger
Tel & Fax: 3 9446 227
Email: mblendinger@cotas.com.bo,
    info@discoveringbolivia.com
Web: www.discoveringbolivia.com
Address: Calle Bolívar, frente al Museo Samaipata,
    Santa Cruz, Bolivia

ACCOM+
SAN CRISTOBAL LODGE

Located in the south of the country in
semi-desert 'puna' at an altitude of 3700
metres. The main attractions of this
immense plateau are the Salar de Uyuni
and the green and red lagoons. The town
and its colonial church, which was disas-
sembled and carefully reconstructed,
were transferred 12km from their original

Contact: Jaime Rubin
Tel: 2 2433 800
Fax: 2 2433 737
Email: jaime.rubin@ascbolivia.com.bo
Web: www.lama-mama.com
Address: Calle Campos 265, Ciudad de la Paz.
    PO Box 13790, Bolivia

location by a mining company. Visitors can hire bicycles to explore the area around the lodge, which has all the necessary amenities for a comfortable stay. Both the lodge and bicycle business are due to be handed over to the community of San Cristobal as the best method for the community to overcome poverty.

TOURS
SERERE SANCTUARY/MADIDI TRAVEL

Madidi Travel offers tours to the Serere Sanctuary. It is a protected area of the Amazon, two and a half hours on the Beni River from Rurrenabaque. You can stay in forest friendly lodges where the owners are working with local people to consolidate their land rights whilst promoting the conservation of the area and offering opportunities

Tel: 00 591 2 245 0069
Fax: 00 591 2 246 1228
Web: www.madidi-travel.com
Address: c/o Jimenez No 806 esq,
   c/o Santa Cruz, La Paz, Bolivia

for the community to benefit, in part, from tourism. Employing the expertise of local guides, tours are tailored around the individuals' chosen activities, whether it is walking, swimming, relaxing or viewing the wildlife which includes reptiles, insects, fish and a great variety of flora.

BRAZIL
International dialling code +55

Brazil is a country of mixed colours, flavours, sounds and cultures. More than 500 years after its 'discovery' by the Portuguese, Brazil is today South America's mega-economy with a regional (left-wing) leader. Even so, unequal income distribution remains a pressing problem. The Brazilian people are known for being friendly, warm and welcoming. Brazil offers an infinite variety of options for tourists (nature, historical, archaeological and modern cities). It has many natural beauties to be seen, but be sure you have sufficient time as Brazil has continental dimensions – it's the fifth largest country in the world.

The north and northeast are the least developed, where there's a strong legacy from colonial times, especially in the architecture of the region. Brazil's African heritage is also best exemplified here. The south and southeast are the wealthiest and most developed, with influences from the migration of Italians and Germans. All this contrast is what makes this extraordinary country endlessly intriguing.

ACCOM/HOST
CAMA E CAFÉ

Cama e Café aims to be the first Brazilian 'bed and breakfast' network. Established in 2003, it now has around 50 hosts registered and concentrated in the Santa Teresa district of Rio, which is a historic, lively and cultural area. It follows the local Agenda 21 and tries to implement sustainable management principles. The aim is to make Santa Teresa into a sustainable tourism area, with plenty of activities on offer in and around the locality.

Contact: Marcela Almeida
Tel: 21 2221 7635/2224 5689
Email: booking@camaecafe.com.br
Web: www.camaecafe.com.br
Address: Rua Progresso, 67, Santa Teresa, Rio de Janeiro RJ, Brazil

ACCOM/HOST/DAY
CASA GRANDE - NOVA OLINDA

Nova Olinda is a village in the Kariri valley, Ceara, one of Brazil's poorest states, in the north-east of the country. It's home to the Casa Grande foundation, working to try to recover the heritage of the local Krui-Kariri people and educate its young. It's regarded as a model of local empowerment keeping the culture alive through educational projects. A museum, radio and television station have been created as part of the project. Their success brings many visitors to the area. Accommodation is usually within the family home. There are 12 different 'pousadas' (guesthouses) on different sites, all of them offering full board, usually on a four-day package. Visitors usually can participate in workshops and interact with the children and young people, and visit archaeological and mythological sites. Part of the income from the tourism project supports the school.

Tel: 88 521 8133/88 546 1333
Email: casagrande@baydejbc.com.br
Address: Rua Jeremias Pereira 444, 63165 000 Nova Olinda, Ceara, Brazil

RAINFOREST
EL NAGUAL RESERVA

The reserve is located 68km from Rio, on the edge of the Serra dos Orgaos National Park, and is a guesthouse with six simple rooms with private bathrooms. There is a hydro energy plant for light and solar for hot water; they grow food organically and produce crafts such as candles and mosaics. Stress is placed on education about the rainforest and there are opportunities to help prepare lunch and to join art and craft courses. Or visitors just relax in the swimming pool.

Contact: Mariana & Erhard Kalloch Devoto
Tel: 21 2630 2625
Cellular: 9977 0569/9853 6069
Email: artnagual@hotmail.com
Web: www.artnagual.com.br
Address: Rua Capitão Antero S/N km 03, 25920-000 Santo Aleixo/Magé , Rio de Janeiro, Brazil

DAY
FAVELA TOUR

Everyone who comes into contact with the founder, Marcello Armstrong, sings his praises. The name tells the story – the three-hour tour (vehicle and foot) takes you round favela districts and you realize that Rio is more than Copacabana, and that the favelas are not all criminal no-go areas. The tours stimulate an understanding of 'the city, its contrasts and paradoxes'. A key weekday component is a visit to a local community school which Favela Tour helps to support.

Contact: Marcello Armstrong
Tel: 21 3322 2727
Cellular: 9989 0074/9772 1133
Fax: 21 3322 5958
Email: info@favelatour.com.br
Web: www.favelatour.com.br
Address: Estrada das Canoas 722, apt, 125. São Conrado, Rio de Janeiro, CEP: 22610-210, Brazil

THE AMERICAS SOUTH

ACCOM
FAZENDA RIO NEGRO

Conservation International bought Fazenda Rio Negro as part of their strategy for the Pantanal region. They are cooperating with local private farmers to develop landscape management alternatives and see ecotourism as a way of wedding conservation and regional economic growth. The Fazenda is in the state of Mato Grasso, about 30 minutes by plane from the state capital, Campo Grande. The eco-lodge offers 'safe, clean and comfortable accommodation' consistent with local conditions. A maximum of 42 people can be accommodated.

Contact: Heloisa Bogalho
Tel: 67 326 0002
Fax: 67 326 0002
Email: a.prado@conservation.org.br
Web: www.fazendarionegro.com.br
Address: Rua Paraná, 32, Jardim dos Estados, Campo Grande/MS, CEP: 79020-290, Brazil

DAY/VOL
IKO PORAN

Iko Poran is a not-for-profit organization with NGO partners in Rio, Salvador and the Amazon. Its mandate is to implement projects and volunteer programmes, promote the concept of cultural exchange and strengthen the NGO presence in Brazil. Iko Poran facilitates community tours that allow participants to experience Rio from a new perspective and see how its problems are being solved.

Contact: Luis Felipe Murray
Tel: 21 3084 2242
Tel weekend: 21 9218 4014
Fax: 21 3084 1446
Email: rj@ikoporan.org, tour@ikoporan.org
Web: www.ikoporan.org
Address: Av. Nilo Peçanha, 50/ 1709 Centro, Rio de Janeiro, RJ, CEP: 20044-900, Brazil

RAINFOREST
MAMIRAUA RESERVA – POUSADA UACARI

This conservation unit, managed by the Mamiraua Institute, uses ecotourism to involve local communities. The floating lodge deep in the Amazon rainforest – an hour by air from Manaus and then a boat journey – was built to minimize any impact on the environment and recycles solar energy and rainwater. It is managed by local people, who also offer guided treks, visits to local villages and crafts. Packages are usually of 3–4 days and include transfers, accommodation and full board.

Contact: Monique Vasconcelos
Tel: 97 3343 4160
Fax: 97 3343 2967
Email: ecoturismo@mamiraua.org.br
Web: www.mamiraua.org.br/ecoturismo
Address: Instituto Mamirauá, Programa de Ecoturismo, Av. Brazil, 197, Bairro Juruá, CEP: 69470-000, Brazil

RAINFOREST
PEDRAS NEGRAS

'Black rocks' reserve is in the Guapore Valley in Rondonia, which is a vital area for the conservation of both the environment and its indigenous people. Stay in adapted rubber tapper housing and walk the collection paths. Members of the 22 indigenous reserve families who live off the harvesting of Brazil nuts, fishing and subsistence agriculture will guide you over the nut collection trails. This is pro-people tourism in practice.

Contact: Carolina Doria Cleo
Tel: 69 224 7870
Fax: 69 224 7870
Web: www.pedrasnegras.com, www.ecopore.org.br, www.wwf.com.br
Address: Rua Rafael Vaz e Silva 3335, Porto Velho/RO, CEP: 78900-000, Brazil

ACCOM/TOUR
PONTA GROSSA

This combination of local family investment, charitable donation and NGO assistance has created a network of guesthouses, overnight accommodation, restaurants and guide services. It's based in the village of Ponta Grossa, 200km from Fortalez, capital of Ceara state in northeast Brazil. The main community income is from fishing so tourism

Contact: Eliabe Crispym
Tel: 88 3432 5001
Cellular: 88 9953 2209
Email: elicrispym@bol.com.br
Address: Astuma, 62810–000 Ponta Grossa, Icapuí, Ceará, Brazil

income is a very desirable economic add-on and everyone involved is self-motivated. The environmental protection area was created at the request of the local people.

RAINFOREST
POUSADA ALDEIA DOS LAGOS (ASPAC)

This pousada is an experimental ecotourism project – the first in the Amazon region – developed by the Silves Association for the Preservation of the Environment and Culture (ASPAC), on Silves Island, 200km from Manaus, in the Amazon lakes region. The 'pousada' consists of 12 rooms with private bathroom and balcony, a restaurant, crafts shop and other facilities

Tel: 92 528 2124
Fax: 92 528 2124
Email: amazonas@viverde.com.br, aldeiadoslagos@terra.com.br
Web: www.viverde.com.br, www.viverde.com.br/aldeia.html

such as laundry and recreation areas. They offer 13 different tours. Revenue from the project helps preserve the lakes and fisheries and improve life in the community. Pousada Aldeia dos Lagos was given technical support by the World Wildlife Fund (WWF).

ACCOM
PRAINHA DO CANTO VERDE

You can relax on the beach in this award winning, beautiful fishing village in northeast Brazil knowing that all the economic benefits accrue to the locals. A local cooperative acts as the incoming operator for guesthouses and restaurants. It is very involved in wider community tourism development, especially with other communities in Ceara, and has a leadership role in promoting the ethos of sustainable community-led tourism.

Contact: Ely Fernandes de Lima
Tel: 88 3413 1426
Fax: 88 3413 1426
Email: fishnet@uol.com.br
Web: www.prainhadocantoverde.org
Address: Caixa Postal 52722, Aldeota, 60.151-970 Fortaleza, Ceará, Brazil

TOUR
PROJETO BAGAGEM

If you want to visit communities that are off the beaten track knowing that each trip is organized in cooperation with local partners, then this NGO offers one-week tours for small groups. Projeto Bagagem is an NGO based in Sao Paulo with a mission to contribute to the sustainable development of Brazilian communities through tourism. They believe tourism is an opportunity for community growth and empowerment and for visitor/local interaction. They set store also by conservation of the environment and ethical behaviour.

Contact: Cecilia Zanotti
Tel: 11 5505 2986
Fax: 11 5505 2986
Email: projetobagagem@hotmail.com
Web: www.projetobagagem.org
Address: Rua Arandu 801, São Paulo SP 04562-031, Brazil

THE AMERICAS SOUTH

ORG
TERRAMAR

Terramar is a campaigning NGO fighting to promote the integrated development of coastal communities in Ceara State. Alongside this work Terramar coordinates and supports the Network of Community-Based Tourism Destinations in Brazil. Their activities include: resisting land grabbing, building village structures, environmental education and the sustainable use of natural resources. The community tourism activities are overseen by Terramar's coastal management programme that supports sustainability, local participation and recognition of the value of local cultures.

Tel: 85 226.2476/226.4154
Email: terramar@fortalnet.com.br
Web: www.terramar.org.br,
    www.soszonacosteira.hpg.com.br
Address: Rua Pinho Pessoa, 86, Joaquim Tavora,
    CEP: 60135-170, Fortaleza, Ceara, Brazil

COLOMBIA
International dialling code +57

Gabriel García Márquez' home country, Colombia, probably does not immediately spring to mind as a place to visit. Frequent reports about murders, kidnappings, narcotics trafficking, drug cartels and endemic corruption are all too familiar. Yet Colombia deserves its fair share of credit. At the northeast tip of South America, Colombia prides itself on its virtually untouched coastlines of more tha 3200km on both the Caribbean Sea and Pacific Ocean with stunning views and pristine beaches. Shielded in the west by three Andes mountain ranges, plains, covered by jungle and savannahs, constitute the bulk of the hinterland before merging into the vast Amazonian forest in the east, Colombia's other natural asset. In the centre lies Bogotá, a vibrant urban mix of old and new, of easygoing flow and aggressive bustle. Similarly to its neighbours, Colombia's population is a rich mix of indigenous peoples, Europeans and Africans, with women enjoying the greatest degree of economic and professional autonomy in Latin America.

Colombia's drug and crime problems have limited its appeal and full potential as a major tourist destination. Once the situation improves, however, this could be a major chance for Colombia to learn from mistakes made by the established tourist destinations in promoting sustainable and community-based tourism.

RAINFOREST
BUENAVENTURA'S MANGROVE

Buenaventura is the second biggest seaport in the country – a three-hour drive from Cali or 30 minutes by plane from Bogotá. Trails have been created in the rainforest for visitors to enjoy the great biodiversity of the area, and cabins built within the forest for them to rest. It is possible to see spotted cat, deer, anteater and armadillo as well as abundant bird life. There are also 12 species of local palm and a variety of orchids. Visitors can go on hiking tours, fish in natural lagoons and take part in local music and dances, enjoying typical meals made with local produce. Buenaventura is run by the FUNDELPA foundation for the economic development of the Pacific coast.

Contact: Flor Maria Yanes Baltan
Tel: 2244 2404/2244 2403
Fax: 2242 5327
Email: fundelpa@hotmail.com
Address: El Valle, Carrera 59, entre calle 6 y 7, Barrio Independencia, Buenaventura, Colombia

RAINFOREST
COHABITATION WITH COMMUNITIES THE COLOMBIAN AMAZON REGION

This programme is in the Amacayacu National Park, in the South Colombian Amazon region, next to the Brazilian and Peruvian frontiers. It is designed to allow visitors to fully immerse themselves in the natural and cultural environment. Interpreters guide tourists who can visit small farms, and take part in sporting events and traditional festivals. There are good opportunities for hiking, night tours, canoeing, excursions to the islands and lakes, fishing, and dolphin and birdwatching. The park features a restaurant and a lodge with accommodation for 51 people. The organizer is Siempre Columbia, which aims to integrate the tourists in local culture while promoting the equal distribution of any returns.

Contact: Jonhy Ochoa
Tel: 1226 6378/1542 6730/1640 8628
Email: siempre_colombia@yahoo.com
Web: www.parquenacionales.gov.co
Address: Calle 100, No. 41, 40 of. 319 - Calle 63. No. 10, 83 local 1086, Bogotá, Colombia

ACCOM+
KAI ECO-TRAVEL

Kai Eco-travel is a community-based venture located in a semi-desert landscape containing exotic vegetation, quiet beaches, large dunes and imposing mountains. Travellers can visit the Macuira hills, a national park with great biodiversity or hike in Wososopo, to the waterfalls in Macuira Hills or to the various beaches. On the way you can also visit Wayuu farms, textile workshops, and attend traditional dance shows, or enjoy a cockleboat tour. Many indigenous tribes still live in Uribia, sustaining their culture and traditions. Accommodation is offered on Wayuu farms, with food prepared in traditional wood ovens. It is also possible to camp in tents and on the beach.

Contact: Rocio Barros Pushaina
Tel: 5717 7173
Email: kai_ecotravel@hotmail.com
Web: www.locombia.net/kai-ecotravel
Address: Diagonal 1B #8 - 68, Barrio Abuchaibe, Uribia, Guajira, Colombia

ACCOM+
SUSTAINABLE DEVELOPMENT WITH BLACK COMMUNITIES OF THE COLOMBIAN PACIFIC IN NUQUI

This project is located on the Pacific coast of Colombia, near the Ensenada de Utria park, one hour by plane from Medellin. The area contains humid tropical rainforest, as well as coastal and marine ecosystems. Visitors can enjoy hiking tours, marine

Contact: Emigdio Pertuz Buendia
Tel: 4682 7001/4682 7233
Email: asoheco@hotmail.com, emigdiopertuz@hotmail.com
Web: www.parquenacionales.gov.co
Address: Calle 4a, No.4-31, Bahia Solano, Colombia

THE AMERICAS SOUTH

diving, whale and dolphin observation, surfing and horse riding, among many activities. The main natural attractions in the area are waterfalls, beaches with high waves, as well as beaches resembling natural swimming pools. Accommodation is available in guesthouses, cabins, eco-lodges, hotels or camping.

ECUADOR

International dialling code +593

1000km

QUITO

Marginally larger in size than the UK, Ecuador is one of the smaller countries in South America. It is the world's number one supplier of bananas. The Andes mountain range runs north to south cutting the country into the hot and humid Amazonian rainforest in the east and the hot and dry Pacific coastal regions in the west. The world-famous Galapagos Islands also form part of Ecuador. High above sea level in the middle of the Andes, Ecuador's capital and main gateway, Quito, is a pleasant and accessible city benefiting from a mild climate throughout the entire year. Once the capital of the mighty Inca Empire, Quito boasts large amounts of Spanish colonial architecture, now a UNESCO World Heritage Site.

The Amazonian rainforest is home to many indigenous Indian tribes such as the Huaorani and the Siona-Secoya. Logging and recent developments in the oil industry coupled with internal migration all disrupt those people's livelihoods, as well as the fragile environment. Similarly, an ever-increasing number of tourist arrivals threatens the Galapagos Archipelagos – that microcosm of unique and bountiful fauna and flora. In tandem with tourism, local and international initiatives have sprung up in recent years not only to help protect these islands and the rainforest but also the traditional habitat of the local communities.

RAINFOREST+/VOL
BELLAVISTA CLOUD FOREST RESERVE & LODGE

This private conservation project and private reserve is in the buffer zone of the Mindo-Nambillo protected forest. Bellavista offers (a maximum of 40 people) adventure, birdwatching, trekking and relaxation. They strive to run a green operation, but, as they say, it's difficult to preach water conservation in a cloud forest. They promise unusual accommodation (includ-

Contact: Jens Larsen
Tel: 2 2901 536/2232 313/9 9490 891
Cellular: 2 2116 047 /2 2116 232
Fax: 2 2903 165
Email: info@bellavistacloudforest.com
Web: www.bellavistacloudforest.com
Address: Jorge Washington E7-23 y 6 de Diciembre, Quito, Ecuador

ing a four-storey, thatched roof, geodesic dome) and gourmet food. There's also a budget hostel, camping and research centre; volunteers can help with conservation activities.

THE AMERICAS SOUTH

ACCOM+
BLACK SHEEP INN ECOLODGE

High in the rural Andes, the two owners not only run the Black Sheep Inn but have also helped make the local village of Chugchilan into a paradigm for community-based tourism. They have encouraged the founding of hostels and sustainable businesses and acted as an award winning role model. The Inn benefits local people directly and indirectly, and all aspects of the operation aim to promote conservation, sustainability and environmentalism. The restaurant offers family-style vegetarian gourmet food and the Inn itself caters for the individual traveller.

Contact: Michelle Kirby
Tel: 3281 4587
Email: info@blacksheepinn.com
Web: www.blacksheepinn.com
Address: PO Box 05-01-240, Chugchilán, Cotopaxi, Ecuador

THE **AMERICAS** SOUTH

RAINFOREST+
BOSQUE NUBLADO SANTA LUCIA

This is a land cooperative (formed, owned and run by 12 former landless campesinos), which is committed to forest conservation and is trying to make a sustainable living out of ecotourism. The ecolodge (maximum occupancy of 20 people) is in the heart of the cloud forest in the Andean lowlands at 1900 metres. There's birdwatching,

Contact: Paulina Tapia
Tel: 2215 7242
Fax: 2215 7242
Email: info@santaluciaecuador.com
Web: www.santaluciaecuador.com
Address: Parroquia Nanegal, Quito, Ecuador.

hiking and learning about sustainable farming – or you can just relax in a hammock. Food is a mixture of traditional and international home cooking and you eat by candlelight (there's no electricity). A very reasonable £25/US$45 per night includes three meals. Proceeds go back into the business and toward conservation and any profit goes to the members.

RAINFOREST+
FOUNDATION INTERNATIONAL SHIWIAR SIN FRONTERAS (FUNSSIF)

This ecotourism initiative by the indigenous Shiwiar people in the remote community (accessible only by air) of Tanguntsa in the Ecuadorian rainforest, near the Peruvian border, offers an unusual experience but may not be for the faint-hearted. You will have day and night guided walks in the rainforest, learn about medicinal plants, see rivers and lakes (and, in winter, go rafting) and just generally soak in the hospitable waters of the

Contact: Pascual Kunchicuy
Tel: 2 887 225
Cellular: 09832 3637/09769 2988
Fax: 2 886 109
Email: shiwiarfund@hotmail.com, ikiamp21@hotmail.com
Web: www.ikiam.info
Address: PO Box 16-01-703, Puyo, Ecuador

Shiwiar culture. The majority of the income yielded by this sustainable alternative tourism goes towards the education and health of the local people. The Shiwiar are struggling to gain ownership of their land, to protect it from exploitation by oil companies. Tourism can help generate funds for the struggle, and bring hope and self-respect.

ORG/ACCOM+/RAINFOREST+/VOL
GOLONDRINAS (Foundation)

Ecotourism and its companion agri-tourism represent only one aspect of the work carried out by this not-for-profit NGO, which is dedicated to the conservation of natural resources, fighting soil erosion and fostering general environmental education in the Rio Mira area between the provinces of Imbabura and Carchi. A maximum of ten people can be accommodated in a choice of three locations, which give the visitor the chance

Contact: Maria Eliza Manteca
Tel: 22 22660/99 012781/62 648679
Email: manteca@uio.satnet.net,
permaviajes@yahoo.com
Web: www.fundaciongolondrinas.org,
www.ecuadorexplorer.com/golondrinas
Address: Calle Isabel la Católica n24-679 y
Cristóbal Gangotena, Quito, Ecuador

to learn about the work being done; it is possible to contribute in a volunteer capacity. Tours into the cloud forest (from one to four days) – on foot or on horseback – are organized by Permacultura, a tour operator that supports the Foundation's activities.

RAINFOREST+
KAPAWI ECOLODGE & RESERVE

The privately owned Kapawi Lodge, on the Peruvian border, was developed with the full cooperation of the Achuar people who receive £2500/US$4500 rent each month for the land on which the lodge is situated; in 2011 the Achuar will become the owners of the lodge without cost. Thus the project provides employment and income for education, health and community development. Kapawi is very remote (accessible

Contact: Aracely Ortega
Tel: 4 2285 711/4 2280 880
Fax: 42 287 651
Email: canodros@canodros.com,
goperaciones@canodros.com
Web: www.canodros.com, www.kapawi.com
Address: Urbanización Santa Leonor MS.
5 Solar 10, Guayaquil, Ecuador

only by air and then canoe), located in mountainous rainforest. Activities, including birdwatching, canoeing and camping, are geared to visitors' tastes and capacities. The 20 rooms on a lake are built with traditional materials.

RAINFOREST+
KUMANII LODGE

A new community lodge (opened in 2005), Kumanii is partnered with UNORCAC Community Lodging (see below) and both are run in association with Latin Trails, which looks after the administrative side of things plus the overland operation and marketing; the local communities run the lodge and local tourism activities, such as guided trekking in the jungle and birdwatching. Kumanii is part of the Kumanii Foundation and is keen to sponsor local sustainable tourism activity. The

Contact: Martha Salazar
Tel: 2 286 6898
Fax: 2 286 7832
Email: reservations@latintrails.com
Web: www.latintrails.com,
www.kumanilodge.com
Address: Av. Rumiñahui 221 y 1ra Transversal
(frente colegio Farina), San Rafael, Quito, Ecuador

lodge, which can accommodate 26 visitors, benefits ten communities in the Choco rainforest region, a biodiversity hotspot. It is a six-hour drive and three hours by canoe from Quito.

RAINFOREST+
LA SELVA JUNGLE LODGE

The privately owned La Selva has been open for some 20 years and employs a range of local staff, some of whom are second generation; they are given reason to feel proud of their involvement in the lodge. A lot of investment goes into local education and health care. There are cosy, thatched cabanas (with hot water) for sleeping, and gourmet meals – tropical ingredients fused with sophisticated cooking skills – for eating.

Contact: Eric Schwartz
Tel: +1 772 225 8884
Fax: +1 772 225 8884
Email: sales@laselvajunglelodge.com, lscentral1@cs.com
Web: www.laselvajunglelodge.com
Address: PO Box 6033, Jensen Beach, Florida 34957 USA

RAINFOREST+/VOL
MAQUIPUCUNA ECOLODGE

The Maquipucuna Sustainable Tourism Programme provides a way in which local people can approach conservation and development sustainably. The Lodge, 80km from Quito, houses up to 34 people in a variety of accommodation; there is also a camping area. The Maquipucuna Foundation manages a 15,000 acre cloud forest reserve with a range of habitats and is a biodiversity 'hotspot' with about 350 bird species, more than 50 mammal species and thousands of invertebrates. The daily rate for the Lodge (a maximum of £40/US$70) includes lodging, three meals and taxes. This is a superb example of a marriage of conservation serving the natural world and ecotourism serving the community.

Contact: Mauricio Caviedes
Tel: 2 250 7200/2/3
Fax: 2 250 7201
Email: Ecotourism@maquipucuna.org, usa@maquipucuna.org
Web: www.maqui.org
Address: Baquerizo Moreno E9-153 y Tamayo, PO Box 17-12-167, Quito, Ecuador

RAINFOREST+
MOMOPEHO RAINFOREST HOME HACIENDA

Basic but comfortable accommodation in a farm, with two rooms for up to four people in each. Prices include full board (breakfast, lunch and dinner). There are plenty of different activities all year around, although some depend on the season: birdwatching, walking, farm work, such as milking the cows and feeding the guinea pigs. It is a private enterprise that helps the local community in education and health. It also develops projects of recycling, water conservation and protection of the fauna.

Contact: Alvaro Moreno Perez
Tel: 9 8309 202/2 2439 460
Fax: 2 2439 460
Email: momopeho@yahoo.com, momopeho@gmail.com
Web: www.momopeho.com

HOST+
RUNA TUPARI NATIVE TRAVEL

Runa Tupari was set up by UNORCAC (the union of organizations of farmers and indigenous people of Cotacachi) in response to discrimination against indigenous people. Visitors stay with local families and partake fully in their lives, experiencing a different lifestyle in a

THE AMERICAS SOUTH

natural and traditional environment. The accommodation is in 12 family-run lodges. Price per person for homestay with transport, breakfast and dinner is £13/US$23 per night. The tours cost extra (£14–34/US$25–60) depending on their type and numbers involved. Visitors receive a code of conduct before beginning a homestay or taking a tour.

Contact: Christian Garzon
Tel: 6 2925 985
Fax: 6 2925 985
Email: nativetravel@runatupari.com, runatupari@hotmail.com
Web: www.runatupari.com
Address: Plaza de los Ponchos Sucre y Quiroga, Otavalo, Ecuador

RAINFOREST+
TROPIC ECOLOGICAL ADVENTURES

An award-winning ecotourism company which specializes in providing visits to Ecuador's most spectacular natural areas in partnership with the remote Huaorani people. One small group a month (eight persons maximum) is taken on a rainforest experience with the full cooperation of the Huaorani. Accommodation is in a camp to which you return each evening.

Contact: Jascivan Carvalho
Tel: 2 2234 594/2 2225 907
Fax: 2 2560 756
Email: info@tropiceco.com
Web: www.tropiceco.com
Address: Av. Republica E7-320 y Almagro, Edf. Taurus Dpto 1-A, Quito, Ecuador

ACCOM+
UNORCAC COMMUNITY LODGE

UNORCAC provides accommodation with Otavalo indigenous families in family-owned lodges (for two people) with private bathroom and living-room in each cabin. Shared family meals (organic produce), trekking, horseback riding and cycling are some of the activities. UNORCAC (an indigenous peoples' organization) community lodging is partnered with Kumanii Lodge (see above) and both are run in association with Latin Trails, which looks after the administrative side of things. Briefings about the local culture and community rules are given. A two-day tour costs £123/US$219 for two people, including lodging, some meals and guide services. It's only a three-hour drive from Quito, the capital.

Contact: Martha Salazar
Tel: 2 286 6898
Fax: 2 286 7832
Email: reservations@latintrails.com
Web: www.latintrails.com
Address: Av. Ruminahui 221 y 1ra Transversal (frente colegio Farina), San Rafael, Quito, Ecuador

RAINFOREST+
YACHANA LODGE

This lodge in the Ecuadorian Amazon region was established by FUNEDESIN, a not-for-profit foundation. Profits from the Lodge help to support community development, education, health and conservation. Yachana is a Quichua word meaning 'a place for learning'; this is the lodge philosophy and learning is a two-way process. The guides for the 3–4 night tours are all local people who were sent to the US to learn English. The operation is as 'green' as possible; for example, the lodge runs on solar energy. Visitors reach the lodge by a 30-minute local flight from Quito to Coca where they are met and taken on the final two-hour river leg by motorized canoe.

Contact: Ivan Martinez or Gabriela Figuero
Tel: 2 252 2791
Fax: 2 222 0362
Email: ivan@yachana.com, Gabriela@yachana.com
Web: www.yachana.com
Address: PO Box 17-17-185, Quito, Ecuador

PERU
International dialling code +51

Three of the most diverse geographic zones on the planet – coast, mountain and jungle – make up this huge and diverse country. The flat coastal lands feature harsh deserts and oases as well as the capital, Lima, which is a mind-boggling feat of fairly unsustainable irrigation. The Andes, which stretch from Colombia and Ecuador in the north down through Chile and Argentina in the south and across to Bolivia in the east, are dotted with Inca and pre-Inca ruins. Away from the mountains, in the Inca capital of Cusco, take a bus through the cloud forests and you may be lucky enough to see the scarlet cock-of-the-rock, the Peruvian national bird, before the warm, moist air of the jungle envelops you. Microclimates reign in Peru, check out the weather in the local area in advance to avoid shocks.

Buses and some night buses are excellent, but do go with reputable companies. Most tours will kick off from a town like Cusco, Lima or Ayacucho, which have shops equal to small-town Europe where you will never be far from a toothbrush, bottled water or a well-stocked chemist. Listen to your guides, and one nice tip – Wellington boots bought in the local market are far more useful than the most expensive technical boots when it comes to jungle walking…

Peru is corrupt and does have a high level of crime, and you will always meet tourists and travellers who have horror stories. However, when these things do happen, it is usually because a traveller has not followed one or more of the golden rules. People are poor, you are rich, and the assumption is you won't really miss your stuff!

HOST+
ALL WAY TRAVEL

All Way is a local operator in the Lake Titicaca area, a private company with half the staff being from rural communities and trained guides. The company is interested in promoting rural educational development, often with volunteer and tourist help, and in providing visitors with a cultural exchange experience. Local families act as hosts. The whole enterprise is truly a cooperative blend of community, company and the guest.

Contact: Vicentina Quispe
Tel: 355 552
Fax: 355 552
Email: allwaystravel@titicacaperu.com
Web: www.titicacaperu.com
Address: Tacna Street 234, Puno, Peru

RAINFOREST+
AMAZONAS LODGE

This 30-room lodge, which offers all-inclusive packages, is a joint venture between the Native Community of Infierno (NCI) and the Peruvian private ecotourism company Rainforest Expeditions (RFE) in Tambopata. The lodge is wholly owned by the NCI but operated jointly. The

Contact: Erika Berrospi
Tel: 1 421 8347
Fax: 1 421 8183
Email: postmaster@rainforest.com.pe
Web: www.perunature.com
Address: Ave. Aramburu, 166 . 2b, Miraflores, Lima, Peru

success of the venture has had a ripple effect socially and economically, and the community is developing projects that link in to tourism, for example, handicrafts and fish farms. RFE are opening two similar lodges in the near future. Tourist activity is controlled in the interests of wildlife; the lodge was built on uninhabited land and the community can be visited only with the permission of the Control Committee.

ACCOM+
ANAPIA & YUSPIQUI

The islands of Anapia and Yuspiqui, with a population of 1200, are located on Lake Titicaca in the part called the minor lake or Winaymarca. In this beautiful area along the Bolivian frontier visitors can share an intercultural exchange, participating in activities such as fishing, agriculture, cattle rearing and preparing tradi-

Tel: 5135 3979/5135 5552
Fax: 5135 5552
Email: awtperu@terra.com.pe
Web: www.allwaystraveltitikaka.com
Address: Jr. Tacna 234, Puno, Peru

tional meals. Boat tours to the various islands on Lake Titicaca are also available. This is a unique opportunity to share the Andean way of thinking, daily life, cultural rites and ancestral knowledge, meeting a kind, enthusiastic community in a wonderful setting.

ARACARI TRAVEL CONSULTING

Aracari is a 'boutique travel company' which organizes high quality tailor-made itineraries throughout Peru, Bolivia and Ecuador and the Galapagos Islands. They aim at offering a sustainable product by means of subcontracting to carefully selected

Contact: Cynthia Caceres
Tel: 1 242 6673
Fax: 1 242 4856
Email: postmaster@aracari.com
Web: www.aracari.com
Address: Ave. Pardo 610 of 802, Miraflores, Lima 18, Peru

ethical operators in areas to which they take clients. They give donations and support non-profit local initiatives, such as a museum and a centre for traditional textiles. They provide medical aid to the Patakancha community with whom they have had a long-standing relationship.

ACCOM/HOST
CIVIL SOCIETY GREEN LIFE

Civil Society Green Life is a non-profitable organization that offers community/family run lodging in small hostels or private houses. It works with associated communities, which can accommodate groups (up to 12 people)

Contact: Andrea Ravaglioli
Tel: 1 2410 559
Fax: 1 2410 559
Email: greenlife@pacaya-samiria.com
Address: Green Life A.C. Elías Aguirre 460 - 201, Miraflores, Lima 18, Perú

or individuals. It also organizes tours through the Andean and Amazonian regions, including archaeological sites. The project helps the local communities' economy, education, health, women and local minorities. Green Life also helps the community on waste management and programmes of fauna protection.

HOST+
EXPLORANDES/TITIKAYAK

This is an alliance of two Peruvian companies, which between them cater for soft adventure seekers and people preferring community-based rural tourism experiences. The profits are split 50/50. About 150 families are currently involved in the community side in aspects like homestays, arts and crafts etc. Titikayak refers to their unique blend of community-based rural tourism experience with sea kayaking on Lake Titicaca. Any donation made by homestay tourists goes to the school and/or the hospital. Clear guidance is given to tourists as to the behaviour expected of them in their interaction with hosts and other local people.

Contact: Vanessa Santos
Tel: 1 445 0532
Fax: 1 445 4686
Email: postmaster@explorandes.com
Web: www.explorandes.com, www.titikayak.com
Address: Aristides Aljovin 484, Miraflores, Lima 18, Peru

ACCOM+/AGRI
GRANJA PORCON

Located in the northern Sierra of Peru, at an altitude of between 3200 and 3850 metres, this project gives visitors the chance to experience the agricultural life of rural Peru. Guests at the Sierra Verde lodging hotel, with its panoramic views of the surrounding area, can enjoy hiking, horse riding and camping in the Granja Porcon. If they wish to, they can participate in milking the cows, visit areas of forest plantation and vegetable seeding in biological gardens or sheep and alpaca kept for wool production. Keen anglers will find an abundance of trout in the local rivers.

Contact: Daniel Valdivia
Tel: 4 4825 631
Fax: 4 4825631
Address: Cooperativa Agraria, 'Atahualpa-Jerusalen', Sr. Daniel Valdivia Jr., Chanchamayo 1355, Cjamarca, Peru

TREK
LAMA TREK

Starting in Olleros, a village in the High Andean plateau, this is a four-day trek accompanied by lamas and local guides. Visitors can also participate in activities such as rock climbing, sailing, cycling, parasailing and enjoying the thermal baths of Monterrey. The trek follows the ancient Inca trail between Olleros and Chavin de Huantar. Visitors will enjoy the beautiful snow-covered landscapes of the Huascaran national park, along the way experiencing a taste of Andean food, music, ritual ceremonies, traditional medicine and natural art, including textile production using lama and alpaca wool. The national park of Huascaran contains an immense variety of flora and fauna, including deer, Andean spectacled bear, vicuna, puma, condor and Andean stag.

Contact: Jorge Martel Alva
Tel: 4472 1266
Fax: 4472 1266
Address: Calle Agustin Loli, No. 43, Plazuela de la Soledad, Huaraz, Peru

THE AMERICAS SOUTH

ACCOM+
LLACHON

The Llachon community is an Andean village located at an altitude of 3810 metres on the shore of Lake Titicaca. Visitors can enjoy exceptional landscapes combining water, sky and snow-capped mountains with white sand beaches. Local guides accompany the visitor in a tour of the main natural and archaeological attractions, including the Carus Sanctuary in the Auki Carus mountain, and by boat to the floating islands of Los Uros. Tourists can also experience Andean ceremonies, traditional handicrafts, going on guided sailing tours of the lake, as well as small-scale fishing and agricultural production. Don Valentin Quispe's house offers rustic but convenient accommodation with panoramic views over Lake Titicaca.

Tel: 982 1392/5135 3979
Fax: 5135 5552
Email: llachon@yahoo.com,
   awtperu@terra.com.pe
Web: www.allwaystraveltitikaka.com
Address: Albergue Corita, Districto de Llachon, Capachica, Puno, Peru

ACCOM+
THE MOUNTAIN INSTITUTE
Andean Programme Inka Naani Project

If you would like to walk the Inca road interacting all the way with local families offering tourism services, this is an excellent opportunity. Ninety members of families from seven communities living along the Inca Camino Real or main highway at Conchucos Valley, Ancash, are involved. At present camping is being used, but the community 'Tambos' or traditional Inca Inns should be ready for 2007. TMI is keen to advance mountain cultures and protect their environments and encourage rural families to manage their own development. To this end it is helping the local NGO, Kuntur, to implement sustainable tourism projects that are truly participative. As the TMI approach is holistic, conservation goes in step with tourism development

Contact: Miriam Torres
Tel: 43 723 446
Fax: 43 726 610
Email: mtorres@mountain.org
Web: www.mountain.org
Address: Instituto de Montaña, Casilla 01-Huaraz, Peru

ACCOM+
THE MOUNTAIN INSTITUTE
Community Tourism Project in Humacchuco

Set up by The Mountain Institute (TMI) with funding from the Dutch embassy in Lima, this project is grounded on selected families in Humacchuco. Four-person tourist lodges have been constructed near their homes where visitors sleep but they eat with their host family; 'it is an intercultural learning experience. Six families are involved, five with a lodge and the sixth concentrating on its area of expertise, guiding. The cost to the visitor is only £17/US$30 per day, and this covers everything except travelling to and from Humacchuco. All the money goes into the community project.

Contact: Guido J. van Es
Tel: 43 723 446/43 722 362
Fax: 43 726 610
Email: guidovanes@mountain.org
Web: www.mountain.org/work/andes/tourism/index.cfm, www.yachaquiwayi.org
Address: Pje. Ricardo Palma nº 100, Huaraz, Ancash, Perú

ACCOM+
THE MOUNTAIN INSTITUTE
Community Tourism Project Invicos

This is another project funded by the Dutch embassy; this one involves a selected group of eight families in Vicos. All the income from tourism visits goes into the families and is shared out according to the extent and nature of their involvement. Part also goes into funding community development work.

Contact: Guido J. van Es
Tel: 43 723 446/43 722 362
Fax: 43 726 610
Email: guidovanes@mountain.org
Web: www.mountain.org/work/andes/tourism/index.cfm, www.yachaquiwayi.org
Address: Pje. Ricardo Palma nº 100, Huaraz, Ancash, Perú

Visitors stay in seven lodge houses, which take four people each and which are next to local family houses. This is another inter-cultural opportunity and experience that breeds a lifetime of memories.

PERU VERDE – INKA NATURA TRAVEL

Peru Verde is a non-profit conservation group based in Cusco running three ecotourism lodges in the Amazon. The Manu Wildlife centre is in the heart of the rainforest and features lakes with abundant wildlife, including giant river otters, macaws and tapirs and up to 13

Contact: Rodrigo Custodio
Tel: 1 440 2022
Fax: 1 440 9225
Email: postmaster@inkanaturatravel.com.pe
Web: www.inkanatura.com, www.peruverde.org
Address: Manuel Bañon 461, San Isidro, Lima 27, Peru

species of monkey. The Cock-of-the-Rock Lodge is set in a forest reserve surrounded by 600 species of birds. The Sandoval Lake Lodge, as its name suggests, is on the shore of a lake where giant river otters live as well as four species of monkeys, macaws and wading birds. From here it is easy to visit the Heath River Wildlife Centre in Bolivia. Peru Verde trains local communities to grow produce and prepare handicrafts, which are sold at the lodge's gift shops. Profits are used to help protect wildlife in the area.

ACCOM+
THE TREASURE OF WINAYMARKA

The aptly named project The Treasure of Winaymarka gives tourists a bracing diet of cross-cultural tourism within the community of Anapia Island, which is one of the islands comprising the archipelago of The Minor Lake. The aim is to show both visitor and locals that tourism could change lives, enhance self-respect and self-esteem and above all improve

Contact: Willy Lopez
Tel: 5135 5552/5135 5979
Fax: 51 35 5552
Email: allwaystravel@titicacaperu.com, sales@titicacaperu.com
Web: www.titicacaperu.com
Address: Jr. Tacna 234, Puno, Peru

local education and health. The cross-cultural exchange makes the local people realize that they should be proud of their culture and what they are. A Sustainable Tourism Association has been set up in Anapia and efforts are made to be environmentally responsible.

ACCOM+
YACHAQUI WAYI

This non-profit association was kick-started by a private donation from a US foundation thanks to Crooked Trails. Their aim is to promote community-based tourism and in time to link up with other community-based tourism projects from the same area and

Contact: Guido J. van Es
Tel: 43 422 362
Fax: 43 426 610
Email: guidovanes@mountain.org
Web: www.yachaquiwayi.org
Address: Avenida Tarapacá 1452, Huaraz, Ancash, Perú

beyond. In Quechua the name means 'house of learning, of exchanging ideas', which fits well the hope of being not just a hotel but also a weavers' shop, a responsible travel agency, an educational centre for all including tourists – really an education and information exchange. The project, which began in July 2005, already has guests booked for the hotel, and sounds extremely interesting.

VENEZUELA
International dialling code +58

1000km

CARACAS

The birthplace of one of South America's greatest independence leaders, Simón Bolívar, and, more recently, of the maverick president Hugo Chavez, Venezuela presents itself as a surprizingly multifaceted and self-confident nation. On the one hand, it has embraced modernity sooner than many of its surrounding neighbours thanks to its important oil reserves making Venezuela one of the founding members of the OPEC and South America's most important petroleum exporter. On the other hand, it is also the most Caribbean country in character in South America. The paradisiacal seaside region in the north is dotted with highlights such as the Los Roques National Park and the Paria peninsula. In striking contrast, Venezuela is also home to the starting point of South America's 'backbone', the Andes, the Los Llanos plains in the centre with a prolific wildlife and La Gran Sabana National Park in the southwest, which offers spectacular landscapes with high plateaus and canyons through which rivers and waterfalls gush. No wonder that Christopher Columbus once called Venezuela Tierra de García (Land of Grace). Finally, together with Brazil, Venezuela is also home to the famous Yanomami people, one of the last Amazonian native tribes to lead traditional lifestyles. A great country to visit, an even greater duty to preserve!

ACCOM
ANDES TROPICALES

The tropical Andes programme of this environmental NGO runs 11 'mucuposadas' or guest houses in the highlands of the state of Merida. The mucuposadas are traditional dwellings reconditioned to offer the visitor food and lodging in a simple and hospitable style. They are located along the Caminos Posaderos Andinos (Andean Inn Routes). The caminos or pathways have varying degrees of difficulty and guides are available. The operation directly benefits the people involved.

Contact: Dayana Muñoz
Tel & Fax: 274 263 8633
Email: mariechris@andestropicales.org,
dayana@andestropicales.org
Web: www.andestropicales.org
Address: Quinta Irma, calle 41 con prolongación Av. 2,
Mérida 5101, edo. Mérida, Venezuela

THE AMERICAS SOUTH

ASIA

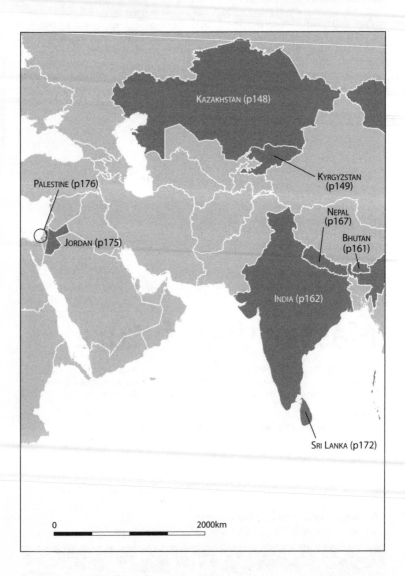

KAZAKHSTAN (p148)

KYRGYZSTAN (p149)

PALESTINE (p176)

NEPAL (p167)

BHUTAN (p161)

JORDAN (p175)

INDIA (p162)

SRI LANKA (p172)

0   2000km

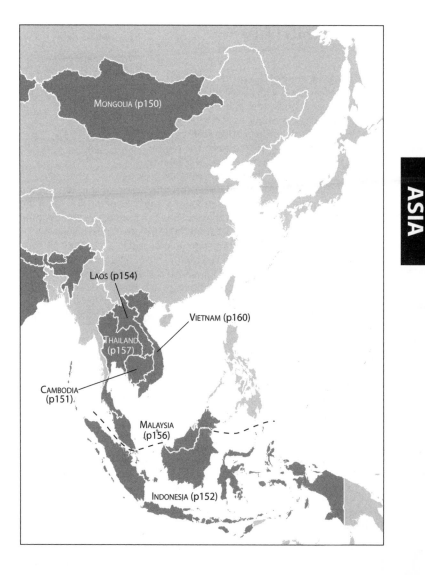

MONGOLIA (p150)

ASIA

LAOS (p154)

VIETNAM (p160)

THAILAND (p157)

CAMBODIA (p151)

MALAYSIA (p156)

INDONESIA (p152)

CENTRAL ASIA

KAZAKHSTAN

International dialling code +7

1500km

ALMATY

Lying along the route of the ancient Silk Road, Kazakhstan fascinates with hospitable people, gorgeous natural landscapes and rare wildlife. As one of the biggest countries in central Asia, Kazakhstan offers endless possibilities to explore its remote and wild corners. The region around the capital, Almaty, carries the beautiful name of Land of Seven Rivers and stretches over five climatic zones, from the mighty year-round glaciers of the Zaili Alatau Mountain range to the 'singing' desert sands at the bank of the Ili River. In the Turkistan region of southern Kazakhstan, one can admire the architectural splendour of the medieval capital of the Turkic people. Kazakhs are passionate hunters and fishermen. Hunting with golden eagles is a favorite pastime and fishing for gigantic specimen like the Ural River beluga and the sheathfish can be a one-time experience for amateur anglers, especially when the catch is thrown back into its habitat and let to live. Horse games are curious events. Look out for the goat-carcass version of polo and the 'kiss-the-girl' game where a boy pursues a girl on horseback trying to kiss her. If he does not succeed, she will turn around and chase him with a whip.

HOST/TOUR/TREK
ECOTOURISM KAZAKHSTAN

Ecotourism Kazakhstan offers homestay guesthouses where visitors are shown traditional hospitality and served meals of fresh, local produce. They can also sleep under the stars in a traditional nomadic yurt. Travellers can explore Kazakhstan, the home of flamingos, wolves and bears, and trek on horseback or foot into the Tien-Shan or Altai mountains. They can discover the culture of rural Kazakhstan through concerts of local music and dance, or see the historical and religious sites of the ancient Silk Road, accompanied by local guides.

Contact: Ainur Suleimenova
Tel: 3272 798146
Fax: 3272 798146
Email: ecotourism.kz@mail.kz
Web: www.ecotourism.kz
Address: 71 Zheltokzan Street, Almaty 050004, Kazakhstan

KYRGYZSTAN
International dialling code +996

Kyrgyzstan is a landlocked and mountainous country at the heart of Central Asia. Some of the highest mountains in the region, the Tien-Shan and the Pamir, span over Kyrgyzstan's territory and make the countryside an adventure to travel through. Outside the capital city Bishkek, life continues the way it has done for centuries. Nomadic families move around with their livestock in a seasonal pattern and are often cut off for months from the rest of the world. That's why they are particularly fond of travellers as they bring news from the outside world. Typical Kyrgyz cuisine is very rich and fatty to help the people survive through the harsh long winter months. An interesting speciality, somewhat awkward to the Western taste, is Kumys, a drink made from fermented mare's milk. During the hot summer months, the greatest pleasure is to cool off at the beaches of the largest lake in Kyrgyzstan, the Issyk-Kul. Locals call it 'hot lake' because it does not freeze in winter, even though it is situated at more than 5000 feet above sea-level.

HOST/TOUR/TREK
KYRGYZ COMMUNITY BASED TOURISM ASSOCIATION (KCBTA)
Hospitality Kyrgzstan

KCBTA offers community-based tourism in Kyrgyzstan. Visitors can stay with rural families in village houses, or traditional yurtas (nomadic tents) in the mountains. They can also enjoy trekking, horse riding tours, local festivals and handicrafts, all of which is organized by and directly benefits the population of rural villages.

Contact: Asylbek Rajiev
Tel: 312 622385/502 540416
Fax: 312 611814
Email: cbt@cbtkyrgyzstan.kg, kcbta@mail.ru, reservation@cbtkyrgyzstan.kg
Web: www.cbtkyrgyzstan.kg
Address: 4, 95, Kievskaya Street, Bishkek city, 720001, Kyrgyzstan

MONGOLIA

International dialling code +976

1500km

ULAN
BATOR

As one of the most sparsely populated countries on Earth, Mongolia is the ideal getaway from Europe's overcrowded and urbanized cities. In the 13th century though, when Genghis Khan united the Mongol tribes and defeated many neighbouring peoples, the Mongolian Empire was at the height of its existence.

Today Mongolia is a land of magnificent steppe landscapes, inhabited by herds of wild antelopes, donkeys and yaks. For centuries Mongols have been herding cattle and horses and still move around the country following the old nomadic way of life. Mongols pride themselves as skilled horsemen, and horse races are a favourite pastime. Nomadic families will travel large distances to attend the biggest games at the annually held Naadam Festival. Mongolian culture is heavily influenced by Tibetan Buddhism and ancient Shamanist practices, with priceless religious artifacts found in newly reopened monasteries after sixty years of Socialist rule. On a trip to Mongolia, one should not dare miss a concert of the mystic and enthralling throat singing. A stay in the round and cozy felt tents of the hospitable nomads will be another unforgettable experience, rounded off with a bowl of warm tea and a hearty lamb dish.

ASIA
CENTRAL

ACCOM+
THREE CAMEL LODGE

Three Camel Lodge is a wilderness ger camp and offers a memorable and rewarding stay in Mongolia's Gobi desert. The staff are from the region and are happy to share their local knowledge and passion for their homeland. Guests can visit ancient petroglyphs near the camp, watch the native wildlife, and visit local families to experience the daily life of the desert nomad. The Lodge arranges performances of traditional Mongolian dancing and throat singing. Visitors can also stay overnight in gers, the traditional felt tents of nomadic herders, each heated by a wood stove and furnished with beautifully painted wood-framed beds. These have washing facilities and toilets a few hundred feet away – although new 'luxury' gers get round this slight problem.

Contact: Mr. Y. Badral
Tel: (11) 313 396/(11) 325 786
Fax: (11) 320 311
Email: info@threecamellodge.com,
info@nomadicexpeditions.com
Web: www.threecamellodge.com,
www.nomadicexpeditions.com
Address: Nomadic Expeditions, LLC, Building 76,
Suite 28, 1-40 000, Peace Avenue
Chingeltei District, Ulaanbaantar, Mongolia

SOUTHEAST ASIA

CAMBODIA
International dialling code +855

In its heyday, over 600 years ago, the city of Angkor located in the north of modern day Cambodia boasted a civilized population of more than a million. At the same time, London was inhabited by less than 35,000. Today, tourists flock to see the remains of the temples that represent Cambodia's main tourist attraction. Khmer people are incredibly proud of their ancient heritage, yet the recent history of this ex-French protectorate shows tragedy not glory. Over 500,000 civilians are estimated to have died during a secret and illegal anti-communist bombing campaign by the US during the second Indochina war. Out of the devastation, in 1975 the Khmer Rouge, led by Pol Pot, managed to take power and impose a brutal four-year regime of extreme socialism, which killed around 1.7 million people.

During the rule of Pol Pot, the UN did not intervene. It was Vietnam in 1979 that overthrew the Khmer Rouge. Despite removing such an evil regime, Vietnamese intervention was unacceptable for some countries. In 1992, the UN eventually entered Cambodia and the country has been in the process of recovery since. Human rights remain a huge issue, with many living and working on the streets. The country also remains notorious for child prostitution and sex-worker exploitation from sex tourism.

Be sure to travel to remote provinces such as Mondulkiri and Ratanakiri with their ethnic minority inhabitants, or Kratie where Irriwadi dolphins can be sighted. Learning some Cambodian will almost certainly guarantee smiles from a people who, despite all that they have been through, have a strong national pride and a good sense of keeping daily life light and fun.

TOURS
CARPE DIEM TRAVEL

Carpe Diem is a UK-based company offering small, tailor-made group and customized trips to Cambodia. They employ local guides and groups of no more than ten, using a wide range of different kinds of transport. They also support local community-based tourism projects and take clients to visit local development projects working with street families and

Contact: Debbie Watkins
Tel: +44 (0) 845 226 2198
Fax: +44 (0) 870 132 7589
Email: mail@carpe-diem-travel.com
Web: www.carpe-diem-travel.com
Address: 68 St. Peter's Street, London N1 8JS, UK

ASIA

SOUTHEAST

AIDS victims, as well as donating a portion of their profits directly to humanitarian development projects within Cambodia. Carpe Diem was created as a social venture and so it remains.

TOURS
SYMBIOSIS EXPEDITION PLANNING

SEP are a Cambodian-based company offering tailor-made holidays and small group expeditions throughout Southeast Asia for travellers concerned about the impact of tourism. SEP run cycle tours, kayaking, trekking, wildlife watching, cookery and other forms of mostly non-vehicle-based tourism. They encourage the use of local guides, and stay at smaller locally owned hotels and guesthouses, which

Contact: Polham Seila
Tel: 845 1232844/23 993092
Fax: 1232845/23220161
Email: enquiry@symbiosis-travel.com
Web: www.symbiosis-travel.com,
www.divingsouteastasia.com
Address: 147a Norodom Boulevard, Phnom Penh 12302, Cambodia

are checked for their environmental policies. They also run periodical charity fundraising expeditions such as the Bangkok to Saigon Cycle Challenge. Guests also get the chance to contribute to a local well-run charitable organization and SEP passes these contributions on via its charity bank account.

ACCOM
TOURISM FOR HELP

Offering accommodation sited near Stung Treng in northeast Cambodia, about 60km from the Laotian border, this project was still being set up as this guide went to press (though it is due to open in 2006, so please use the contact details below for latest information). The organizers are keen that their

Contact: Isabelle Lanfranconi
Tel: +41 22 793 10.94
Email: infos@tourismforhelp.org
Web: www.tourismforhelp.org
Address: 81, Route de St Georges, 1213 Pt Lancy, Geneva, Switzerland

plans for a maximum of ten bungalows, with a 60-person capacity, should be backed up by environmentally friendly technologies (for example, solar power) and that the operation should be a driver for the development of sustainable tourism practices in the Stung Treng region.

INDONESIA
International dialling code +62

Indonesia consists of over 17,000 islands, about 6000 of which are inhabited. The islands are located on the edge of a tectonic plate and are therefore subject to earthquakes (also having 400 volcanoes, 130 of which are active – including one with a drive-in crater!). Stretching between Southeast Asia and Oceania, Indonesia has 34,000 miles of coastline with some superb (but endangered) coral reefs and some of the world's best surf.

Covering an area of 780,000 square miles, Indonesia has an immense variety of flora and fauna including tropical rain forests (disappearing at an alarming rate), mangroves (threatened by prawn farming and other coastal industries), orchids, orang-utans, rhinos, komodo dragons, tarsiers and birds of paradise.

With a population of over 240 million from over 350 ethnic groups, the culture is as varied as the nature. From the world's largest Buddhist temple/monument, Burbodur, to Hindu temples and megaliths, a huge range of architectural styles is complemented by flourishing music, art, dance, puppetry, theatre, textiles, wood carving and so on.

While over 80 per cent of the population profess to be Muslims most are not extremists and many are not practising. On some islands other religions predominate, for example, Hindus on Bali, Catholics on Flores, Protestants on Sumba, etc. Whatever their religious background, in nearly all areas 'conservative dress' is appreciated. Forty-five per cent of Indonesians are employed in agriculture and almost a third live below the poverty line, thus due consideration of your relative wealth should be borne in mind. Nearly all Indonesians (except the very old) speak Indonesian. Learning a little of this very easy language will go a long way in relating to local people outside the tourist zones.

ACCOM/TREK
KANDORA LODGE

Located south of Rantepao, in southern Sulewesi, Kandora Mountain Lodge is owned by a local NGO. It offers an opportunity to spend one or two nights exploring local

Tel: 423 27344
Email: kandora@toraja.net, info@ladybamboo.org
Web: www.toraja.net

culture and history and trekking in the magnificent scenery with local Torajan guides. Lodge costs are very reasonable and income generated goes to benefit the local community at Sandalla village.

ORG/DAY
MITRA BALI

Mitra Bali is an NGO run by Balinese people that aims to improve the lot of rural handicraft producers through fair trade programmes promoting their products. About 800 craftspeople throughout Bali are involved. Additionally they are transforming Abuan into a Fair Trade Handicraft Village, which groups (15 maximum) can visit, meet villagers, have lunch with them and see how crafts are made – encountering the production end of the fair trade process.

Contact: Komang Redana
Tel: 361 295010
Fax: 361 295616
Email: agungalit@mitrabali.com
Web: www.mitrabali.com
Address: Jl. Gunung Abang, Banjar Lod Sema,
Lod Tunduh, Ubud, Bali, Indonesia

ASIA SOUTHEAST

LUX
NIHIWATU RESORT

The operators describe their operation as 'an upmarket…resort'. One can only agree, and add as well that they have put a great deal of money into helping the community of Sumba Island. Since 2001 their guests have donated over £250,000/US$450,000 to the work of The

Contact: Claude Graves
Tel: 361 757 149/816 570 520
Email: claude@nihiwatu.com
Web: www.nihiwatu.com

Sumba Foundation, which the operators set up. The expenditure focuses on water provision, health clinics and primary education. Nihiwatu is committed to helping alleviate poverty on the island of Sumba as well as providing an excellent service to guests.

ACCOM+
SUA BALI

This is a privately owned small hotel on Bali, the driving force of which is the local philosophy known as Tri Hita Karana, which teaches the virtue of maintaining a balance between human nature and spiritual life, because if this is done then taking care of other people comes automatically. Not unnaturally they try to do the right thing by the environment and the local community by being a socially responsible destination. All activities take place within the community.

Contact: Alit Suwarsawan
Tel: 361 941050
Fax: 361 941035
Email: info@suabali.com
Web: www.suabali.com
Address: Kemenuh Village district
Gianyar, Bali, Indonesia

LAOS
International dialling code +856

600km

VIENTIANE

Dominated by the Mekong and its tributaries, which cut through rugged jungle-covered mountains, Laos, for so long obscured by its more powerful neighbours, is today beginning to assert itself as a must-see destination. Isolated by its terrain and its rudimentary infrastructure Laos has retained a slow pace of life that affords the visitor a glimpse of a bygone age. In towns such as Luang Prabang crumbling colonial shop fronts are punctuated with ornate Buddhist temples, outside which sit saffron-robed monks shading from the sun and, in the countryside, where 85 per cent of the population are subsistence farmers, life has changed little in the last hundred years.

Landlocked and sandwiched between Vietnam and Thailand and with a population comprising over 68 ethnic groups this diminutive land hides a tragic recent history. Laos has the unfortunate distinction of being, during the Vietnam War, the most heavily bombed nation. In an attempt to destroy north Vietnamese supply routes, the US waged an illegal and secret war in Laos, in which it dropped more bombs than were dropped in the entire

Second World War. This had catastrophic implications for Laos, where today unexploded ordnance litters the land.

One of the world's few remaining communist states, the Maoist administration (the Pathet Lao) came to power in 1973 establishing the Laos Peoples' Democratic Republic and sweeping away 600 years of monarchy. Following the collapse of the Soviet Union, on which Laos was heavily dependent, the country opened its borders in the early 1990s to investors and tourists. Subsistence farming provides 55 per cent of GDP and half the country's budget comes from overseas aid.

The 21st century is fast encroaching on this once sleepy backwater and although the government is keen for Laos to preserve its customs and way of life this cannot be solely determined by those in power and the next few years will be crucial.

ACCOM+
THE BOAT LANDING GUEST HOUSE

The owners of this Guest House are trying hard to assist the surrounding community of diverse ethnic groups in Luang Namtha, by putting guests in touch with people who provide services to tourists, for example, boatmen, taxi drivers and guides. Offering varied activities, including bike tours, they also advise other local guesthouses and restaurants in areas like

Contact: Sompawn Khantisouk
Tel: 86 312 398
Fax: 86 312 239
Email: theboatlanding@yahoo.com
Web: www.theboatlanding.com
Address: PO Box 28, Luang Namtha, Laos

marketing and presentation. They are working hard at spreading the word as to how much communities can benefit from tourism and at raising money for the village school and an animal conservation project – the Black Cheeked Gibbon. In 2004 they purchased local goods and services to the tune of £22,000/US$39,000 out of a total spend of £25,000/US$45,000 – which indicates their commitment to the area.

ACCOM+
MEKONG TOURISM DEVELOPMENT PROJECT

This is a project implemented via the National Tourism Administration through four provincial tourism offices. In Luang Namtha, Luang Prabang, Khammouane and Champassak provinces three new community-based ecotourism projects are being developed. The villages at each location own their project and the villagers provide the services directly or through a private company or guide service. All

Contact: Mr Sounh Manivong
Tel: 21 212 251
Fax: 21 217 910
Email: snh_manivong@yahoo.com
Web: www.ecotourismlaos.com
Address: PO Box 3556, Lanexang Avenue, Vientiane, Laos

aspects of the visitor's experience are community-rooted, which gives a unique insight into Lao life. Operations are made as green as possible and great stress is placed on educating villagers and ensuring that they reap the economic harvest yielded by tourism. All the local people involved in any one project are indigenous to that area and many are members of an ethnic minority.

ASIA

SOUTHEAST

TREK
NAM HA ECOTOURISM PROJECT

The Nam Ha Ecotourism Project offers treks varying in length from one to four days. Overnight treks stay in village guesthouses of four different ethnic minority groups. Each trek has at least one English-speaking guide, as well as other guides familiar with the local terrain, which varies from mountain to forest to agricultural fields. A boat trip is also offered along the Nam Tha River, visiting riverside villages and with great opportunities for swimming.

Contact: Mr. Bounta Chalurnsok
Tel: 86 21534
Cellular: 20 7790423
Fax: 86 312047
Email: namhacenter@hotmail.com
Web: www.unescobkk.org
Address: Provincial Tourism Office,
PO Box 07, Luang Namtha, Lao PDR

MALAYSIA
International dialling code +60

Split between the Malay Peninsula and its two Borneo states of Sabah and Sarawak, this historic trading route from Europe to China and India is a cultural melting pot of Malays, Indians and Chinese. These peoples bring with them a wealth of culture through their Islamic, Buddhist, Taoist and Hindi religions, festivals and varied cuisine. Malaysia boasts a rapidly developing economy with major cities like its capital, Kuala Lumpur, hosting modern hotels and shopping malls. Closer investigation into cities like Georgetown on Penang Island in the north reveals Chinese and Indian cultural districts.

Away from the cities the natural beauty of the country can be explored from popular, beautiful islands like Palau Langkawi to the inner regional rainforests and their hidden caves, waterfalls and canopy walkways offering glimpses of its illusive wildlife and primary rainforest for the determined trekker. Sabah can offer spectacular interactions with nature including the world's largest flower (Rafflesia). An accessible tourist route ascent of the highest peak in Southeast Asia, Mount Kinabalu, presents the opportunity to take in the sun rising across the region. To the east, Sepilok offers an opportunity to experience our close cousins the orang-utan. Palau Sipadan is a popular dive destination with everything from turtles to sharks. For the more adventurous, Sarawak can offer river rides to interact with local indigenous peoples; however, one should note that tribes like the Penan in this area are threatened by encroaching development and logging.

RAINFOREST
BORNEO ADVENTURE/ULU AI PROJECT

Ulu Ai is a traditional longhouse in the Iban heart-land, situated in the remote interior of Borneo. A trip to Ulu Ai offers a glimpse into the lifestyles of the local tribes, who for centuries have lived simply, following schedules imposed only by the cycles of nature. The surroundings are idyllic, with clear, clean streams, waterfalls and treks along rainforest trails. Accommodation is at the Borneo Adventure Lodge,

Contact: Carsten Jensen
Tel: 82 245 175
Fax: 82 422 626
Email: sales@borneoadventure.com
Web: www.borneoadventure.com
Address: No 55 Main Bazaar, 93000, Kuching, Malaysia

which provides simple, clean lodging with western-style toilets. Visitors can go trekking or travel upriver by longboat. They can visit the longhouse and surrounding farms, as well as participate in the daily activities of the Iban people. The enterprise works with and helps the local community by, for example, building a sanitary system to improve health and by setting up a scholarship fund.

DAY/TOUR
BORNEO TOUCH ECOTOURS

This is a one-family business offering a range of activities like mountain biking, rafting, climbing, hiking and caving within the national parks. The company has good relations with the indigenous tribes who benefit from tourist spending and they also receive a proportion of the profits and interest-free loans. They hope to develop an eco-lodge and to organize stays in traditional longhouses.

Contact: Mr Lim Chong Teah
Tel: 085 211 515
Email: sales@borneotouch.com/ borneotouch@yahoo.ca
Web: www.borneotouch.com
Address: P.O. Box 10, Limbang, Sarawak, 98700, Malaysia

THAILAND
International dialling code +66

Bangkok is unfortunately well known for its Patpong district with its neon lights and sex trade, which can throw a bad light on Thailand. There is much more to this city, however, including a vibrant culture and the amazing architecture like the King's Grand Palace and an impressive procession that marks his official birthday on December 5th, a national holiday. Away from the capital, Thailand's ability to cater for western desires are demonstrated on islands like Ko Pangan with its Full Moon parties set along the island's southern beaches.

Tourism development in Thailand has been rapid since the late 1970s and often uncontrolled, leading to some coastal pollution, and golf courses, which compounds water shortage problems, even with the country's long rainy season between May and October. The tsunami in 2004 heavily affected the western coast, including popular tourist destinations like Phuket and Phi

Phi island. These areas have been quick to rebuild and publicize that business is back to normal, with pristine beaches and shark diving. There are, however, questions around the displacement of local peoples to make way for some new development sites.

Dominant Theravada Buddhism with its spectacular ornate temples across the country demonstrates a strong cultural unity among a people who have experienced historically unstable political governance. A popular northern city to explore from is Chiang Mai. Here you can learn to cook energizing Thai food, practise Thai massage or hire motorbikes. You can also venture out on trekking trips with rafting, elephant rides and visit mountain peoples. It is well worth exploring the inner regions of the country where a large welcoming rural population still make a living growing rice. For those seeking even quieter destinations try beaches and islands further east like Ko Chang or take time to reflect at a Buddhist retreat.

TOUR
AKHA HILL TRIBE

About 23km from Chiang Rai in the mountains of northern Thailand (at a height of 1500 metres, so you should be out of mosquito range) you can stay with the Akha in a project bungalow and know that all the profit from what you are paying is going into the community, its school and education. And anyone

Contact: Jennifer Newton
Tel: 9 997 5505
Fax: 53 715 451
Email: apeahouse@hotmail.com
Web: www.akhahill.com

who does well at school is helped financially to go and study further elsewhere. You will go on guided jungle walks, catch fish, stay overnight in a banana leaf house and meet other hill tribes. Please note, tourism is the only source of income since the government banned slash and burn farming.

ACCOM+/AGRI
GECKO VILLA

Gecko Villa nestles amongst paddy fields in Thailand's Isaan plateau in the northeast of the country. It is a locally owned spacious villa with a pool, offering guests the chance to experience rural Thailand at first hand. This includes taking an interest in rice farming, water buffalo, local village traditions and crafts, temples, wetlands, extraordi-

Contact: Ten
Tel: 1 9180500
Email: info@geckovilla.com
Web: www.geckovilla.com
Address: 126 Moo 13, Baan Um Jaan,
A. Prjak Sinlapakom, Udon Thani, Thailand

nary local cuisine, or simply relaxing and enjoying the slower pace of rural Thailand. All proceeds from the rentals stay in the local village and contribute to this sustainable tourism project.

HOST+
LAMAI HOMESTAY AND VILLAGE TOURS

A homestay, for up to six people in a rural northern Thai village, offering a choice of activities. Most guests opt for a cultural/historical tour of the Khmer ruins at Phimai or Phanom Rung and the archaeological site at Ban Prasat. Also on offer is participating in a range of rural craft activities including a half-day course in spinning or weaving silk, a morning of Isan cookery lessons, an afternoon of raffia mat and basket-making or even rice planting or harvesting, depending on the season. Accessible by bus, train, air or motorway. Accommodation is available from as little as £4/US$7.

Contact: Ann Moore
Tel: 62585894/1970 871464
Fax: 1970 871995
Email: annmoore@quik.com
Web: www.thailandhomestay.com
Address: 23/1 M003, Ban Ko Phet, Bua Yai, Khorat, Thailand

TREK
POOH ECO TREKKING

An environmentally conscious trek in a small group of four to six people in a Pwo Karen hill tribe village in Mae Hong Son province in northern Thailand. Visitors learn about hill tribe culture, go camping, caving, wade up rivers and learn how to cook naturally and organically in the tradition of the hill tribe people. To minimize the environmental impact, all waste is brought back. Pooh eco trekking also helps the local people by providing money for

Contact: Pooh or Tee
Tel: 53 208 538
Cellular: 50 414 971
Fax: 53 208 538
Email: remimin@loxinfo.co.th
Web: www.pooheco.com
Address: 59 Rajchapakinai Rd, Muang, Chiang Mai 50200, Thailand

transportation to hospital, and has educated the villagers to recycle waste and run a cooperative shop where the profits are distributed among local families.

ORG/TOUR/HOST
RESPONSIBLE ECOLOGICAL SOCIAL TOURS (REST)

REST is a Thai NGO aiming to use community-based tourism as a tool for sustainable community development. REST offers tailor-made tours using local guides and REST's multilingual tour facilitators. Travellers are invited to share the lives of their hosts; all tours include a homestay with a local family. Activities could include jungle-trekking, traditional arts, weaving, herbal medicine or rice-wine making. Visitors are

Contact: Peter Richards
Tel: 2 938 7007
Fax: 2 938 5275
Email: rest@asiaaccess.net.th
Web: www.ecotour.in.th
Address: 109/79 Mooban Yucharoen Pattana, Ladprao Road, Soi 18, Ladyao, Chatuchak, Bangkok 10900, Thailand

encouraged to experience the rich, living relationship between local people and the natural world, and may be invited to join their hosts planting rice, trees or even orchids.

ORG/ACCOM+
TELL TALE TRAVEL

Tell Tale Travel offer either a bespoke service to Thailand where you put together your perfect trip from a range of handpicked elements or choose their ready made service including cultural home stays, Thai cooking and family adventures.

Contact: Chris Bland
Tel: +44 (0)20 7659 5432
Email: guests@telltaletravel.co.uk
Web: www.telltaletravel.co.uk
Address: 28 Bruton Street, London W1 6QW

ASIA

SOUTHEAST

VIETNAM
International dialling code +84

It is hard not to let first impressions of Vietnam be characterized by images of the Vietnam War, and yet the country has a lot more to offer than a history of atrocities and bloodshed. This long, thin stretch of land, flanked by Laos and Cambodia on the west and 3000km of coastline on the east, boasts bleached white beaches, paddy fields dotted with the ubiquitous conical hat-clad farmers, heaving head-spinning cities, jungle treks and mist enfolded pagodas. Despite a decade of war and a legacy of trade embargoes and international isolation, the country is rapidly reinventing itself and is finally beginning to shake of its more damaging communist stereotypes of the past. Today there are few visible reminders of the conflict that saw over 5 million tonnes of bombs dropped, accounting for the loss of 2.2 million hectares of forest. The craters that still pockmark the country are slowly being refilled or used as fish farms or small-scale irrigation systems. Vietnam is a country of growing biodiversity and home to a number of rare and endangered species including the Javan rhino, thought only to exist in Indonesia, until a recent discovery in 1989, and the previously unknown Soala, a species of ox. A trip into the hill country of the north may lead to an invitation into one of the traditional communal longhouses where you can experience unrivalled hospitality and elaborate displays of age-old customs, complete with tribal costumes and rice wine. Alternatively, a foray into Hanoi, Vietnam's northern capital, or Ho Chi Minh City, the largest city of the south, encourages you to explore the country's cultural heritage at a slightly more frantic pace.

TOUR
FOOTPRINT

Footprint is a tour operator owned and run by three Vietnamese guides. They organize responsible travel packages and community-based tourism, designed in agreement with and in cooperation with the local population. They also have an education programme to teach local children to prevent disease from water and daily activities. Footprint run a community-based project in Quan Ba Ha Giang. By cooperating with the local population, they are able to train them to manage and operate their own projects, so they directly participate and benefit from tourism rather than feel it is imposed upon them.

Contact: Mr Dien Dang Quang
Tel: 933 2844
Cellular: 913 55 1852
Fax: 933 2855
Email: son@footprintsvietnam.com, footprint@hn.vnn.vn
Web: www.FootprintsVietnam.com
Address: #6 Le Thanh Tong, Hanoi 10000, Vietnam

ASIA SOUTHEAST

SOUTH ASIA

BHUTAN
International dialling code +975

The King of Bhutan decided not to follow neighbouring Nepal's example and allow unrestricted tourism, with all its detrimental effects on the local culture and environment. Tourist numbers are limited by the relatively high cost of visiting Bhutan. All visitors must book and pay for all services – transport, guide, accommodation, meals and admission costs – in advance, for a set amount (around £140/US$250 per person per day). The profit pays for free health care and education for all Bhutanese. Individual travellers are treated as small groups, and are accompanied everywhere by a guide. As well as visiting the many Mahayana Buddhist monasteries and picturesque towns with wooden chalet-style houses, trekking in the mountains is increasingly popular. The modern world has been kept at bay in Bhutan until very recently – the wearing of national dress is mandatory, and television and mobile phones were only introduced in 1999. The national sport of archery is still the most popular male pastime. The determination to maintain the purity of Bhutanese culture culminated in the 1990s in ethnic Nepalese migrant workers being ordered to adopt Drukpa culture and prove citizenship entitlement based on residency. Large numbers who did not qualify have been in refugee settlements since then.

TOURS
NATURE TOURISM

Nature Tourism provides guided tours to visitors on different aspects of biodiversity in Bhutan. Visitors choose from a whole range of programmes such as birdwatching, botanical tours, entomology and fungi. Nature Tourism is closely involved with local communities, making informal visits to villages to exchange views on issues of biodiversity. It also mobilizes funds for community forestry projects, and cleaning up degraded rivers and streams. The bottom line is the intention to build conservation awareness within local communities.

Contact: Karma Jamtsho
Tel: 2 327355
Fax: 2 327356
Email: nattouri@druknet.bt
Web: www.naturetourism-bhutan.com
Address: Kelwang Building, Post Box 673, Thimphu, Bhutan

TOURS
SNOW WHITE TREKS & TOURS

Snow White Treks and Tours are a small company based in Bhutan offering tourists activities such as attending festivals, staying in farm houses with local communities, culture tours, trekking and birdwatching. They want to offer a homely service and give the travellers a memorable experience. State policy imposes a uniform tariff on Bhutan tourism companies so holidays there are not cheap, but that income goes towards free health care and education.

Contact: Ms. Kencho Wangmo Dorjee
Tel: 2 323028
Fax: 2 321696
Email: snowwhite@druknet.bt, kenchod@yahoo.com
Web: www.snowwhitetours.com.bt
Address: Phendey Lam, Post box 1123, Thimphu, Bhutan

INDIA
International dialling code +91

India never fails to astonish: her powerful contrast between old and new, poverty and extravagance, efficiency and chaos guarantee the visitor a roller-coaster ride of adventure. Humanity presents itself in a vibrant and creative diversity of cultures, religions and landscapes. But India's deep cultural roots entwine her people inseparably as one. India is the world's sixth largest country and, with almost one billion citizens, is the second most populous. It has one of the most ancient civilizations, dating back to 4000BC, yet it is India's modern history that preoccupies most visitors: astonished by Britain's detrimental role in shaping the India we see today.

British occupation of India was born out of international trade, giving way to British supremacy in 1852. Mahatma Ghandi is the popular face of Indian independence. However, despite India technically winning independence in 1930, it was not the united India that Ghandi had dreamt of: in 1948 the creation of the separate Muslim state of Pakistan resulted in extreme conflict and violence that persist to this day. Whilst Indians never tire of paying homage to the British institutions of cricket and the railways, feelings about British imperialism are deep seated and complex and sadly are not restricted to the past: today's corporate-led globalization is now widely viewed as neo-colonialism.

Eighty per cent of Indians follow Hinduism and the remainder are Muslims, Christians, Buddhists and Jains. Women visitors should respect the tradition of covering shoulders and legs – this is an Indian, rather than Muslim tradition; men should refrain from wearing shorts. The handshake is a British tradition so visitors should greet Indians by placing their hands together in a prayer like gesture – especially women greeting Indian men, as the handshake has become somewhat of a ruse for Indian men, with heavy sexual undertones.

ACCOM/TOUR/HOST
ALTERNATIVE TRAVELS
Small group tours exploring rural life in Rajasthan, including homestays. Designed to show and share the lives of people who are not the princes of Rajasthan! Hiking is on offer in Arawali hills, together with horse riding and cycling. There is also a peaceful, organic eco-lodge in Shekhawati between Delhi and Jaipur that helps to safeguard Shekhawati's extraordinary architectural heritage and support sustainable development projects.

Contact: Ramesh C Jangid
Tel: 01594 22239/01594 24061
Fax: 484 3099520
Email: rcjangid@yahoo.com
Web: www.apanidhani.com,
www.alternativetravelsindia.com

DAY/TOUR
BILLION STAR HOTEL
Billion Star Hotel offers camel safaris in the Thar Desert of far west Rajasthan near Jaisalmer. Run by a local camel driver cooperative, guests can write their own holiday. You are collected from your hotel and driven by jeep to the entrance of the Desert National Park. There you are picked up by your guides and can enjoy a camel trek of anything from two hours to three weeks, sleeping under the

Contact: Rosie Jardine
Tel: +61 421 499 409
Fax: +61 3 9876 7137
Email: rosie@billionstarhotel.com
Web: www.billionstarhotel.com
Address: 34 Smedley Road, Park Orchards, 3114 Victoria, Australia

billion stars beside a campfire in the desert. Customers pay the camel drivers direct; this income goes to families and is used for their very real needs (for example, food and medicines).

ACCOM/TOUR
COCO PLANET TOURS & TRAVEL
Coco Planet Tours specialize in backwater tourism in Kerala, southwest India. They offer eco-friendly houseboats featuring well-furnished bedrooms, but leaving the traditional character of the boats intact. The boats are run through solar power, and the crew prepare

ASIA SOUTH

all the food in the traditional way using mud pots. Despite their speciality houseboats, they can also organize package tours with guided service throughout Kerela and to the Maldive Islands; tell them your budget and number of people, and they will provide a tailor-made package. The tours give employment to ten families.

Contact: Mr.Biju
Tel: 477 2239904/223 9903
Fax: 477 223 9903
Email: cocoindiagroup@yahoo.com
Web: www.beautifulkerala.com
Address: Near Nehru Trophy Finishing Point, Thathampally post, Alleppey 688013, India

ORG
ECO-KERALA

This is a state initiative for sustainable tourism in Kerala. Kerala has carved a

Web: www.keralatourism.org/sidenews/ecokerala/Eco.htm

niche for itself as a destination of immense natural appeal with its backwaters, beaches, hill stations, wildlife, Ayurveda and cuisine. The high population density and fragile ecosystem of Kerala call for a pragmatic approach towards the conservation of resources and heritage for a sustainable tourism development and thus they have launched a Kerela Tourism Eco initiative. As part of this they are offering local communities training on environmental conservation and support to local self-help groups.

HOST
HIMALAYAN HOMESTAYS

Himalayan Homestays is one of the initiatives developed by the Snow Leopard Conservancy (SLC), which promotes community-based stewardship of the snow leopard and its environment. This entails a marriage of conservation and the interests

Contact: Dr Rodney Jackson
Tel: +1 707 935 3851
Email: rodjackson@mountain.org, uncia@vam.com
Web: www.himalayan-homestays.com

of local people and their domestic livestock. As a visitor you will be offered a comfortable room, traditional meals, clean solar boiled spring water to drink, a clean dry composting toilet and the opportunity to enjoy the rhythm of life in a village where farming and livestock herding has been the way of life for centuries.

TOUR
INSIDER TOURS

Insider offers tailor-made guided tours throughout southern India and Sri Lanka, with weddings and honeymoons being a speciality. The entire operation is embedded in the local people and the company's relationship with them. The company prefers

Tel: +44 (0) 1233 811 771
Email: info@insider-tours.com
Web: www.insider-tours.com
Address: Insider Tours Ltd, 8 The Close, Chequers Park, Wye, Kent, TN25 5BD, UK

to use homestays and lodges, and small locally owned hotels. To this end the tours are built around regions or projects that benefit the community so that visitors can support the local economy, travel less and relax more and absorb the local culture.

HOST
KABANI
The other direction

Kabani is the non-profit initiative of a group of young people in Kerala. Its twin aims are sustainable socio-economic development of local communities and the conservation of natural resources. There is a network of homestay providers – you stay with local people and learn from them, and they from you. All the profits will go to the local population and into community development work. The stimulus for Kabani was the realization that a community-based network has a very real chance to walk the stage in the theatre of tourism.

Contact: Nirmal Joy
Tel: 4936/247414
Cellular: 09447 887396
Email: info@kabani.org
Web: www.kabani.org
Address: 'Thottamariyil', PO Meenangadi, Wayanad, Kerala, India. Pin Code 670 645

TOUR
KOLAM RESPONSIBLE TOURS

With many years of experience behind them, this husband and wife team of Ranjith and Rani Henry run fair trade, small group and customized tours primarily around southern India and Tamilnadu, visiting development projects as well as exploring contemporary life in the country. Tours can be arranged with or without personal guidance and cultural activities are an integral part of most itineraries.

Contact: Ranjith Henry
Tel: +44 2490 0939
Cellular: 98401 76656
Fax: +44 2491 5767
Email: kolam@vsnl.com
Web: www.kolamtravel.com
Address: Ranjith and Rani Henry, F1 Kgeyes Iswarya, Plot No 48 Rukmani Road, Kalakshetra Colony, Besant Nagar Chennai 600 090, India

VOL/HOST
KURMANCHAL SEVA SANSTHAN/RURAL ORGANIZATION FOR SOCIAL ELEVATION (KSS/ROSE)

KSS/ROSE is an NGO based in the small village of Kanda, situated in the Kumoani Hills of Uttaranchal, India, at the base of the Himalayas. KSS/ROSE encourages responsible, volunteer-based tourism. Visitors stay with families and everyone eats together. They can help plant seedlings of local oak and pine to help avoid deforestation, assist in maintaining water filtration and irrigation systems and get to know the people of this region and their fascinating culture, bringing with them their skills and knowledge to help on various rural development projects.

Contact: Jeevan Lal Verma
Tel: 59632 41081/59632 41097
Email: Jlverma_rosekanda@yahoo.co.in
Web: www.rosekanda.info
Address: Village-Sonargan, PO-Kanda, District-Bageshwar, State-Uttaranchal 263631, India

ACCOM
ROOFTOP RETREAT GUESTHOUSE

Rooftop Retreat is a comfortable, homely self-contained apartment ten minutes by bus or auto-rickshaw from the centre of Mysore, located in a quiet hillside suburb, providing a convenient base to explore the city in an area well off the tourist track. Guests enjoy contact with a local family without giving up their independence. The accommodation comprises a

ASIA SOUTH

light airy bedroom with one king-size or two single teakwood beds (with mosquito nets), toilet, and shower with hot water. Guests can prepare their own drinks and snacks, while a western breakfast and Indian-style evening meals can be cooked to order.

Contact: Ashley Butterfield
Tel: after 7 pm only (India)- 0821 2450 483
Email: butterfieldashley@yahoo.co.uk
Web: www.itarsi2000.org
Address: 165 Gopal Printers Road, Gayathripuram 2nd stage, Mysore, Karnataka, India

RAINFOREST
SUNDERBANS/MANAS JUNGLE CAMPS

A community-based tourism project offering ethnic accommodation, conservation centres, protection camps and a cultural and education centre. Activities are run and controlled by local people in a forest rich in wildlife, including endangered species such as the Bengal tiger and the Asiatic one-horned rhinoceros. Both jungle camps are located in national parks and host communities, and visitors are able to learn from each other. Stress is placed on environmental sensitivity, social responsibility and community ownership of the project.

Contact: Mr Abhra Bhattacharya/Mr Kaushik Ghosh
Tel: 33 24550917/24854584/353 2433683/2535893
Cellular: 0098310 31980/94351 49066/ 93318 60213/98320 66626
Fax: 33 24853275 to 77
Email: kalighat@vsnl.net, Garumara@yahoo.co.uk, helptourism@sancharnet.in, info@actnowornever.org
Web: www.helptourism.com, www.actnowornever.org, www.manas100.com
Address: 67A,Kali Temple Road, Sadananda Kuthi., Kolkata- 700 026, West Bengal, India or PO Box-67, 143,Hill Cart Road, Malati Bhawan, Siliguri- 734 401, West Bengal, India, or 122/1, Ganapati Apartments, Flat-6, Toot Sarai, Malviya Nagar, New Delhi- 110 017, India

DAY
TENMALA ECOTOURISM

This ecotourism project in and around the Shenduruney Wildlife Sanctuary in Kerala offers trekking and birdwatching trails as well as cultural activities. Ensuring that the local people benefit is key to this operation.

Tel: 471 2329770/475 2344800
Fax: 471 2337037
Email: info@thenmalaecotourism.com
Web: www.thenmalaecotourism.com
Address: Thenmala PO 691308 Kollam District, Kerala, India

TREK
WILD KERALA TOUR COMPANY

WKTC offers two days trekking and camping ecotourism programmes inside the national parks and wildlife sanctuaries of Kerala. Visitors experience various different habitats such as evergreen, semi-evergreen, moist deciduous and dry deciduous forest with a vast variety of flora and fauna.

Contact: Pramod KG
Tel: 484 3099520/484 9846 62157
Fax: 484 3099520
Email: mail@wildkeralatours.com
Web: www.wildkeralatours.com
Address: VI/480, KVA Buildings, Bazaar road, Mattancherry, Cochin, Kerala, India PIN 682 002

Guides come from the local indigenous community, and are accompanied by an experienced naturalist who can help interpret the various sounds of the jungle. WKTC is committed to responsible tourism and minimum impact on the environment. Ten per cent of the turnover goes towards conservation and local communities.

ASIA SOUTH

THE HIMALAYAN TOURIST CODE

By following these simple guidelines, you can help preserve the unique environment and ancient cultures of the Himalayas:

- **Protect the natural environment.**

- **Limit deforestation** – make no open fires and discourage others from doing so on your behalf. Where water is heated by scarce firewood, use as little as possible. When possible choose accommodation that uses kerosene or fuel-efficient wood stoves.

- **Remove litter** – burn or bury paper and carry out all non-degradable litter. Graffiti are permanent examples of environmental pollution.

- **Keep local water clean** and avoid using pollutants such as detergents in streams or springs. If no toilet facilities are available, make sure you are at least 30 metres away from water sources, and bury or cover wastes.

- **Leave plants alone** to flourish in their natural environment – taking cuttings, seeds and roots is illegal in many parts of the Himalayas.

- **Help your guides and porters** to follow conservation measures.

- **Respect privacy when taking photographs** – ask permission and use restraint.

- **Respect holy places** – preserve what you have come to see, never touch or remove religious objects. Shoes should be removed when visiting temples.

- **Do not give money to children** – it encourages begging. A donation to a project, health centre or school is a more constructive way to help.

- **Follow local customs** – you will be accepted and welcomed. Use only your right hand for eating and greeting. Do not share cutlery or cups, etc. It is polite to use both hands when giving or receiving gifts.

- **Respect local etiquette** to earn respect locally – loose, lightweight clothes are preferable to revealing shorts, skimpy tops and tight-fitting action wear. Hand-holding or kissing in public are disliked by local people.

- **Observe standard food and bed charges** but do not condone overcharging. Remember when you're shopping that the bargains you buy may only be possible because of low income to others.

Remember – you are a guest. As a guest, respect local traditions, protect local cultures, maintain local pride. Be patient, friendly and sensitive. Help local people gain a realistic view of life in western countries.

THE HIMALAYAS MAY CHANGE YOU – PLEASE DO NOT CHANGE THEM

ASIA

SOUTH

NEPAL
International dialling code +977

From being a Mecca for hippy backpackers in the 1960s, Nepal has evolved into a tourist destination with something for almost every kind of tourist, including coach tour parties – the latter being more prevalent than hippies nowadays. Nepal's main appeal today is for lovers of the outdoors, who can join a group for mountaineering, hiking in the foothills of the Himalayas and the National Parks, trekking and visiting different ethnic tribes, and white-water rafting. Cultural tourism is also popular, with the the many beautiful Hindu temples and ancient carved wooden architecture. Shoppers can find everything from pashminas, silks, handmade books, wooden carvings and metalwork, Nepalese and Tibetan religious artefacts, to equipment for camping, climbing and hiking. There is every kind of accommodation from backpacker hostels to deluxe hotels in converted ancient palaces. The best times to visit are spring and autumn. Maoist rebels cause disruption to everyday life as well as tourism from time to time, blockading key roads and bombing buildings in the centre of Kathmandu – including some of the major tourist hotels. In such cases warnings are usually given. Although tourists are not their targets, they can be inadvertently caught up in such attacks.

Tourism Concern is proud to have produced a responsible tourism code for trekking in the Himalayas together with ACAP (see 'The Himalayan Tourist Code' box on previous page). In addition we have produced a code for tour operators so that they can properly employ the porters carrying the baggage up the mountains (see 'Trekking Wrongs' box on page 47 for further information about this). Please make sure that any trekking company that you use adheres to these important practices. Too many porters die or are injured on treks because of inadequate clothing and gear. The International Porters Protection Group (IPPG) is also well worth contacting for full up-to-date information about porters' issues (see www.ippg.net).

ORG/TREK
ANNAPURNA CONSERVATION AREA PROJECT (ACAP)

This project was established in 1968 under the guidance of the King Mahendra Trust for Nature Conservation. It encompasses the entire Annapurna range, an area of 7683km². The ACAP programme relies on the participation of the local people and emphasizes

Tel: 1 5526571/5526573
Fax: 1 5526570
Email: info@kmtnc.org.np
Web: www.kmtnc.org.np
Address: PO Box 3712, Jawalakhel, Lalitpur, Nepal

environmental education and conservation for development. Tourism is integrated into wider poverty alleviating programmes such as agriculture. ACAP is supported by a fee of 2000 Nepalese rupees (£17/US$30) collected from all visiting trekkers. One of the attractions of the Annapurna Region is the opportunity to make a short trek ranging from a few

ASIA SOUTH

hours to a week. Many fine short treks begin and end near Pokhara. Throughout this region a main attraction is the dense rhododendron forest and spectacular views of mountains, waterfalls, terraced farms and villages.

TREK
COMMUNITY ACTION TREKS

This company specializes in the Himalayas and other mountain regions. Founded by Doug Scott, the mountaineer, to help improve labour conditions in the trekking industry, it is the UK arm of the fundraising charity Community Action Nepal. After covering running costs all the proceeds go to fund community development projects in the areas to which they take trekkers. Everything is done in cooperation with the local communities and they fund projects such as water provision, schools, health posts and income generating schemes.

Contact: Doug Scott
Tel: +44 (0) 1228 564488
Email: info@catreks.com
Web: www.catreks.com

TOUR/DAY/TREK/VOL
DREAM NEPAL TRAVEL & TOURS

Dream Nepal offers activity holidays such as trekking and white-water rafting, as well as nature and birdwatching tours, and visits to Buddhist monasteries in the Kathmandu Valley. Its sister organization, the NGO Discover Nepal, arranges health camps, sends volunteers to teach English and conducts awareness programmes in Nepalese villages.

Contact: Mr Bijaya Pradhan
Tel: 1 4413690
Fax: 1 4255487
Email: stt@mos.com.np, bijayapradhan@hotmail.com
Web: www.dreamnepal.com.np
Address: GPO Box 20209, Kathmandu, Nepal.

TREK
INDEPENDENT TREKKING GUIDE GROUP

The ITGG is an independent trekking guide group, organized by local people, based in a region 70km northwest of Kathmandu. They hope to use income from tourists to develop transport and health infrastructure, build schools, improve water supplies and arrange work schemes for the unemployed young people of their community. Eighty per cent belong to the Tamang ethnic group who rely predominantly on agriculture.

Contact: Jagat Lama
Cellular: 10 98510 76386
Email: l_jagat@hotmail.com
Web: www.independent-trekkingguide-nepal.com
Address: GPO Box 5827 Kathmandu, Nepal

ORG
INTERNATIONAL PORTER PROTECTION GROUP (IPPG)

The IPPG is a voluntary organization, which promotes awareness of porters' needs and vulnerability and runs training for them. They build porter shelters in remote areas, also employ one Sherpa in Nepal to run the Porter Shelter and

Contact: Dr Jim Duff
Tel: +44 (0)12295 86225
Fax: +44 (0)12295 86225
Email: info@ippg.net
Web: www.ippg.net
Address: 53 Dale Street, Ulverston, LA129AR Cumbria, UK

ASIA

SOUTH

Rescue post at Machermo. All other workers are volunteers and consequently 99 per cent of donations go directly into their projects, as there are no offices or other overheads.

ORG
KEEP – KATHMANDU ENVIRONMENTAL EDUCATIONAL PROJECT

Keep is a non-profit organization aiming to provide important information to independent travellers. They operate Travellers' Information Centres for visitors at Sermanthang (Helambu/Langtang), Salleri (Solu Khumbu), Royal Bardia National Park as well as in Kathmandu – offering non-commercial, unbiased advice on all aspects of trekking, including important

Tel: 1 4412 944
Fax: 1 4413 018
Email: keep@info.com.np
Web: www.keepnepal.org
Address: PO Box 9178, Tridevi Marg, Thamel, Kathmandu, Nepal

information regarding mountain safety and altitude sickness. You can learn how to minimize your impact and help protect the fragile Himalayan environment and culture while trekking. At the Travellers' Information Centres in Jyatha, Thamel and Kathmandu you'll also find a reference library of materials on Nepal and the Himalayas, notice boards, displays, embassy registration forms for trekkers, lectures, and slide shows. At the Green Cafe you can also enjoy a real cappuccino.

ORG/TREK/VOL
THE NEPAL TRUST

A Scottish charity that helps develop health, education, renewable energy and other community projects in northwest Nepal. It runs annual treks that incorporate work on community projects such as building a health clinic or installing micro-hydro or solar systems. The Trust is now developing a separate trekking company and can arrange trips throughout Nepal to suit people's interests. Profits from treks will support Nepal Trust projects.

Tel: + 44 (0) 1343 810358
Fax: + 44 (0) 1343 810359
Email: admin@nepaltrust.org
Web: www.nepaltrust.org
Address: 4 Marina Quay, Lossiemouth, Moray IV31 6TJ, Scotland
In Nepal:
Tel: 1 472 1112
Fax: 1 472 0224
Email: ntrust@mail.com.np

TOUR
RELIANCE TRAVEL & TOURS (RTT)

This project is based on, run by and is for local people. The aim is to improve their health and better their education if at all possible. In this context a primary focus is the women and children both from the ethnic minority and the indigenous

Contact: Mr Prabal Thapa
Tel: 1 4424614
Fax: 1 4424615
Email: info@reliancenepal.com
Web: www.discoverhimalayas.biz
Address: PO Box 8974, CPC 249, Thamel, Kathmandu, Nepal

population. What the visitor will get is cultural tours with the Tharu, Magar and Gurung, with a focus on local culture, language and tradition. What you take away will be the memory of a 'wonderful and memorable stay'. The local communities benefit to the tune of 15 per cent of the total net profits and they are the true owners of the project.

ASIA SOUTH

TREK
ROLWALING ECOTOURISM DEVELOPMENT PROJECT (RETP)

RETP is a non-profit developmental agency operating in a highly scenic but little visited area of Nepal's northern Dolakha district. The RETP offers trekking holidays in this impoverished rural area, with all proceeds going to the local community and all activities and infrastructure benefiting the local community directly. Of all RETP staff, only one is non-Nepali, the remaining 15 are from the project area itself and have been trained by RETP.

Contact: Max Petrik
Tel: 1 4414714
Fax: 1 4437304
Email: oekomax@ecohimal.org
Web: www.ecohimal.org

TOUR
RURAL EDUCATION AND DEVELOPMENT (READ)

READ is a non-profit organization based in the US that constructs community centres in rural areas of Nepal, with libraries at the hub. The aim is to improve education and literacy, as well as increase local infrastructure. Travellers see a variety of libraries in the mountains, valleys and jungles of Nepal. In addition guests meet Nepalese from all walks of life, getting a unique perspective on the country, often having the opportunity to attend lectures by noted authors and politicians.

Contact: Dr Antonia Neubauer
Tel: +1 775 832 5454
Fax: +1 775 832 4454
Email: travel@mythsandmountains.com
Web: www.mythsandmountains.com
Address: Myths and Mountains,
976 Tee Court, Incline Village,
NV 89451, USA

TOUR
SOCIALTOURS.COM

Socialtours.com is a locally based tour operator offering popular and off the beaten track tours with responsible travel in mind. The tours are environmentally and culturally sensitive, with a strong commitment to contributing to the local economy. The most popular trips are trekking and jungle safaris, as well as visits to Tibet. The company also organizes tours to Bhutan and northern India.

Contact: Prerna Gurung
Tel: 1 4412508/1 4700452
Fax: 1 4435207
Email: info@socialtours.com,/
raj@socialtreks.com
Web: www.socialtours.com,
www.socialtreks.com
Address: GPO Box 1663, Tridevi Marg, Thamel,
Kathmandu, Nepal

ACCOM+
TIGER MOUNTAIN POKHARA LODGE

Tiger Mountain offers visitors the chance to relax and de-stress in a rural community setting in the foothills of the Himalayas. The lodge provides a range of wildlife and cultural walks led by local guides who will informally explain issues about cultural sensitivity that may cause offence. A range of complementary activities such as reiki, hara and shiatsu massage, and yoga lessons are also available. Seventy-five per cent of the profit is repatriated into the local community, its health and schools.

Tel: 1436 1500
Fax: 61 531316
Email: marcus@tigermountain.com
Web: www.tigermountain.com/pokhara
Address: GPO Box 242, Kathmandu, Nepal

TREK
TOURISM FOR RURAL POVERTY ALLEVIATION PROGRAMME (TRPAP)

TRPAP is a government model tourism project aiming to reach out to some of Nepal's poorest areas and promote sustainable rural tourism. They offer various treks from 3–21 days, supply local guides and porters, homestays, hotels/lodges, community-owned campsites, museums and handicraft outlets. Local people

Contact: Mr Rabi Jung Pandey
Tel: 1 4269768/ 4256909
Fax: 1 4269770
Email: info_trpap@ntb.org.np
Web: www.welcomenepal.com/trpap
Address: PO Box 107, Kathmandu, Nepal

are given training to become guides, manage hotels, to cook and make handicrafts. The focus of the programme is always towards those living below the poverty line, using tourism as a vehicle to reduce poverty.

SRI LANKA
International dialling code +94

Sitting just above the equator, Sri Lanka is the pearl of the Indian Ocean, because this small island has everything a traveller could wish for. Tropical golden palm-fringed beaches stretch for over a thousand miles around the coastline, and the tourism industry is gradually recovering after the devastation of the Asian tsunami in 2004. The cool highland interior features lush green landscapes of paddy fields and its world-famous tea plantations, along with scenic water-falls and mountain passes. The 'Cultural Triangle' is rich in historical interest, encompassing ancient ruined capitals, rock fortresses, cave temples, giant Buddha and the sacred city of Kandy. Then there's the abundant and varied wildlife – you're practically guaranteed to see a wild elephant (or even a herd) if you know where to go, and could catch sight of an elusive sloth bear or leopard. And it is an absolute dream for bird lovers. Throw in the chance to lose your head with adventure and water sports, eat yourself stupid on exotic dishes, experience colourful festivals and indulge in the national obsession, cricket (if that's your cup of tea!), and you'll understand why a visit to this country forever sticks in the mind.

But, of course, Sri Lanka also has a protracted and bloody civil war, which simmers under the surface despite the current ceasefire. Tourists should avoid the most affected parts of the country, but your visit to other areas will be something to savour, and, since the tsunami, more vital than ever to the Sri Lankan economy.

TOUR/VOL
THE DIFFERENT TRAVEL COMPANY
The Different Travel Company is a UK-based company, which, as the name suggests, organizes holidays with a difference. They offer the comfort and relaxation of high quality accommodation with the opportunity to work on local humanitarian, social and environmental projects. These vary from building houses to offering child

Contact: Sarah Yalland
Tel: 02380 669903
Email: info@different-travel.com
Web: www.different-travel.com
Address: 3 Maritime Avenue, Marchwood, Hampshire, SO40 4AN, UK

care, working in local hospitals, orphanages and care homes or removing debris from the seabed. There is plenty of time for sightseeing and relaxing on the beach and many post-project travel options. Most of the projects so far have been based in Sri Lanka, but they aim to expand to other countries.

TOUR
INSIDER TOURS
Insider offer tailor-made guided tours throughout southern India and Sri Lanka, with weddings and honeymoons being a speciality. The entire operation is embedded in the local people and the company's relationship with them. They prefer to use

Tel: +44 (0)1233 811 771
Email: info@insider-tours.com
Web: www.insider-tours.com
Address: Insider Tours Ltd, 8 The Close, Chequers Park, Wye, Kent, TN25 5BD England, UK

homestays and lodges, and small locally owned hotels. To this end the tours are built around regions or projects that benefit the community so that visitors can support the local economy, travel less, relax more and absorb the local culture.

ACCOM+
RANWELI HOLIDAY VILLAGE
At Ranweli Holiday Village guests can enjoy birdwatching and nature walks, cycling tours, kayaking, canoeing and surfing in the marine estuary, where mangrove forests and rivers converge to meet the sea. Its 72 bungalows and 12 family rooms are just 18km from Colombo's international airport on the west coast of the country.

Contact: Wimal Dassanayake
Tel: 11 2423236
Fax: 11 2438704
Email: ranweli@sri.lanak.net
Web: www.ranweli.com

Ranweli aims to promote tourism based on environmental conservation and respect for the welfare of the local community. Modelled on a traditional Sri Lankan village and built using locally sourced biodegradable materials, water is heated using solar power, there are extensive recycling facilities, kitchen waste is used to irrigate and fertilize the organic garden.

ACCOM+
SEWALANKA FOUNDATION
A community-based ecotourism project, offering visitors the opportunity to interact with a marine environment, guided by local fishermen. The Pottuvil Lagoon Ecotour introduces the concepts of mangrove reforestation and visits a mangrove nursery

Contact: Raheem Haniffa
Tel: 63 2248 189/11 2545 362 5/11 2861 013
Fax: 11 2545 166
Email: oddfish@slt.lk/sewahq@sri.lanka.net
Web: www.sewalanka.org, www.arugambay.lk
Address: Colombo Road, Boralesgamuwa, Sri Lanka

ASIA SOUTH

on the east coast. The Arugam Bay Sea Safari provides information on the surrounding coast and marine life, including whales and dolphins. The ecotours are promoted through a partnership with a locally owned hotel, the Arugam Bay Hillton, and provides an additional source of income to the fishermen who continue to obtain their main source of income from fishing.

HOST/ACCOM/TOUR

SRI LANKA ECOTOURISM FOUNDATION (SLEF) & SRI LANKA ECO TOURS (SLET)

SLET is a registered travel agency, the tourism business arm of SLEF. They promote homestays and community-owned eco-lodges in rural Sri Lanka. SLET also promotes camping in protected areas, rainforests and mountainous regions. All of these are focused on assuring economic benefits and improving living standards of local communities, many of which have been hard hit by the tsunami. They offer tours from seven to ten days on a half-board basis; 75 per cent of the proceeds going to the local community.

Contact: Ms L. D. Tennekoon
Tel: 11 2764253/11 2706433
Fax: 777 631334
Fax: 11 2763324
Email: sleco@sltnet.lk, sletf@sri.lanka.net
Web: www.ecotourismsrilanka.org,
www.srilankaecotours.com
Address: 17, Atsumi Holiday Resort, Thuduwa,
Madapatha, Sri Lanka

ACCOM+

WOODLANDS

A guesthouse run along ecotourism principles offering visitors an escape from crowded beaches and cities. Guests can enjoy the Sri Lankan countryside at Bandarawela in Uvo Province, stay overnight in local villages and even take part in cookery lessons. Woodlands Network is a non-profit organization that aims to support local community projects with revenue from tourists.

Contact: Sarojinie Ellawela
Tel: 57 2232328/2232668
Fax: 57 2232862
Email: haas@sltnet.lk, woodlands@sltnet.lk
Address: 38/1c, Esplanade Road, Bandarawela.
90100. Sri Lanka

SOUTHWEST ASIA

JORDAN
International dialling code +962

Don't be surprised when you get to Jordan and a Bedouin invites you to his tent for a cup of sweet tea. The hospitality and warmth of the Jordanian people is just one of the many surprises you'll experience in the Hashemite Kingdom.

From north to south, Jordan's landscape is full of beautiful surprises, with archaeological riches from neolithic man and relics from many of the world's great civilizations. In the north, you'll stand on hills covered with olive and pine trees that overlook the historic Sea of Galilee. Heading south, you'll come to the lowest place on earth, the Dead Sea with its healing, mineral-laden waters. The salty sea is located in the subtropical Jordan Valley where bananas, tomatoes and watermelon grow year round. Further south is Petra, a registered UNESCO World Heritage site and Jordan's most popular tourist destination. With good reason: the amazing workmanship of the Nabateans and Romans feature amphitheatres and temples, tombs and elaborate buildings cut out of solid rock. Just south lies Wadi Rum, where Lawrence of Arabia was filmed, with its majestic mountains and vast desert. The southern tip of the country lies on the Red Sea where Aqaba offers a dream location for avid scuba divers.

The tourism industry has been affected by regional instability in the past several years. Despite these difficulties, Jordan is committed to developing a sustainable tourism industry and is implementing a national tourism strategy. The strategy aims to celebrate Jordan's amazing landscape and tourist sites while showing the rest of the world what hospitality really means.

ACCOM+
AMMARIN BEDOUIN CAMP

If you want to support the development of local community-based sustainable tourism and visit Petra, the 'rose red city half as old as time', then this Bedouin camp, owned jointly by the Beidha Tourism Cooperative and Ziad Hamzeh and Co., should be of interest. The company supplies the know-how, infrastructure and marketing and the entire local community supports the camp activities, be

Contact: Ziad Hamzeh
Tel: 79 5667771
Fax: 6 4616787
Email: info@bedouincamp.net,
ziad@bedouincamp.net
Web: www.bedouincamp.net
Address: PO Box 285 Wadi Mousa, Jordan

ASIA

SOUTHWEST

they hospitality, catering, music or dance; it is the only stakeholder. Sit under the stars by night and wonder what you did to deserve it, and remember that each and every dollar you paid will benefit this hospitable Bedouin community.

ORG/ACCOM+
THE ROYAL SOCIETY FOR THE CONSERVATION & NATURE (RSCN)

The Jordanian Royal Society is an NGO devoted to environmental protection. It has established protected areas or nature reserves and supports local communities by providing work opportunities rooted in its work and ethos. The ecotourism and handicrafts dimensions are managed entirely by the local communities living in and around the reserves, who benefit to the tune of 65 per cent of the price charged. There are five trails and campsites in the country and a Wild Jordan shop and café in Amman, which offers lots of information and advice.

Contact: Ghada Al-Sous
Tel: 6 4616 523
Fax: 6 4616 483
Email: tourism@rscn.org.jo
Web: www.rscn.org.jo
Address: PO Box 1215, Jubaiha 11941 - Jordan

PALESTINE
International dialling code +970 (but this is often not recognized and the Israeli dialling code of +972 should generally be tried first)

Although Palestine does not yet exist as an independent country, it is generally accepted that its heartland lies in the West Bank, covering 6000 square kilometres west of the Jordan River. The Israeli occupation is tangible in some 120 illegal Jewish settlements, military outposts and checkpoints, the wall separating the West Bank from Israel, and in the numerous Palestinian refugee camps that bear witness to the unresolved conflicts.

Yet the area also attracts tourists and pilgrims, eager to see its many ancient and biblical sites. Among the best known in the arid southern hills of Judea, the town of Bethlehem is the birthplace of Jesus; Hebron contains the Tomb of the Patriarchs, the burial place of Abraham, revered by both Muslims and Jews; and the palm-fringed city of Jericho, the oldest and lowest town on earth, includes the spectacular remains of Hisham's summer palace. The northern greener area of ancient Samaria is home to Nablus with its fascinating Old City, and the summer retreat of Ramallah. However, it is Jerusalem that lies at the political and cultural centre, with the Palestinian eastern side and the Old City containing the most interesting – and contested – sites, including the Church of the Holy Sepulchre, the site of the crucifixion, the Dome of the Rock and the Western (Wailing) Wall.

Palestine also includes the Gaza Strip, on the Mediterranean coast between Israel and the Egyptian Sinai, from which Israeli settlements and military have recently withdrawn. As 'home' to some 900,000 Palestinian refugees, it is one of most densely populated areas on earth, and its tourist sites and facilities are yet to be developed.

ORG
ALTERNATIVE TOURISM GROUP (ATG)

ATG is a not-for-profit Palestinian NGO headquartered in Bethlehem and owing its birth to the belief that conventional pilgrim-oriented tourism gave no voice to contemporary Palestinian culture or political realities. It provides study and educational tours to Palestine and Israel, which address

Contact: Samer Kokaly
Tel: +972 2 277 2151
Fax: +972 2 277 2211
Email: info@atg.ps
Web: www.atg.ps
Address: PO Box 173, Beit Sahour, Palestine

the culture, history and politic of Palestine and which are geared to the specific require-ments of groups and individuals. Another target is local development – for example, 30 rooms have been restored in people's homes in the Bethlehem area to facilitate bed and breakfast programmes. A further aim is to encourage tourists to stay within Palestinian areas so that their spending will create revenue streams by their use of local tourist infra-structure, for example, hotels, homes, restaurants etc. There is a very real desire to foster human encounters between the local community and visitors and to create a better understanding of the situation of the Palestinians.

TOUR+
ALTERNATIVE TOURS

Founded by the manager who operates out of the Jerusalem Hotel in that city, Alternative Tours has a two-pronged approach: to raise awareness about the plight of the Palestinian people and also to help visitors to discover the West Bank and experience its most inter-

Contact: Abu Hassan
Tel: +972 522 864205
Fax: +972 2 6283282
Email: abuhasan@alqudsnet.com
Address: PO Box 20754, Jerusalem, via Israel

esting and beautiful places. The usual tourist attractions come along with contemporary political insights – the best of both worlds. They will take care of you but anywhere that can only be reached with 'difficulties' is off limits.

ACCOM+
THE INTERNATIONAL CENTRE OF BETHLEHEM
Authentic Tourism Programme

The programme is wholly owned by the ICB. It is inspired by a new theology of pilgrimage being socially responsible travel, which offers a holistic approach to visiting the Holy Land. The ICB is committed to combating unemploy-ment in the hospitality industry in Palestine and is also licensed to train

Contact: Mr. Shawky Awad
Tel: +972 2 2770047
Fax: +972 2 2770048
Email: info@annadwa.org
Web: www.annadwa.org
Address: PO Box 162, Paul VI St. 109, Bethlehem, Palestine

ASIA SOUTHWEST

Palestinian guides. A degree in tourism is planned from 2006 at the to-be-opened Dar al-Kalima Academy. The ICB is headquartered in the heart of Bethlehem and the guesthouse can house 26 people who receive opportunities to visit all the usual religious sites and also to visit present day faith communities and experience life in contemporary Palestine with its problems but also its joys. The cuisine on offer is delicious, traditional Palestinian.

TOUR+
OLIVE CO-OPERATIVE

This worker-run cooperative and limited company works via independent contractors and partners such as the Alternative Tourism Group in Beit Sahour. There are two strands to their bow in that they deal in fairly traded goods, such as olive oil, and operate tours specifically aimed at contributing to the Palestinian economy. Both on the ground and in the UK office they run an environmentally friendly operation. The tours (a maximum of nine people each time for safety reasons) are designed to 'tell it like it is' politically and to support Palestinian fair trade produce. You will stay in local hotels or with families. If the Olive Co-operative's work has to be categorized then it can be said to be targeted at people working for a just peace.

Contact: Mary Horbury
Tel UK: +44 (0) 161 273 1970/0845 456 1472
Email: info@olivecoop.com
Web: www.olivecoop.com
Address: Olive Co-operative Ltd, Bridge 5 Mill,
    22a Beswick Street, Manchester M4 7HR, UK

ASIA

SOUTHWEST

Join our

online community

and help us save paper and postage!

www.earthscan.co.uk

Join the Earthscan website and enjoy these benefits –

✓ Membership is free!

✓ 10% discount on all books online

✓ Invitations to high-profile book launch events

✓ e-newsletters and e-alerts delivered directly to your inbox, keeping you informed but not costing the Earth

✓ Special offers and discounts from New Consumer, New Internationalist, The Ecologist and more

✓ Academics – request inspection copies

✓ Journalists – subscribe to advance information e-alerts on upcoming titles – write to info@earthscan.co.uk for more information about this service

✓ Authors – keep up to date with the latest publications in your field

Join now?
Join Earthscan now!
name
surname
email address

Earthscan Member
[Your name]
My profile
My forum
My bookmarks
All my pages

Click to Change

How? – Become a member in seconds!

>> Visit **www.earthscan.co.uk** and add your name and email address to the sign-up box in the top left of the screen – you're now a member!

>> On your new member's page, you can subscribe to our monthly **e-newsletter,** choose **e-alerts** in subjects of interest, control the amount of mail you receive and unsubscribe yourself if you want to.

ASIA SOUTHWEST

www.earthscan.co.uk

OCEANIA

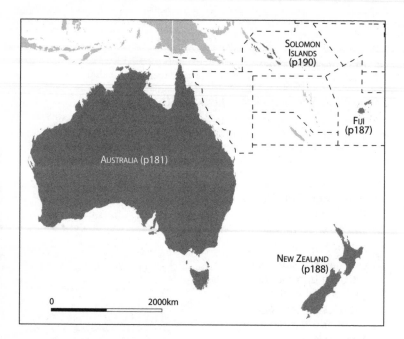

SOLOMON
ISLANDS
(p190)

FIJI
(p187)

AUSTRALIA (p181)

NEW ZEALAND
(p188)

0   2000km

AUSTRALIA
International dialling code +61

Australia is a sunburnt country, there's no doubt about it. The vast two million square miles of 'outback' is inhospitably dry most of the time. No wonder the majority of Australians hug its coastline, facing the rolling sea. But there's more than surfing dudes and outback Aboriginals to this beautiful island continent. There are snowy mountains, ancient rainforest, the largest coral reef in the world and spectacular geological phenomena. Combine this with a laid-back city life, where time on the beach or at outdoor cafes is as important as that in the office, and you have, possibly, the perfect destination. No wonder Australia often tops the polls of places to visit. From expensive tropical island hideaways to backpackers' lodges in bohemian seaside towns, there is something for every budget.

Aboriginal Australia is an increasingly popular holiday experience. In Queensland's Daintree Rainforest – the oldest rainforest in the world – you can take a tour with clans that have been the traditional owners for millennia. At Uluru, an interpretive centre explains the religious significance of the world's largest monolith, which its traditional owners would prefer you not to climb. Even in Sydney's harbourside botanical gardens, there are guided walks explaining traditional medicinal uses of the plantlife.

DAY/TOUR
ABORIGINAL CULTURAL TOURS
Aboriginal Cultural Tours will take you to rarely seen areas of Adjahdura Land (Yorke Peninsula). This is an opportunity to walk the country with direct descendants of the traditional owners, to live with, talk with and experience at first hand their rich culture. Tours vary from one to five days.

Tel: (0) 429 367 121
Email: info@diversetravel.com.au
Web: www.diversetravel.com.au,
www.aboriginalaustraliatravel.com

DAY
ANANGU TOURS
An aboriginal owned tour company based in Uluru Kata Tjuta National Park in Australia's Northern Territory. Anangu Tours offers daily cultural tours to Uluru (Ayers Rock) and Uluru Cultural Centre. Visitors can opt for a morning half-day tour including a sunrise viewing, or afternoon, including sunset. There are also self-drive touring options, and the opportunity to experience Inma, traditional song and dance. All tours are guided by Aboriginal guides with an Aboriginal language interpreter.

Contact: Anthea Hamilton
Tel: 8 8956 2123/8 8950 3032
Fax: 8 8956 3136/8 8953 7493
Email: reservations@anangutours.com.au,
administration@anangutours.com.au
Web: www.anangutours.com.au
Address: PO Box 8483, Alice Springs,
NT 0871, Australia

OCEANIA

DAY
AYERS ROCK RESORT – CAVE HILL SAFARIS
Desert Tracks

The Cave Hill tour is the result of a unique partnership between Odyssey Tours & Safaris and Desert
Tracks. Visitors are taken to Cave Hill, from Uluru, the
heart of the Red Centre to the small aboriginal
community of Cave Hill. The Yankunytjatjara custo-
dians then explain the significance of the

Tel: 2 8296 8010/2 6286 9033
Fax: (02) 6286 8368
Email: travel@voyages.com.au,
   info@deserttracks.com.au
Web: www.ayersrockresort.com.au/bookings

surrounding landscape and how it relates to Tjukurpa, their system of values, beliefs and
lore. The remarkable thing about these myths is that they appear in countless other
cultures – anywhere, it seems, where people gaze in wonder at the stars. The art at Cave
Hill portraying their adventures is considered to be among the most spectacular in the
region. Training, education and direct financial benefits are essential outcomes for the
partners. Desert Tracks is wholly owned and operated by the Pitjantjatjara People of Central
Australia. Established in 1988 as a cross-cultural tour to the homeland of Angatja,
Nganyinytja's country. The tours have since expanded to encompass several other
homeland destinations.

DAY
BLUE MOUNTAINS ABORIGINAL WALKABOUT

Inspiring and adventurous, this Australian
Aboriginal owned walkabout will provide visitors
with a deep connection to country and culture. This
stunning, educational Aboriginal tour is as easily
accessed by train as Sydney. It is neither commercial nor touristy but a thought-provoking traditional

Contact: Evan Yanna Muru ▲
Tel: (0) 408 443 822
Email: walkaboutguide@yahoo.com
Web: www.bluemountainswalkabout.com
Address: PO Box 519 Springwood NSW 2777

walkabout following a songline along an 8km challenging off-track walk through secluded
Blue Mountains wilderness where visitors are invited to enter their dreaming with stories
and activities. Tour available everyday all year round! 'We walk rain, hail or shine (cave fire if
desired). *Quai da ngalaringi nangami* – Welcome to our dreamtime'.

TOUR
BOOKABEE TOURS (ex Adelaide)

Escape to the spectacular Flinders Ranges for a
relaxing holiday with a unique Aboriginal cultural
experience and share a cultural experience 40,000

Tel: (08) 8235 9954
Email: bookabeetours@optusnet.com

years in the making. Listen to Adnyamathanha Creation stories at traditional significant
sites and see ancient paintings and engravings. Learn about the history of the area in the
beautiful Ranges landscape, with rugged mountains, scenic gorges, ruins of early settlement and abundant wildlife. Your chauffeured 4WD tour is an all inclusive package with
everything catered for – including Aboriginal cultural stories from your Aboriginal tour
guide. Tours range from 2–5 days and full accommodation is included.

TOUR
BUNGOOLEE TOURS (ex Broome)

Bunuba people are the traditional owners of one of the Kimberley's natural wonders of
Windjana Gorge, formed where the Lennard River cut through the old reef system, Tunnel

OCEANIA

Creek, Western Australia's oldest cave system, and Gieke Gorge. This area, in the late 19th century, was the scene of bloody conflict when local Aboriginal people put up fierce resistance to the inland movement of the European settlers. Tourism provides an opportunity to introduce visitors to traditional and contemporary issues affecting Aboriginal lifestyle, providing an Aboriginal perspective on the landscape and history of the people.

Tel: (08) 8303 3422
Fax: (08) 8303 4363
Email: info@diversetravel.com.au
Web: www.diversetravel.com.au,
www.aboriginalaustraliatravel.com

ACCOM+
CAMP COORONG RACE RELATIONS & CULTURAL EDUCATION CENTRE

This is a Ngarrindjeri community-run organization, two hours southeast of Adelaide (10km south of Meningie), which offers accommodation that includes dorms, cabins and camping and cultural tours focused on Dreaming stories, bush tucker/ bush medicine, cultural museum, ecology and contemporary issues. Rates for accommodation range from AU$25 (£11/US$19) for dorms to AU$70 (£30/US$55) for a cabin.

Tel: 08 8575 1557
Fax: 08 8575 1448
Email: nlpa@bigpond.com
Address: PO Box 126, Meningie SA 5264

ACCOM+
COORONG WILDERNESS LODGE

The Ngarrindjeri people from the Coorong Wilderness Lodge in southeast Australia welcome guests to the Coorong. This haunting landscape of wild untamed beaches, sheltered bays and inlets and towering dunes plays host to an amazing array of migratory birds. The Ngarrindjeri people look forward to sharing the magic of the Coorong and their culture during the three-day tour. Included is a guided bushwalk where visitors can experience the wonders of the Coorong's flora and fauna and an opportunity to kayak along the beautiful waterways to the sand dunes and small islands. There is considerable bird life to watch from the Lodge. Basic en suite cabin accommodation available, and powered or unpowered camping spaces.

Tel: (08) 8575 6001
Fax: (08) 8575 6041
Email: info@diversetravel.com.au
Web: www.diversetravel.com.au,
www.aboriginalaustraliatravel.com

OCEANIA

TOURS
DIVERSE TRAVEL

Diverse Travel Australia (DTA) has been operating for eight years specializing in developing and promoting authentic Aboriginal tourism experiences both domestically and internationally. They have created close alliances with Aboriginal people and communities across Australia and have been involved in assisting many of them with developing and growing their businesses. Most indigenous tour businesses are specialized niche market operations and the mainstream travel industry has very limited ongoing knowledge, understanding and contact with the diversity and spread of indigenous experiences available. Diverse Travel is the only tour operator dedicated to developing and promoting indigenous tourism. People can find it difficult to access national Aboriginal experiences and often come to Diverse Travel to

Tel: (08) 8303 3422
Fax: (08) 8303 4363
Email: info@diversetravel.com.au
Web: www.diversetravel.com.au,
www.aboriginalaustraliatravel.com

assist them in developing innovative and memorable itineraries that incorporate Aboriginal experiences with mainstream activities. They offer a very personal service and can tailor any experience to suit your needs and budget.

TOUR+
GUURRBI TOURS QUEENSLAND

This tour includes a visit to three rock art sites including the Great Emu Cave, and provides a fascinating introduction to Aboriginal culture and society, as well as the traditional survival techniques of the Nugal-warra people.

Tel: (07) 4069 6259
Email: info@diversetravel.com.au
Web: www.diversetravel.com.au,
    www.aboriginalaustraliatravel.com

TOUR+
IGA WARTA – SOUTH AUSTRALIA

Iga Warta in the Northern Flinders Ranges offers visitors an opportunity to experience Adnyamathanha culture and to share the bush. Visitors have the ability to become part of the environment and learn first hand the importance

Tel: (08) 8648 3737
Fax: (08) 8648 3794
Email: enquiries@igawarta.com
Web: www.igawarta.com

of this area to the Adnyamathanha people. Tour options include: plant tour artefact making, visiting painting sites, immersing oneself in one of the world's oldest cultures, cultural cookout, and social history. Accommodation available in safari tents or cabins or swag camping.

DAY
JACK'S TOUR AND STORY TELLING

Kojonup is a small town in the southwest corner of Australia, surrounded by unique bush reserves, historical landmarks and significant sites. Jack Cox is famous for his storytelling, billy tea and damper

Contact: The Kodja Place Visitor Centre
Tel: 08 9831 0500
Email: kodjaplace@bigpond.com

and his knowledge of bush tucker and bush medicine. Jack's vision is to promote his birthplace Kojonup to visitors. Jack is most at home in the bush and has planned a series of tours in local reserves where he shows visitors how the bush is used to provide shelter, food, recreation and health. This will lead to sustainable economic development opportunities, increased responsibility and respect for Aboriginal elders from their families and the wider community.

ACCOM+
KOOLJAMAN at CAPE LEVEQUE

220km by dirt track from Broome in Western Australia is this 'unique wilderness style luxury camp'. It is wholly owned and run by the Bardi People who try to ensure that their visitors enjoy themselves but also learn about the indigenous customs, culture and traditions of the land and ocean. Seven accommodation types cater for all budgets and what you pay goes either into improv-

Contact: Claire Prendergast
Tel: 8 9192 4970
Fax: 8 9192 4978
Email: leveque@bigpond.com
Web: www.kooljaman.com.au
Address: PMB 8, Cape Leveque, Via Broome,
    WA 6725, Australia

ing facilities or directly back to the communities. This holiday provides an Aboriginal experience and superb beaches. Booking essential.

DAY/RAINFOREST
KUKU YALANJI DREAMTIME WALKS

Organized and run by the aboriginal community of Mossman Gorge, Dreamtime Walks offers an indigenous cultural experience. Visitors experience a one and a half hour walk through the rainforest, with guides explaining the traditional use of plants for food and medicine, telling local stories, and showing cave paintings and places of significance. After the walk, billy tea and damper are served, and

Contact: Colin Brook
Tel: 7 4098 2595
Fax: 7 4098 2607
Email: tours@yalanji.com.au
Web: www.yalanji.com.au
Address: PO Box 171, Mossman, Queensland, 4873, Australia

there is an opportunity to talk to the guides, finishing with a didgeridoo performance. There is also a well-stocked gallery selling authentic Kuku Yalanji arts and crafts.

ACCOM+
LOMBADINA

Lombadina is an Aboriginal community of about 60 people, where Basil and Caroline Sibosado and their family are working towards self-sufficiency

Tel: (08) 9192 4936
Email: lombo@comswest.net.au

through community ventures that include a general store, artefact and craft shop, a bakery and tourism. Visitors can watch as artefacts are made from local materials or charter a boat to explore the bays and lagoons, fish, sightsee or simply relax. There is a lot to explore in an area rich in natural beauty as well as joining in hunting and gathering the Aboriginal way. Lombadina is more a retreat for people to come and share an indigenous lifestyle rather than a resort – an Aboriginal way of life you can experience for yourself. It is open April to October in the Dampier Peninsula north of Broome.

TOUR+
MIMILI MAKU TOURS

Mimili Maku Tours offer an authentic indigenous tourism experience to small groups of visitors who are seeking an opportunity to understand the landscape of the Everard Ranges and the ancient indigenous culture of the Pitjantjatjara

Tel: (08) 8956 7935
Fax: (08) 8956 7601
Email: information@mimilimakutours.com.au
Web: www.aboriginalaustraliatravel.com

Yankunytjatjara people. Mimili Maku Tours is managed and operated by local people, Mimili and traditional owner homelands with the assistance of sympathetic non-indigenous Australians. It seeks to be fully self-sustaining. There is a range of cultural experiences on offer including visits to sites to hear stories of the Dreaming; bush tucker – learning how to find and dig for maku (witchetty grubs) or tjala (honey ants); and bush medicines – learn how Anangu people traditionally made and used medicines from plant and animal sources.

OCEANIA

TOUR
NIPBAMJEN ARNHEM LAND ABORIGINAL TOUR

This two-day tour is run by Odyssey Tours & Safaris in association with Manyalluluk Aboriginal Tours and Gecko Canoeing. It offers a special opportunity to visit remote Aboriginal lands in small intimate

Tel: 8 8984 3540
Email: info@odysaf.com.au
Web: www.odysaf.com.au/bookings

groups and spend time with a local Aboriginal guide to learn about traditional lifestyles, hike in pristine wilderness, swim in natural waterholes and soak up the tranquil surroundings. Accommodation at Nipbamjen is in a twin-bed safari hut in a comfortable yet simple bush camp. Guests are picked up and returned to the nearest town, Katherine.

DAY
RAINBOW SERPENT TOUR – QUEENSLAND

This walk will take you through a dramatic landscape to six rock art sites, including an ancestral Birth Cave and the Reconciliation Cave, where you will hear the stories behind the paintings, and why this art is so important to present and future generations of Nugal-warra people.

Tel: (08) 8303 3422
Fax: (08) 8303 4363
Email: info@diversetravel.com.au
Web: www.diversetravel.com.au,
   www.aboriginalaustraliatravel.com

DAY/TOUR
TRIBAL WARRIOR ASSOCIATION

A non-profit community organization initiated and directed by Aboriginal people with Aboriginal Elders. Offers unique and memorable scheduled cruises and corporate charters on Sydney Harbour aboard the Tribal Warrior and the Deerubbun as well as cultural tours.

Tel: 02 9699 3491
Fax: 02 9699 3491
Web: www.tribalwarrior.org
Address: PO Box 3200, Redfern
   NSW 2016, Australia

DAY/DIS
VALLEY OF THE GIANTS TREE TOP WALK

Based in Western Australia, the Tree Top Walk is an ambitiously designed elevated walkway that lifts visitors 40 metres above the forest floor through the forest canopy. Designed to preserve the forest of 400-year-old giant red tingle trees, which were under threat from the pressure of visitors, this award winning project gives visitors a unique perspective as they watch birds fly below them. The project has full community involvement and is wheelchair accessible.

Contact: Trevor Burslem
Tel: 8 9840 8263
Fax: 8 9840 8132
Email: ttw@calm.wa.gov.au
Web: www.naturebase.net/tourism
Address: c/o- Department of CALM,
   South West Highway, Walpole,
   WA, 6398, Australia

DAY
WARDAN ABORIGINAL CULTURAL CENTRE

The Wardan Aboriginal Cultural Centre is an indigenous tourism project that was 12 years in the making. It is owned and operated by the Bibelmen Mia Aboriginal Corporation and Josh Whiteland is head guide and tour manager. Josh is a cultural custodian of the Wardandi people who lived in the region bordered by the southern Western Australia coastline to the Capel River in the southwest. From childhood stories told to him by his grandmother and mother, to frequent bush walks with his grandfather and father, Mr Whiteland has an excellent knowledge of the plants and animals of his cultural heritage.

Tel: (08) 9756 6566
Email: wardan@westnet.com.au
Web: www.wardan.com.au
Address: Injidup Springs Rd, PO Box 30, Yallingup, WA 6282, Australia

FIJI
International dialling code +679

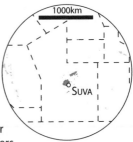

Fijians are some of the friendliest people on the planet. When you see their heavenly country, you understand why. This South Pacific nation consists of several hundred volcanic and coral land masses scattered across turquoise seas. It is an increasingly popular playground for Australians and New Zealanders, with hotels for every budget. From tiny sandy atolls to jagged, jungle-covered mountains, there's more than enough to do for a month. If it's the tropical island experience you want, then head for the Mamanuca or Yasawa island groups, or, if you have more time, to the outlying, flat atolls of the Bau group. On the main island of Viti Levu, you can hike to the top of Mount Batilamu in Koroyanitu National Park or go white-water rafting. On Taveuni – 'the garden island' – you can hike into the rainforest to search for one of the world's rarest flowers – the tagimaucia. On Kadavu, people grow the best kava – a root made into a narcotic, peppery brew and drunk as a welcome ceremony.

But it is the people that you will remember most from a visit to Fiji: their cheery 'Bula' greeting, wide smiles and infectious laughter. A highlight of any visit should be some time with a family in a simple thatched 'bure' home stay or in a village-run guesthouse. It may not be the smoothest operation, but relaxing to the rhythm of island life is life-changing.

HOST+
FIJIIBURE.COM/FIJIAN VILLAGE HOMESTAYS

Visitors can experience a truly traditional village homestay. When they arrive they are adopted into the community and can participate in traditional village life. This may include ceremonies, daily activities and sharing traditional Fijian foods caught by the villagers. Children especially have an unforgettable time as they are instantly absorbed into the large group of youngsters who live there. Scott Balson, who personally meets the village Elders and arranges the homestay with them, runs the

Contact: Sarah White
Tel: +11 617 3892 7333
Fax: +11 617 3892 5333
Email: info@fijibure.com
Web: www.fijibure.com
Address: PO Box 91, Wellers Hill, 4121 Queensland, Australia

OCEANIA

project. A large percentage of the income is placed in a village fund, which has resulted in the development of community halls and building of guesthouses. FijiBure.com handles the marketing and bookings.

NEW ZEALAND

International dialling code +64

700km

WELLINGTON

Ancient Maori myth places volcanoes at the very core of New Zealand's identity; they are as much a part of the uniquely New Zealand way of life as they are a fiery force in its landscape. New Zealanders' innate sense of environmental sustainability and inner spirituality is manifested in the numerous towns making claim to zero waste and their pride in their 'greenness' awards. If it is a love of nature that is drawing you to New Zealand you will be delighted by the myriad opportunities that present themselves.

But while it is easy to feel you are really at one with nature, for example, by experiencing the wilderness along the 130km Heaphy track in the South Island's northwest corner, tourist hot spots such as the South Island's glacial region have been ravaged by tourists and their insatiable desire for new experiences. The constant whirring of helicopters and small planes, giving visitors an aerial view of Fox Glacier, do not let you forget this.

Protest seems ingrained in the Kiwi psyche, which is perhaps due to their earlier victory against the nuclear industry. Whilst visiting New Zealand you are bound to stumble across at least one inspiring local struggle.

White New Zealanders have a respectful attitude towards the indigenous Maori culture: many government signs are bilingual and the Maori language is widely taught in schools.

DAY
BUSH & BEYOND GUIDED WALKS

This is a conservation-based guided walking company working in New Zealand's Kahurangi National Park. They are determined to do nothing to compromise the park's wilderness qualities, which includes limiting their own growth as a business to what is sustainable. They

Contact: Maryann Ewers
Tel: 3 528 9054
Fax: 3 528 9054
Email: Bushandbeyond@xtra.co.nz
Web: www.naturetreks.co.nz
Address: 35 School Road, RD 3 Motueka, New Zealand

support a community conservation project, Friends of Flora Inc, that aims to eradicate non-native predators from the park to protect the bird population. Conservation before economics – not a bad gospel to follow.

OCEANIA

RAINFOREST+/VOL
CATLINS WILDLIFE TRACKERS

Catlins are to be found two hours drive from Dunedin in the South Island. On offer are in-depth ecotours of the forests and southeast coast of the South Island. At the moment they can accommodate eight people at any one time plus another eight in self-catering. The latter costs NZ$120–150 (£45–58/US$82–105) per night and the former NZ$345 (£135/US$235) per person for a two-day/two-night experience all-inclusive. They have plans to develop but in a way that respects the physical and cultural environment.

Contact: Mary Sutherland
Tel: 3 4158 513
Fax: 3 4158 613
Email: info@catlins-ecotours.co.nz
Web: www.catlins-ecotours.co.nz
Address: Papatowai, RD 2 Owaka, Catlins, New Zealand

ACCOM+
FRENCH PASS SEA SAFARIS & BEACHFRONT VILLAS

Located at the end of a two-hour spectacular drive from Nelson this 13-year-old operation offers accommodation and tours of marine interest – watching (and maybe swimming with) dolphins, seals and whales. The owners have been working for years to bring back native bird life by eradicating alien pest predators and to establish marine reserves. French Pass itself is a small seaport on the Western Marlborough Sound. The accommodation is self-contained. Prices for a double room range from NZ$180 (£70/US$125) per night in high season to NZ$140 (£65/US$95) in the low season and tours begin at NZ$70 (£27/US$48) per person.

Contact: Danny Boulton
Tel: 3 5765 204
Fax: 3 5765 204
Email: adventure@seasafaris.co.nz
Web: www.seasafaris.co.nz
Address: Rd 3 Rai Valley, Marlborough Sounds, New Zealand

LUX+
KNAPDALE ECO-LODGE

The Lodge was opened in 2004 and plans to offer tranquil, home and farm-based hospitality and dining. They endeavour to live off the land and to leave as small an ecological footprint as possible. They work with the local Maori community to give the visitor a unique and authentic cultural experience – there are Maori historical sites on the property and visits to them are mediated by Maori people. The setting is extremely rural being about four hours drive from Gisborne (see the website map). At the moment there are only two rooms priced at NZ$300 (£115/US$205) and NZ$250 (£97/US$170) respectively per night for dinner, bed and breakfast.

Contact: Kees Weytmans
Tel: 6 8625 444
Fax: 6 8625 006
Email: eco-experience@knapdale.co.nz
Web: www.knapdale.co.nz
Address: 114 Snowsill Road, Waihirere, Gisborne, New Zealand

ACCOM+/BUDGET
TUKU WAIRUA CENTRE AND MAINSTREET BACKPACKERS LODGE

This Maori-owned cultural centre and lodge in the far north of the country organizes many activities and tours that enable visitors to get closer to Maori culture. You can get to meet the 'rangatani' (young people) at the Whakairo (carving) or join in other Maori craft

OCEANIA

workshops. You can wander through beautiful native bush, learn Maori Marae protocol, traditions and legends and immerse yourself as fully as you wish into the culture.

Tel: 94 084884
Email: twnt@xtra.co.nz, tall-tale-touris@extra.co.nz, mainstreet@extra.co.nez
Web: www.tall-tale.co.nz, www.taitokerau.com
Address: 237a Commerce Street, Kaitaia, New Zealand

SOLOMON ISLANDS
International dialling code +677

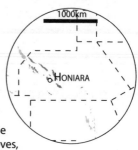

The Solomon Islands were so named, because when the Spanish explorer, Mendana, 'discovered' them, he thought the islands so beautiful, they must be the location of King Solomon's gold mines. Although they've since had to contend with mining and logging, the islands are still exquisite, with rainforest, mangroves, pristine reefs and volcanoes. Outside the few urban areas, people lead a semi-subsistence lifestyle: fishing from dug out canoes and making their homes in palm-leaf and wood houses, sometimes built on stilts over the lagoons.

Marovo Lagoon is the longest in the world. Rennell Island has the South Pacific's largest lake, which has World Heritage listing. Throughout the islands, the diving is some of the best on the planet. The culture is enormously varied: there are people who still wear 'grass' skirts and worship sharks. Yet, due to a troubled history of tribal fighting, poor air links and infrastructure, tourism has never taken off.

This is not somewhere to visit if you are in a rush or want everything to run smoothly. But if you are keen for an adventure and have plenty of funds, a visit to this diverse island nation (which is larger than Fiji) will be an unforgettable experience. There are extremely basic guesthouses, some run by church and community groups and aimed mostly at visiting officials, and a few intended for resident expats and the rare tourist.

ORG/ACCOM
ST DOMINIC'S RURAL TRAINING CENTRE – VANGA POINT

This operation is administered by the local Catholic Diocese and run by the Marist Brothers. The Centre opened in 2004 and now has about 120 students selected from the poorest and most neglected areas of the country. A wide

Contact: Maria Ketiro
Fax: 60121
Email: marist-vanga@pipolfastaem.gov.sb
Web: www.siartc.org.sb/RTCS/dominic.html
Address: PO Box 22, Gizo Western Province, Solomon Islands

range of skills is taught (too many to list here) with the aim of sending people back to their villages equipped to help their communities, including the training required to establish home stay village-based tourism. Simple accommodation is available for up to eight persons who have the chance to observe this 'school without classrooms' in action.

ACCOM/HOST
TETEPARE ECOLODGE

Tetepare, the largest uninhabited island in the Solomons, has an eco-lodge founded and operated by members of the Tetepare Descendents' Association

Contact: Allan Tippet Bero
Email: tetepare@solomon.com.sb/wwf@solomon.com.sb
Web: www.tetepare.org

(TDA). The lodge provides most of the income for the TDA whose mission is to preserve the island from commercial logging. Village-stay accommodation is also possible. The TDA is active in education, health and sustainable livelihood facilitation for many Solomon communities in return for a commitment to conservation on their behalf. What's on offer: pristine forest, coral reefs, amazing marine life, turtles, and more.

OCEANIA

EUROPE

0   2000km

Sweden (p202)

Russia (p199)

Croatia (p194)

Slovakia (p201)

Bosnia & Herzegovina (p193)

Serbia & Montenegro (p200)

Italy (p197)

Portugal (p198)

Greece (p195)

BOSNIA & HERZEGOVINA
International dialling code +387

Bosnia and Herzegovina is heart shaped. This tiny central Balkan state has long been the crossroads of east and west. It is here that eastern Byzantine and Ottoman powers met and mingled with the western influences of Rome, Venice and Austria. Bosnia and Herzegovina is, for the first time since the fifteenth century, an independent state once again. In many ways this new country struggles for an identity of its own, having been embraced by its larger and more powerful neighbours for over a half millennium. Covering no more than 52,000km² it's amazing to find both alpine and Mediterranean climates as well as a rich array of cultures and traditions.

Sarajevo epitomizes this sacred melange of Islam, Christianity and Judaism. This quickly changing city has been reborn into one of the most fascinating cultural bastions in southeast Europe. The Sarajevo film festival, jazz fest, alternative theatre and dozens of other cultural manifestations have attracted curious guests from every corner of the globe.

Tourism has been very much a building bridge in Bosnia and Herzegovina. It has enabled fractured communities to come together again and to rekindle ancient ties. Whilst travelling in Bosnia and Herzegovina, make an effort to get off the beaten path. Visit the ancient villages where people and nature still live in harmony and where guests are treated like members of the family. Local foods are organically grown in most villages and the hospitality will have you wanting to come back for more. Responsible tourism is key to improving the social and economic conditions, particularly in the rural areas. Bosnia and Herzegovina is an inexpensive, new and exciting destination – one of the few remaining unexplored destinations of Europe.

TOUR
EASTERN EUROPE HOLIDAYS

Eastern Europe Holidays offer tailor-made tours for small groups of two to ten persons. Each group has a dedicated guide and driver and unlimited use of a private vehicle for the duration of the tour. The tours can vary from skiing and rafting to historical and cultural adventures. The company hopes to play a part in the revitalization of this wonderful but forgotten region of Europe.

Contact: Ben Robinson
Tel: 6198 4458
Email: brobinson@e-europeholidays.com
Web: www.e-europeholidays.com
Address: Vase Pelagica 34 C/V, Banja Luka, 78000, Bosnia - Herzegovina

HOST/TOUR
GREEN VISIONS

Green Visions is a tour operator dedicated to promoting and preserving the cultural and natural heritage of Bosnia and Herzegovina. It sees ecotourism as a way to protect the highland communities of the Central Dinaric Alps. It follows a low trace, no

Contact: Vesna Pranjic
Tel: 33 717 290
Fax: 33 717 291
Email: Sarajevo@greenvision.ba
Web: www.greenvisions.ba
Address: Radnicka bb, Sarajevo 71000, Bosnia - Herzegovina

impact policy organizing small group mountain tours to the 'old world European villages' throughout Bosnia and Herzegovina. Green Visions provides accommodation, transport, guides, meals and activities. These can vary from hiking, walking, biking, rafting, wildlife observation, medicinal herb picking to skiing or snow-shoeing. Visitors stay in rustic but cosy home-stays in the mountain villages, enjoying traditional organic food, with a real chance to mingle with the local population. Guests leave with a true understanding of the environment they have experienced, having connected with the social issues, cultures and traditions of the host community.

CROATIA
International dialling code +385

300km

ZAGREB

Croatia borders on the Adriatic Sea – a part of the Mediterranean with good seawater quality, clean beaches and rich coastal flora and fauna. Twenty-two of Croatia's beaches and marinas have been awarded the International Blue Flag certificate for exceptional quality of the environment. The coastline is varied with hundreds of uninhabited or abandoned islands to see and discover. If you prefer the plains and the mountains, you can try a bike tour on the numerous bike routes stretching throughout the country. Horseback riding, rafting, canoeing, kayaking or balloon trips are all adventure tours on offer in the beautiful Croatian countryside. Other places of interest include the 900-year-old capital city Zagreb and the Old Town of Dubrovnik with the small authentic villages surrounding it. Dubrovnik – or the 'Jewel of the Adriatic' as it is sometimes referred to – was built in the 13th century and has remained virtually unchanged to the present day. A former independent merchant republic, Dubrovnik has lost nothing of its bustling and jovial flair, and one of the greatest pleasures for visitors is to sit in a local café with the splendid view of the Mediterranean.

EUROPE

DAY/TOUR
ADRIA ADVENTURE – ADRIATIC SEA KAYAKING

Founded in 2003 by two self-confessed addicts of all things marine, Adria offers one-day and multi-day sea kayaking excursions. They can handle up to 20 people and clients stay in local accommodation. They are very keen to keep the Adriatic clean – if you see plastic floating en route you retrieve it and take it for recycling.

Contact: Ivana Grzetic
Tel: (0) 9842 8888/(0) 9850 0309
Email: info@adriatic-sea-kayak.com
Web: www.adriatic-sea-kayak.com
Address: Gorica Sv Vlaha 159, 20000 Dubrovnik, Croatia

GREECE
International dialling code +30

500km

ATHENS

Greece has for many years been a favourite package holiday destination. With warm weather from April to October, sandy beaches and turquoise seas in abundance, it is easy to see why it continues to be so popular. With its endless past, from ancient temples to Byzantine churches to Crusader castles, it is a place of pilgrimage for historians of every era. But the more intrepid traveller can also find plenty to discover. With more than 1400 islands, only 169 of which are inhabited, island hopping can still bring a sense of adventure. From Crete, the largest island, once home of the Minoan civilisation, with a mountainous interior and fierce sense of identity, to Mykonos, with its 365 churches existing alongside a hedonistic nightlife. The mainland also has much to offer. Athens, bristling with self-confidence after the successful Olympic Games is a lively, vibrant if smoggy city. The Parthenon rests on the Acropolis as a beacon and symbol of the city's past glory, but modern Athens with its numerous bars, cafes and restaurants is an exciting destination in itself. Much of the mainland is comparatively little visited but is ideal for exploring on foot, containing a great variety of landscape, from the extraordinary monasteries precariously built on rocks at Meteora, to Mount Olympus, home of the gods and still a place to inspire awe.

ORG
ECOCLUB

An award-winning website forms the centre of ECOCLUB's worldwide ecotourism network. This is an international clearing house for ecotourism information that individuals and eco-lodges can join, and they provide

Contact: Antonis B. Petropoulos
Tel: 210 671 9 671
Fax: 210 671 9 251
Email: a@ecoclub.com
Web: http://ecoclub.com/lodges.html, www.ecoclub.com
Address: PO Box 65232, Psihico, Gr-154 10, Athens, Greece

support, guidance and promotion for the latter. No charges are made either to lodges or to their visitors; you can book your stay in genuine eco-lodges at lower rates and no commission is charged to tourists or lodges.

ACCOM
LEVENDIS ESTATE

Are you tempted by lotus-eating overlooking the wine-dark sea surrounding Homeric Ithaca, by the prospect of informal luxury in family friendly accommodation? This is for you. Everything Levendis does is geared to the health of an environmentally fragile island. Your

Contact: Marilyn Raftopulos
Tel: 6944 169 770
Fax: 2674 031 648
Email: levendis@otenet.gr
Web: www.levendisestate.com
Address: P O Box 23, Vathy, 28300, Island of Ithaca, Greece

spending on the island will benefit local families and businesses. And you can even buy trees to offset the carbon emissions of your flight to Greece. The project has quality and hospitality as its hallmarks.

ACCOM
MILIA RESTORED TRADITIONAL CRETAN SETTLEMENT

'Peace and quiet in prodigious amounts' are promised if you stay in one of the 14 restored guesthouses that offer 'simplicity, good taste and basic comforts'. You need not cook – there is a restaurant and the food is either home-grown or sourced locally. Solar power, recycling, sensible water use: this project has it right. And something in the air (or is it the ethos?) fosters communication among guests and between them and the locals.

Contact: Tassos Gourgouras
Tel: 28210 46774/28220 51569
Cellular: 69447 44136
Fax: 28210 46774
Email: milia@cha.forthnet.gr
Web: www.milia.gr, www.i-escape.com,
www.atg-oxford.co.uk
Address: Milia, Vlatos - Kissamos, 73012 Chania, Crete, Greece

ACCOM+
NIKKI ROSE SEMINARS/CULINARY SANCTUARIES

If you're a foodie and you love the Med, Greece especially, and you're into the slow food movement, look no further than Crete's Culinary Sanctuaries (CSS), particularly if you want an experience that gives you all this and tells you that your

Contact: Nikki Rose
Tel: 28410 42797
Email: nikkirose@cookingincrete.com
Web: www.cookingincrete.com
Address: Elounda Post T.K. 72053, Elounda, Crete, Greece

presence is helping to preserve local skills and trades. Taste buds are compulsory, as is the desire to learn about Crete's agriculture, history, nature and cuisine. See organic olive oil production, beekeeping, wine making, cheese making, as well as visiting villages off the map and taking walks in magnificent, wild nature.

EUROPE

ITALY
International dialling code +39

From Julius Caesar to the Pope, from Leonardo da Vinci to Mussolini – Italy's history is peppered with both famous and infamous characters. Rich in artistic tradition, steeped in culture and awash with stunning architecture, from Mediterranean coastline to Alpine mountains this country has something to offer everyone. Italy did not become a unified country until 1861, consequently more cultural identity is attached to the nine regions of the country than to the nation as a whole. This is expressed through very distinct dialects, culinary habits and different standards of living. There is a strong north/south divide: the north is a rapidly growing industrialized society, while the south suffers from low literacy rates, economic and social depression and still operates under a pseudo-feudal system. However, it is the central regions that perhaps characterize the essence of the best of Italy. The rolling landscape of Tuscany not only offers great opportunities for trekking but also boasts more classified historical monuments than any other country worldwide. A visit to Venice can satisfy all your romantic yearnings with its shady canals, hidden alleyways and echoing churches. The middle of the day is siesta time, an age-old tradition of the Mediterranean, followed by the obligatory 'passeggiata', the evening stroll enjoyed by young and old alike. The Italians are known for their enjoyment of the 'dolce vita', and no visit would be complete without indulging in fine wine, fine food and fine fashion.

ACCOM+
ECOVILLAGE TORRI SUPERIORE

Torri Superiore dates from the 13th century and consists of eight levels of stone-built structures. There are three main buildings separated by partly covered alleys, in all, the complex has about 160 rooms, which are linked by a maze of stairways, terraces and alleys.

Contact: Lucilla Borio
Tel: 184 215504
Fax: 184 215914
Email: info@torri-superiore.org
Web: www.torri-superiore.org
Address: Via Torri Superiore 5, 18039 Ventimiglia (IM) Italy

In the 1990s a group of people set out to save this amazing place from a slow death. Today this cooperative owns part of the village with the rest owned by individuals. Visitors are welcome; there are 18 beds in total in a variety of rooms.

Summing up the project is difficult, but if the idea of living in a caring eco-community and eating good home-sourced food around a communal table but being able to retreat to your own space appeals then this could be a rewarding experience.

EUROPE

PORTUGAL
International dialling code +351

250km

LISBON

Although small in size, dwarfed by its neighbour Spain, Portugal is rich in both culture and variety of landscape. Most visitors flock to the Algarve, the Mediterranean strip of coastline on the southern edge of Portugal. Though fine for a sun, sand, sea and golf package holiday, there is little to distinguish this part of the country from the Spanish costas.

More interesting, but much less explored, is the western coastline, wilder and more charismatic but, with the cold Atlantic waters, admittedly not ideal for swimming. In the Serra da Estrela it is possible to ski in the winter, but it is great for walking throughout the year. The Alentejo in the centre is the agricultural hub of Portugal, beautiful but little visited. Throughout the country are dotted hotels known as pousadas, some converted from castles and palaces, but relatively inexpensive for luxury accommodation.

Portugal's past, from Magellan to John the navigator, has left the country with a rich architectural heritage. There are numerous towns throughout the country, such as Coimbra and Braga, worth visiting for their fortress-like granite cathedrals and architecture ranging through Gothic, Renaissance and baroque. In the north is the stately city of Porto on the River Douro, home of Port wine, and in the south the vibrant, cosmopolitan city of Lisbon, with its lively nightlife in the Bairro Alto, and home to fado, the melancholic, nostalgic songs of regret. No visit to Portugal would be complete without sampling bacalhau, the national dish of salted cod, which allegedly had as many ways to prepare it as there are days in the year.

ACCOM+
CEGONHA BRANCA

Cegonha Branca organizes accommodation with two different communities; in Sintra and Vaiada Ribatejo, placed between mountains, seaside and the River Tejo Valley. Fluvial transfers to the destinations from Lisbon and different activities such as trekking, abseiling, mountaineering, canoeing, visits to local organic farmers, local craft shops and wine cellars, yoga, scuba-diving, surfing and bodyboard can also be organized. Cegonha Branca supports local communities by providing training for local people to enable them to work closely with the environment and use the best recycling practices.

Contact: José Luís Felix
Tel: 21 3867021
Fax: 21 7931557
Email: cegonhabranca@mail.pt
Address: A Va, Conde Valbom, 116-7° -1070-050 Lisboa - Portugal

AGRI/ACCOM/DIS
QUINTA DA COMENDA

This agri-organic lodging in the mountainous region of Porto has five double rooms, one triple and one flat equipped for disabled people; breakfast is included. It helps the local community with employment, recycling and eco-preservation

Contact: Maria Susana Beirao
Tel: 226179889/966701997
Fax: 226183491
Email: quintadacomenda@sapo.pt
Web: www.quintadacomenda.com
Address: Av. da Boavista nº 2600, 4100-119 Porto – Portugal

techniques for the surrounding environment. A completely organic farm, with swimming pool, table games, gardens and walking, guests can also take part in grape harvesting or fruit picking.

RUSSIA
International dialling code +7

One probably needs more than a lifetime to travel to all corners of Russia. Just look at the famous Trans-Siberian railway. It spans almost 6000 miles from the capital, Moscow, to Vladivostok and cuts across an array of untouched natural landscapes and ethnically and culturally diverse regions. Europe's highest peak, Mount Elbrus, is situated in the Russian Caucasus and presents a serious challenge even to experienced mountaineers. For those interested in wildlife, ecological and scientific tours offer a peek into the habitats of the rare Siberian tiger. Watching seals in the Baikal Lake, the biggest freshwater lake on earth, as well as Beluga whales in the White Sea present exquisite and unique encounters with nature. After years of Soviet party politics Russians began to rethink their magnificent cultural heritage. Christian-orthodox monasteries are being restored and those turned into Gulags under Stalin's rule, like the Solovki Islands, are being re-established as museums. Ethnic Muslim and Buddhist minorities readily celebrate their old traditions and gladly invite travellers to join in. While St Petersburg experiences a reinvigoration of its splendid Tsarist palaces and its centre revives its 19th-century flair, Moscow is becoming ever more modern, cosmopolitan, fast-paced and most beautifully illuminated at night.

EUROPE

TOUR
FIRN TRAVEL

Firn Travel runs cultural and ecological tours and implements projects to promote sustainable tourism in the Lake Baikal region of Eastern Siberia. It was founded by Club Firn, a not-for-profit local NGO, whose mission is the solution of local problems through the development of civil society. Many kinds of tour are on offer: nature, historical, ethnographic, active (kayaking, walking, cycling etc.) and all centred on the area of Lake Baikal, which is a natural phenomenon nonpareil being the biggest, deepest and oldest lake in the world. As for ornithologists or birders – you'll be excused for thinking you've died and gone to heaven when you see the Seelenga Delta in the migration season. Firn operates all year – but you might need your Damart undies for the Winter Wonderland tour.

Contact: Larisa Batotsyrenova
Tel: 3012 21 62 50/3012 21 67 23
Fax: 3012 21 62 50
Email: info@firntravel.ru/larisa@firnclub.ru
Web: http://firntravel.ru
Address: 670017 Russia, Buryatia, Ulan Ude, PO Box 4204, Firn Travel

SERBIA & MONTENEGRO

International dialling code +381

Serbia and Montenegro are the two last remaining 'united' republics of the former Yugoslavia, but future referendums will most likely leave them both independent states. As they offer different tourism experiences, we shall deal with them individually.

Despite a negative image that has dogged Serbia, the largest of the former Yugoslav republics, tourism is making a steady comeback. Known for its kind hospitality and love of history, the region is quickly developing many sectors within the tourism industry. The two largest cities of Belgrade and Novi Sad are attractive, exciting and inexpensive destinations. Belgrade is a hopping capital city teeming with cafes and bars. Novi Sad is one of the most multi-ethnic provinces in the whole former Yugoslavia with Serbian, Croatian, Hungarian and German influences in cuisine, traditions, architecture and language. Both the cultural scene and the nightlife will pleasantly surprise most guests.

However, Serbia offers much more. The newly refined wine tours through the heart of Serbia not only give a fascinating peek into rural life but the wine production (and the local 'rakija' – plum brandy) has significantly improved over the last decade. The western area of Serbia features spectacular rural villages connected with the famous filmmaker from Sarajevo, Emir Kusturica. The ancient Orthodox monasteries, often in serene nature settings, have been fundamental to Serbian spiritual life since the early middle ages. And Kopaonik to the southwest is the best mountain resort in the country with skiing, hiking and a fine taste in traditional foods.

The ecological mountain country of Montenegro is said to be the oldest 'state' in the western Balkans. It is here that mountains meet the sea in what must be one of southeast Europe's most stunning nature destinations. The seaside resorts and tourist towns are well known to tourists for their crystal clear Adriatic seawater with breathtaking mountain views towering just behind. The resorts of Sveti Stephan, Herceg Novi, the Bay of Kotor, Bar and Budva are amongst the Adriatic's best. Peel away just one layer of mountain, though, and a magical world opens up. Lake Shkoeder is a gorgeous bird reserve and a great place for boat rides and fishing. The ancient capital of Montenegro, Cetine, is still the cultural backbone of the country.

Durmitor National Park gets a high rating for its vast wilderness. Perhaps the most exciting experience in Montenegro is the three-day white-water rafting adventure on the Tara River, Europe's deepest river canyon. The northern pocket around Plav has an interesting ethnic mix of Orthodox, Slavic Muslims and Albanians. This area is rather poor and underdeveloped, but equally beautiful.

DAY
UNPD LO PODGORICA

This United Nations Development Programme (UNDP) project is implementing a sustainable tourism programme in the Durmitor National Park under its global initiative 'Unleashing entrepreneurship'. Durmitor is a World Heritage site. The project represents a partnership between the National Park, the local community and local entrepreneurs and NGOs. The

Tel: 81 231 251
Fax: 81 231 644
Email: sanja@undp.org, bojanic@undp.org, tomica.paovic@undp.org
Web: www.undp.org.yu/montenegro, www.destination-durmitor.org, www.durmitor.com
Address: Beogradska 24b, 81000 Podgorica, Montenegro and Serbia

aim is to promote and upgrade two sustainable tourism services, rafting and hiking. The area is attainable by road but the route is more than a little 'iffy' in winter months. You should note that the rafting takes place on the Tara River in the Tara canyon, which is the second deepest in the world. It is reckoned that rafting alone brought a million euro to three communties along the river. UNDP is not directly involved in tourism but is happy to post appropriate contact details on the Durmitor web site.

SLOVAKIA
International dialling code +421

As one of the newest members of the European Union, Slovakia has become an insider tip for a short and inexpensive weekend getaway. Its capital, Bratislava, is a youthful and vibrant city, but without the annoying side effects of other European capitals, such as congestion, commercialism and hoards of tourists. The countryside is full of majestic mountains, lush river valleys and historical towns and castles. Nature lovers should definitely visit some of the numerous Slovak nature parks. Caving and spa tourism are other popular forms of recreation, and thermal spring water may get as hot as 92°C. For young adventurers a good way to explore Slovakia is

EUROPE

through hitchhiking. It is a relatively safe mode of transport and you may pass places off the beaten track and get to know the locals better. Slovaks are happy and generous people and always ready to help. The most popular dishes are made of some basic ingredients – potatoes, wheat flour, goat's or sheep's cheese, onion, cabbage – and have a wonderful, nostalgic peasant touch.

TOUR/DAY
SLOVAKIA GREEN TOURS

This is a partnership between the operator Slovakia Green Tours and a group called Green View who specialize in environmental services. This is a new project (operational since January 2005) but a range of five- and one-day ecotours is already on offer. The canvas they are working on is composed of the birds and other natural phenomena of the country, and they also work closely with local authorities and local craftsmen and guides. The fundamental aim is conservation both of the things of nature and the threatened skills of local people and to this end they endeavour to raise public awareness.

Contact: Ms. Petra Drahosova
Tel: 2 5249 1641/908 989 069
Fax: 2 5249 1651
Email: Petra@Slovakiagreentours.com
Web: www.slovakiagreentours.com
Address: Radlinskeho 27, 811 07, Bratislava, Slovakia

SWEDEN
International dialling code +46

This country in the north of Europe is a haven for responsible travellers. Swedes care very much about the natural environment and are some of the most ecologically responsible people on the planet. Sweden is a mountainous country situated on the Scandinavian Peninsula between Norway and Finland. To the south it is connected to mainland Europe via the ultra-modern Oresund Bridge. In Sweden's most northern town, Kiruna, located 250km beyond the Arctic Circle and a 16-hour train ride away from Stockholm, the Northern Lights can be observed and admired. The north of the country is populated by the Sami people, who in the beginning of the 21st century still manage to preserve their own language, centuries-old customs and their belief in pagan gods. The diverse accommodation base ranges from residing in romantic castles, wild camping sites and inexpensive hostels through to sleeping in a tree house, in an ice hotel or in a 19th-century converted prison. If you happen to visit Sweden in the month of August, definitely take part in the loud, jovial and silly crayfish parties.

600km

STOCKHOLM

EUROPE

TOUR
THE SILENT WAY

The clue is in the name: this is about snow, mountains and dog-sledding – mountain tours lasting 5–16 days in Europe's largest nature reserve, Vindelfjallens. There are about 10/11 long tours each year and each can accommodate five guests. If you like winter, snow and ice and want to learn how to mush a team of huskies then this is vacationing at the sharp end for an inclusive cost of 18,400 kroner (£1350/US$2400) per person. They look after everything, you will be clad properly, and they make their guests feel 'at home'. They hold the first national ecotourism quality label in the northern hemisphere, 'Natures Best'.

Contact: Catrine Anderback
Tel: 95152043
Fax: 95152043
Email: info@silent-way.com
Web: www.dogsledding-adventures.com,
www.silent-way.com
Address: Umnäs 48, 92397 Lapland, Sweden

EUROPE

TOUR OPERATORS

The following tour operators (and one travel agency) are challenging the dominance of mainstream operators. All of them are committed to supporting local communities. Often they are small businesses and are specialists, passionate about the destinations they go to and wanting to ensure that both you – the guest – and those acting as hosts have a good time and benefit from the experience. Thus you should expect a quality, personal service. All of these operators offer journeys to more than one country. Those that are country specific are identified in the country listings. Many of the hotels and tours listed in this guide can be booked through these operators.

UK OPERATORS

BAOBAB TRAVEL

Baobab Travel is a UK-based specialist tour operator, born out of a combination of a love of Africa and travel, and a desire to actively work with and support local communities in the developing world. Baobab holidays are designed to show visitors the real places, nature and culture in Africa, avoiding resorts that have been 'manufactured' for tourists.

Contact: Chris Morris
Tel: +44 (0) 0870 382 5003
Fax: +44 (0) 0870 382 5004
Email: info@baobabtravel.com
Web: www.baobabtravel.com
Address: Old Fallings Hall, Old Fallings Lane, Wolverhampton, WV10 8BL, UK

BEES ABROAD

Bees Abroad is a charity which organizes beekeeping projects in Nepal, Cameroon, Malawi and Kenya. These projects employ local people, with an emphasis on the inclusion of women, minority groups and disabled people wherever possible. Beekeeping offers a means of poverty alleviation through the sales of honey and beeswax products. Bees Abroad holidays offer visitors a chance to visit the projects. A typical 14-day trip includes mainstream tourist activities as well as the chance to visit beekeepers and their local communities. The holidays are mostly organized by volunteers to enable the maximum contribution to be given to the charity for project funding.

Contact: Nicola Gilbert
Tel: +44 (0) 7986 978 822
Email: nicola.gilbert@talk21.com
Web: www.beesabroad.org.uk
Address: 8 Derby Avenue, Harrow Weald, Middlesex, HA3 5JU, UK

CALEDONIA LANGUAGE

Established in 1994, Caledonia specializes in cultural tourism, language and adventure holidays in Europe, Latin America and the Caribbean. Trips include French and Kayaking in Guadeloupe, Spanish and Salsa in Cuba, Italian and Cooking in Tuscany or French and Diving in Nice. Language courses for teenagers, adults and special interest groups. All ages, all levels and all year round.

Tel: +44 (0)131 621 7721
Fax: +44 (0)131 555 6262
Email: courses@caledonialanguages.co.uk
Web: www.caledonialanguages.co.uk
Address: The Clockhouse, Bonnington Mill, 72 Newhaven Road, Edinburgh EH6 5QG, UK

DISCOVERY INITIATIVES

Discovery Initiatives has a mission to offer inspirational small group and tailor-made travel programmes in cooperation with some of the world's leading conservation organizations. Thus guests gain a privileged, behind the scenes insight into local cultures and wildlife around the world. The company has fair

Tel: +44 (0) 1285 643 333
Fax: +44 (0) 1285 885 888
Email: enquiry@discoveryinitiatives.com
Web: www.discoveryinitiatives.co.uk
Address: The Travel House, 51 Castle Street, Cirencester, Gloucestershire, GL7 1QD, UK

trading partnerships with the agencies and local community enterprises visited, and challenges the conventional approach to nature or wilderness travel. They go to 35 countries, working with over 25 International, UK and local agencies such as The Orangutan Foundation and IRDNC in Namibia, contributing over £390,000/US$695,000 to conservation initiatives and agencies across the world in their first five years of business.

DRAGOMAN OVERLAND

Dragoman Overland, a leading adventure travel company, now has something for everyone. They will take you through the landscape and culture of Latin America, Africa, Central Asia and the Far East. Don't miss their exciting talks when you can share the experience of 40 years of adventure and discovery.

Tel: +44 (0)1728 861 133
Fax: +44 (0)1728 861 127
Email: kathy@dragoman.co.uk
Web: www.dragoman.com
Address: Camp Green, Debenham, Suffolk, IP14 6LA, UK

EQUATORIAL TRAVEL

Equatorial Travel operates mainly in Morocco, Ecuador and Rajasthan (India). It is a small specialist company operating often in areas untouched by other tour operators. Working on fair trade principles, the company runs group and tailor-made tours for all ages, including walking tours, arts and crafts tours, music tours, cultural and wildlife tours and family tours.

Tel: +44 (0) 1335 348 770/350 161
Fax: +44 (0) 1335 350 161/300 485
Email: tours@EqTravel.co.uk
Web: www.EqTravel.co.uk
Address: 1 Clergy House, Mappleton, Ashbourne, Derbyshire, DE6 2AB, UK

TOUR OPERATORS

EXPERT AFRICA

Expert Africa, (part of the Sunvil Group) specializes in tailor-made trips to Southern and East Africa, and offers superb value for money with unrivalled expertise. Their trips are individual and highly flexible, catering for free-spirited and discerning travellers. By offering quality trips that support small establishments and local guides, they also try to minimize any environmental damage and help the communities that you visit.

Tel: +44 (0) 20 8232 9777
Fax: +44 (0) 20 8758 4718
Email: info@expertafrica.com
Web: www.expertafrica.com
Address: 10-11 Upper Square,
Old Isleworth, TW7 7BJ, UK

EXPLORE!

Central to the Explore ethos is to bring the traveller closer to the local people, to be a positive benefit to the communities visited and to minimize the impact on the environment. In addition Explore supports a wide variety of environmental and humanitarian charities and projects.

Contact: Fran Hughes
Tel: 01252 760 200
Fax: 01252 760 201
Email: info@explore.co.uk
Web: www.explore.co.uk
Address: Nelson House, 55 Victoria Road,
Farnborough, GU14 7PA, UK

GUERBA WORLD TRAVEL

Guerba operates in the field of worldwide adventure and discovery holidays. The Kenyan arm is co-owned by local management and the UK parent company. Its Guerba for Good UK charity helps fund grass roots charities in Africa and they help on the ground with community projects in East Africa. If something 'feels right' they do it. Their big project is the Amani

Contact: Ian Ripper
Tel: +44 (0) 1373 858 956
Fax: +44 (0) 1373 858 351
Email: res@guerba.co.uk/info@guerba.co.uk
US email: info@adventurecenter.com
Australia email: anna@naturalfocussafaris.com
New Zealand email: SPritchard@travelplan.co.nz (ref Guerba)
Web: www.guerba.co.uk
Address: Wessex House, 40 Station Road, Westbury,
Wilts. BA13 3JN, UK

Children's Home in Moshi, Tanzania, and they offer discounts for travellers willing to fundraise for the Home. They have a strict porters' policy in place for the Kilimanjaro trips. Their clients are given advice on codes of behaviour before they travel.

INTOAFRICA UK

This is a small (and happy to be so) company specializing in fairly traded treks and safaris in Kenya and Tanzania. Its fundamental principle is to benefit local communities, and this is backed up by fair trading practice and direct donations. The operational foci are cultural tourism, wildlife safaris and mountain trekking. They offer neither luxury lodges nor run-of-the-mill adventure safaris. They aim to combine the wildlife and the scenery with genuine insight into local people's lifestyles and environ-ments. Local communities benefit to the tune of 15 per cent of a holiday's cost as payment for their services.

Contact: Chris Morris
Tel: +44 (0) 114 255 5610
Fax: +44 (0) 114 255 5610
Email: info@intoafrica.co.uk
Web: www.intoafrica.co.uk
Address: 40 Huntingdon Crescent,
Sheffield, S11 8AX, UK

INTREPID TRAVEL

Intrepid Travel operates small group trips through Asia, the Middle East and Europe. All their various trip styles share a common philosophy of experiencing a country, rather than just seeing it, meeting local people and gaining cultural understanding. They use small-scale locally owned accommodation and local transport where available. The Intrepid Foundation supports local charitable projects.

Tel: +44 (0)20 7354 6169
  0800 917 6456 (toll free)
Email: info@intrepidtravel.com
Web: www.intrepidtravel.com
Address: 76 Upper Street,
  London N1 0NU, UK

JOURNEY LATIN AMERICA

Journey Latin America, UK's specialist in the region, offers tailor-made trips, group tours, flights and language courses. JLA has evolved carefully through 25 years of operating there. As true specialists, we understand the ecological and social issues particular to Latin America. We use small groups, local guides and, where possible, public transport.

Tel: +44 (0)20 8622 8416
Fax: +44 (0) 20 8995 7710
Email: info@journeylatinamerica.co.uk
Web: www.journeylatinamerica.co.uk
Address: 12/13 Heathfield Terrace,
  London W4 4JE, UK

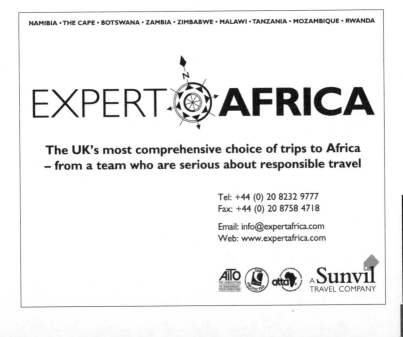
TOUR OPERATORS

LAST FRONTIERS

Last Frontiers is a small tour operator specializing in tailor-made holidays to Latin America, and most of our staff have lived and worked in the region. They recognize their responsibility to ensure the long-term sustainability of their operations and continually monitor environmental and cultural issues.

Tel: +44 (0) 1296 653 000
Email: info@lastfrontiers.com
Web: www.lastfrontiers.com

MUIR'S TOURS

Muir's Tours is a UK-based tour operator specializing in holidays involving, for example, dog sledding and polar bear viewing. The bulk of clients go trekking in the Himalayas, Peru and Chile, dog sledding in Lapland, horse riding in Mongolia, and wildlife watching in Tanzania and Canada. The Nepal Kingdom Foundation, a UK-based charity, is the major benefactor from Muir's Tours' activities. In Nepal, local people are employed on their terms: they are asked how much they need and so far have been given what they asked for. Muir's Tours continues to pay them even if there is no work to do.

Contact: Maurice Adshead
Tel: +44 (0) 118 950 2281
Email: info@nkf-mt.org.uk
Web: www.nkf-mt.org.uk,
   www.tibetantraders.org.uk
Address: Nepal House, 97A Swansea Road,
   Reading, England, RG1 8HA, UK

NORTH SOUTH TRAVEL

North South Travel is a unique travel agency offering global discount fares with excellent personal service. The owner of North South Travel is the NST Development Trust (registered charity 1040656), and all profits from the sale of tickets are donated to grass roots charities worldwide.

Tel: +44 (0) 1245 608 291
Email: reservations@northsouthtravel.co.uk
Web: www.northsouthtravel.co.uk
Address: Moulsham Mill, Parkway,
   Chelmsford, CM2 7PX, UK

RAINBOW TOURS

Africa and Indian Ocean specialist offering some tours but mostly tailor-made, up market itineraries to Southern and East Africa, as well as the most comprehensive programme to Madagascar. Rainbow Tours features many community-partnership lodges and B&Bs. Voted 'Best Tour Operator' in the Guardian/Observer Travel Awards 2004 and 2005. ATOL bonded, AITO member.

Tel: +44 (0) 20 7226 1004
Email: info@rainbowtours.co.uk
Web: www.rainbowtours.co.uk
Address: 305 Upper Street, London N1 2TU, UK

TOUR OPERATORS

SADDLE SKEDADDLE

Saddle Skedadle has a joint venture with Traidcraft's People to People Tours. Traidcraft has run tours for years, but this partnership gives fair trade supporters the chance to go behind the products and meet the people making them and see their homes and communities. All aspects of the tours are organized so as to maximize the benefits, both economic and personal, for the hosts. The tours don't include flight costs. Destinations include Cuba, India, Thailand, Bangladesh, Philippines, South Africa, Kenya.

Contact: Paul Snedkar
Tel: +44 (0) 191 265 1110
Fax: +44 (0) 191 265 1110
Email: paul@skedaddle.co.uk
Web: www.peopletopeopletours.com
Address: Ouseburn Building, East Quayside, Newcastle upon Tyne, NE6 1LL, UK

THE NEPAL TRUST
A New Tourism For A New Millennium

Since 1993 Nepal Trust Himalayan Travel & MAD (Make a Difference – Treks) have run 'Treks To Build' to the 'Hidden Himalayas' to construct renewable energy, health, education and heritage preservation projects. We offer journeys of hope and progress in Nepal – adventure and exploration in Tibet, Bhutan and India. Profits support village-based projects.

Contact: Jim Donovan at The Nepal trust
Tel: +44 (0) 1343 810 358
Fax: +44 (0) 1343 810 359
Email: admin@nepaltrust.org
Web: www.nepaltrust.org
Address: The Nepal Trust, 4 Marina Quay, Lossiemouth, Moray IV31 6TJ, Scotland, UK

Contact: Tony Cook at Himalayan Travel
Tel: +44 (0) 1304 620 880
Fax: +44 (0) 1304 620 880
Email: info@himalayantravel.co.uk
Web: www.himalayantravel.co.uk
Address: Himalayan Travel, 12 Woodland Way, Woodnesborough, Sandwich, Kent CT13 0NG UK

Contact: Lhakpa Sherpa at MAD
Tel: +977 1 472 1112
Fax: +977 1 472 0224
Email: info@madtreks.com, ntrust@mail.com.np
Web: www.madtreks.com
Address: MAD, GPO 8975 - EPC 4131, Chundevi, Maharajgunj, Kathmandu, Nepal

TRAVELROOTS

Travelroots offers responsible ecotourism holidays to destinations across the world with one thing in common: all holidays contribute positively to the holiday areas. This means Travelroots holidays do good to both destination environments and local communities, thus offering a better holiday that doesn't cost more.

Tel: +44 (0) 20 8341 2262
Fax: +44 (0) 208 341 4821
Email: info@travelroots.com
Web: www.travelroots.com
Address: 52 Avenue Road, London N6 5DR, UK

TRIBES

Tribes, the Fair Trade Travel company, arranges quality, tailor-made and small group holidays in Botswana, Ecuador, India, Jordan, Morocco, Namibia, Nepal, Peru, South Africa, Tanzania, Uganda and Zambia. This award winning company is run on ethical and responsible principles, and promotes local community tourism initiatives.

Tel: +44 (0) 1728 685 971
Email: info@tribes.co.uk
Web: www.tribes.co.uk
Address: 72 The Business Centre, Earl Soham, Woodbridge, Suffolk IP13 7SA, UK

TOUR OPERATORS

US OPERATORS

ALOK HOLISTIC HEALTH COMMUNITY

This is health tourism angled thus: tours combining yoga, health, nutrition and ecology. They aim to introduce people to new cultures without impinging on them: 'we leave no trace behind us'. If you are deeply into vegetarianism and ecological living this might be up your alley. Donations are made to non-profit animal-rights and environmental organizations. Check out the website for more, but if you're into crystals this could be you.

Contact: Zemach Zohar Wilson
Tel: +1 347 563 2118
Email:info@alokhealth.com
Web: www.alokhealth.com
Address: 37 Madison Avenue,
Hasbrouck Heights, NJ 07604, USA

CROOKED TRAILS

Founded by two women in Seattle (still the only employees), the company offers tours that combine responsible travel with homestay and work projects. Most programmes are centred on Peru but they also offer access to a wide range of other countries, including Nepal, India, Thailand, Chile, Bolivia and Kenya. A great deal of effort is put into educating clients about responsible travel and behaviour, and a pre-departure package outlines cultural, economic and environmental etiquette rules.

Contact: Chris Mackay
Tel: +1 206 372 4405
Fax: +206 320 0505
Email: info@crookedtrails.com
Web: www.crookedtrails.com
Address: PO Box 94034, Seattle,
WA 98124, USA

ECO INN EXPERIENCES

Eco Inn Experiences wants to be a management and financing partner for locally owned and operated eco inns and lodges on a worldwide basis, but mainly in the South. It aims to become a global brand and its franchise is to become a sort of kite mark for eco-accommodation so that travellers will be able to expect a socially enriching experience with minimum environmental impact, without 'having a shock' when it comes to food and service.

Contact: John Ganzi
Tel: +1 919 933 3610
Fax: +1 919 933 1352
Email: jganzi@ecoinn.org
Web: www.ecoinn.org
Address: PO Box 6517, Chapel Hill, NC 27516-6517, USA

GO NATIVE AMERICA

Go Native America offers visitors an insight into the history, lands and cultures of Native People, guided only by indigenous people, with the goal of making fair trade the standard for tribal tourism on the Northern Plains. Visit the homelands of Sitting Bull, Crazy Horse, Red Cloud; legends of Native America.

Tel: +1 924 840111
Email: info@gonativeamerica.com
Web: www.gonativeamerica.com
USA address: 821 N 27th St, #120, Billings, MT 59101, USA
UK address: 2nd Floor, 145 -157 St John Street, London, EC1V 4PY, UK

IBIKE TOURS

Based in Seattle, USA, Ibike Tours offer unique and affordable (their words) two and four week village-based cultural immersion ecotours in Africa, Asia, South America. All ability levels are catered for and all the programmes focus on cultural diversity and socio-economic complexity of the locales involved. The main mode of travel – no surprise – is by bicycle.

Contact: David Mozer
Tel: +1 206 767 0848
Fax: +1 206 767 0848
Email: ibike@ibike.org
Web: www.ibike.org/ibike
Address: 4887 Columbia Dr S, Seattle, WA 98108, USA

REALITY TOURS & GLOBAL EXCHANGE

Global Exchange is a non-profit human rights organization working for global political, environmental and social justice. Their 'Reality Tours' educate the public about international issues through socially responsible travel. They travel to over 20 destinations throughout Africa, Latin America, the Middle East, Central and Southeast Asia, Europe and US domestic tours.

Tel: +1 415 575 5546
Fax: +1 415 255 7498
Email: realitytours@globalexchange.org
Web: www.globalexchange.org
Address: 2017 Mission St. #303, San Francisco, CA 94110, USA

RELIEF RIDERS INTERNATIONAL

RRI is a humanitarian-based adventure travel company that organizes horseback journeys through breathtaking areas in developing countries around the world. With up to 15 participants per ride, they bring relief supplies to communities in need. Working in joint partnership with the Red Cross, they set up medical

Contact: Alexander Souri
Tel: +1 413 329 5876
Email: info@reliefridersinternational.com
Web: www.reliefridersinternational.com
Address: 304 Main St, Suite 3-B, Great Barrington, MA 01230, USA

TOUR OPERATORS

camps, distribute livestock to families living in poverty, organize an HIV/Aids awareness programme and hold paediatric camps. They also donate educational material to five schools they travel to in the desert of Rajasthan, India.

TERRA INCOGNITA ECOTOURS

The company pledges to engage in 'responsible travel to natural areas that conserves the environment and improves the well-being of local people'. At each destination they cooperate with a different conservation partner and part of the cost of a tour goes to that partner – normally ten per cent. Local communities benefit to the tune of about 70 per cent of the cost. Destinations include Belize, Costa Rica, Nicaragua, Rwanda and Uganda.

Contact: Gerard "Ged" Caddick
Tel: +1 813 289 1049
Fax: +1 813 289 1049
Email: ged@ecotours.com
Web: www.go-explore.com
Address: 4016 West Inman Ave, Tampa, FL 33609, USA

NON-UK/US OPERATORS

ECHOWAY

This French organization has been working since 2003 to promote a tourism which respects both the environment and people. Their website will give you the low-down on all the

Tel: +33 (0) 1 4373 5187
Email: info@echoway.org
Web: www.echoway.org
Address: 75, avenue Philippe-Auguste, 75011 Paris, France

projects they have embraced that conform to all their criteria of ethical, ecological, and fairly traded tourism. They have specialized in Mexico and Central America but they do encompass the world in their search for good tourism practice.

INTREPID TRAVEL

See under UK Operators for Intrepid's main listing. They also have a major office in Australia, and contact telephone numbers for ethical tourists based anywhere in the world.

Tel: +61 3 9473 2656
Mobile: 0417 591 942
Fax: +61 3 9419 5878
Email: jcrouch@intrepidtravel.com
Web: www.intrepidtravel.com
Address: PO Box 2781, Fitzroy DC, Victoria 3065, Australia

Europe tel: (+44) 207 354 6170
North America tel: +1 866 847 8192

New Zealand tel: 0800 174043
Rest of the world tel: (+61) 394732673

RAM (ITALY)

Ram is a fair trade operator running tours to Nepal, India, Thailand, Bangladesh and The Gambia.

Contact: Renzo Garrone
Tel: +39 (0) 185 773061
Email: orzonero@hotmail.com

MUIR'S TOURS is committed to travel with concern for the environment, the indigenous people and YOU.

We partner with local communities and small localised tour operators to offer you a deeper insight to the culture or to provide you with the benefit of local knowledge that may prove helpful on wildlife trips in particular. Western guides on some trips, otherwise expert local guides.

Cultural Immersion, **Activity holidays** of all levels plus **wildlife watching** in Asia, Africa & the Americas.

Email: info@nkf-mt.org.uk
Tel: 0118 950 2281

Websites: www.nkf-mt.org.uk
and www.muirstours.org.uk
And for something a little different www.salsaparty.org.uk

VISION DU MONDE

Vision du Monde operates mainly in Mauritania, and to a lesser extent in Morocco and Peru. The holidays offered are constructed on sharing local lifestyles and staying in the community. Groups are 12 maximum. Vision interests itself principally in projects linked with health, education and access to water. Each year they hold a reunion weekend when new and old clients can exchange memories and discuss what they have seen and done.

Contact: Laurent Besson
Tel: +33 47443 9182
Fax: +33 47443 9142
Email: contact@visiondumonde.org,
bsavariau@tele2.fr
Web: www.visiondumonde.org
Address: 3, route de Chambery,
38300 Bourgoin-Jaillieu, France

VOLUNTEERING

This Guide is focused on holidays, some of which have a volunteering aspect and are included in the country listings. However, during the course of our research we came across worthwhile organizations not focused on holidays, which we have included. We are conscious of many more such volunteering opportunities throughout the world but suggest that readers wishing to know about them be guided by relevant books and websites.

AZAFADY

This UK-registered charity working in partnership with an NGO in Madagascar recruits volunteers from around the world. They work with the 65 local Malagasy staff on integrated conservation and development projects intended to improve health, reduce environmental degradation, and bettering the livelihood prospects for the poorest rural people. Such volunteers, besides helping directly, can also help to spread the word about the needs and the beauty of Madagascar.

Contact: Mal Mitchell
Tel: +44 (0) 20 8960 6629
Email: mal@azafady.org
Web: www.madagascar.co.uk

BLUE VENTURES

The rationale of this UK-registered charity is to support community-centred marine conservation initiatives in the developing world. The main focus of activity is a community-run marine protected area in the village of Andavadoaka, southwestern Madagascar. The commitment is to identifying environmental issues vital to the community and then addressing them with appropriate conservation, education and research plans. Research volunteers (13 max at present) can specialize because of the breadth of the Blue Ventures programme. It costs £1780/US$3170 for a six-week expedition, which reduces to £1380/US$2460 without the optional diving training.

Contact: Tom Savage
Tel: +44 (0) 208 341 9819
Fax: +44 (0) 208 341 4821
Email: tom@blueventures.org
Web: www.blueventures.org
Address: 52 Avenue Road, London, N6 5DR, UK

THE DIFFERENT TRAVEL COMPANY

Different Travel combine the comfort and relaxation of a high quality discovery holiday with opportunities to spend part of the two week break working on development programmes in the host country. Projects currently exist in Sri Lanka, Tibet, Nepal and Thailand.

Tel: +44 (0)2380 669 903
Email: info@different-travel.com
Web: www.different-travel.com
Address: 3 Maritime Avenue, Marchwood, Hampshire, SO40 4AN

DREAM PROJECT

The Dominican Republic Education and Mentoring Project is a non-profit organization, which provides the structure necessary to support philanthropic tourism. The Project aims to develop sustainable educational opportunities for underprivileged children in rural areas and small communities in the Dominican Republic. They offer volunteers the opportunity to make tangible differences in the lives of the underprivileged and change the destinies of children's lives through an experience of cultural immersion that benefits all parties: visitors, the local communities and children.

Contact: Patricia Thorndike Suriel
Tel: +809 571 0497
Fax: +809 571 9551
Email: info@dominicandream.org
Web: www.dominicandream.org
Address: Plaza el Patio, Calle Principal, Cabarete, Republica Dominicana

GLOBAL VISION INTERNATIONAL

GVI offer pioneering conservation, wildlife research and community education projects worldwide. GVI and selected partners run expeditions that include marine conservation in Mexico and the Seychelles, wildlife research in the Amazon, Costa Rica, Kenya and South Africa, community development in Mexico and remote exploration in Patagonia. Training is provided.

Tel: +44 (0) 870 608 8898
Fax: +44 (0) 870 609 2319
Email: info@gvi.co.uk
Web: www.gvi.co.uk
Address: Amwell Farmhouse, Nomansland, Wheathampstead, St Albans, Herts, AL4 8EJ, UK

GOXPLORE

GoXplore is perhaps best described as a recruitment agency that places volunteers in independently operated wildlife projects, mainly in South Africa but also elsewhere. The variety of programmes is very wide, ranging from the direct hands-on care for sick or wounded animals to the equally essential activities of data gathering, such as counting the numbers at water holes and observational research into animal behaviour. The cost to volunteers depends on the type of project to which s/he is assigned.

Contact: Tracey Jones
Tel: +27 31 765 1818/1889/4780
Fax: +27 31 765 4781/1818
Email: wildlife@goxploreafrica.com
Web: www.goxploreafrica.com
Address: PO Box 436, Hillcrest, 3650, KwaZulu-Natal, South Africa

YOUTH ASSOCIATION OF ZAMBIA (YAZ)

This is not where you go if you want to sip wine under a million stars and dream of the Big Five tomorrow. This is a work and study camp organization that gives volunteers the chance to visit tourist sites during excursions. You will be working mainly on environmental outreach programmes and offering your skills to support their take-up

Contact: Evans Mambwe Musonda
Tel: +260 97 75 94 44
Email: yazinfor@yahoo.com, musonda5@yahoo.com
Web: www.youth.unesco.or.kr/volunteer/nation/ 2005/Zambia2005.htm
Address: PO Box 31852, Lusaka, Zambia

and you will be having an intercultural experience beyond measure. YAZ offer volunteers an orientation workshop on arrival (which you pay for) and this ensures you receive 'a less shock if any' during your stay. Volunteers have the opportunity to be given a wide choice of camps in Zambia, which can be extended worldwide as YAZ is a member of many global work camp networks.

RESOURCES

Books

Cater, E. and Lowman, G. (eds) (1994) *Ecotourism: A Sustainable Option?*, John Wiley & Sons, Chichester
Some very good chapters on the impacts of ecotourism.

Clark, D. (2004) *The Rough Guide to Ethical Shopping*, Rough Guides Ltd, London
Balanced and non-prescriptive.

Duffy, R. (2002) *A Trip Too Far; Ecotourism, Politics & Exploitation*, Earthscan, London
Duffy's trenchant monograph leaves one in no doubt that abuses can sail under an ecotourism flag of convenience and thereby remain undetected. She is very good on the impacts on host communities.

Eber, S. (ed.) (1992) *Beyond the Green Horizon: Principles for Sustainable Tourism*, WWF UK, Godalming
A discussion paper commissioned from Tourism Concern by WWF UK, which may now be a little old but which remains one of the best surveys of all the relevant issues.

The Green Guide, Markham Publishing, Wisbech
As this guide went to press, the *Green Guide* series was in the process of being extensively revised. There will be nine editions, each one covering a different region of the UK. The chapters of each guide range over pertinent issues such as Transport & Travel, and Leisure, Activities & Holidays. The indexing is good, enabling easy navigation. There is a good database at greenguide.co.uk.

Harrison, R. et al (2005) *The Ethical Consumer*, Sage, London
The author investigates, and tries to understand, the rise in ethical consumption.

Hickman, L. (2005) *A Good Life: The Guide to Ethical Living*, Guardian Books Ltd, London
The title indicates the content.

Hickman, L. (2005) *A Life Stripped Bare: Tiptoeing Through the Ethical Minefield*, Bantam Press, London
At the request of the *Guardian*, Hickman spent some months attempting to live a more ethical life – this is his diary of the struggle.

Higgins-Desbiolles, F. (2005) *Hostile Meeting Grounds: Encounters Between the Wretched of the Earth and the Tourist Through Tourism and Terrorism in the 21st Century*, Perspectives in Tourism, No. 4, ECOT China, Hong Kong SAR
This is a 'must read' for anyone concerned with the interaction between the tourist from the north and inhabitants of the south, although admittedly the author has an agenda as the quote from Frantz Fanon in the title testifies.

Honey, M. (1999) *Ecotourism and Sustainable Development. Who Owns Paradise?*, Island Press, Washington, DC
Although a little old now, Honey's is still one of the best surveys of the issues, which she follows up with an analysis as to how these manifest themselves in various countries in all their sometimes ugly glory.

Khaneka, P. (2004) *Do the Right Things! A Practical Guide to Ethical Living*, New Internationalist Publications Ltd, Oxford
This is committed campaigning material – but put together with style and humour.

Krippendorf, J. (1989) *The Holidaymakers*, Butterworth-Heinemann, London
It has been said that if you read only one book about what drives modern tourism then this should be it. He makes one examine one's own lifestyle.

Luck, M. and Kirstges, T. (eds) (2003) *Global Ecotourism Policies and Case Studies: Perspectives and Constraints*, Current Themes in Tourism, Channel View Publications, Clevedon
Academic – but not excessively so, with, for example, accessible chapters on Latin American eco-tourism, examining whether the Maasai can benefit from conservation, and community involvement in tourism around national parks.

Mann, M. (2000) *The Community Tourism Guide*, Earthscan, London
Mann's book was pioneering and he had the gift of being able to teach and to inform without seeming to talk down to his audience.

Mowforth, M. and Munt, I. (2004) *Tourism & Sustainability: Development and New Tourism in the Third World*, 2nd edition, Routledge, London
This is an extremely good survey of all the issues.

Pattullo, Polly (2005) *Last Resorts: The Cost of Tourism in the Caribbean*, 2nd edition, Latin America Bureau, London
Analysing the image of the Caribbean as a tropical paradise and revealing the real impact of tourism on the people and the landscape, the book examines the seamy underbelly of a corrupted society and a culture that has become a pitiful parody of its true self. A quote that forms part of one of the chapter titles is chillingly accurate: 'Like an Alien in We Own Land'.

Smith, M. and Duffy, R. (2003) *The Ethics of Tourism Development*, Contemporary Geographies of Leisure, Tourism and Mobility, Routledge, London
Rights, sustainability, ethics of travelling, codes of conduct, host/guest relations – it is all here.

Weaver, D.B. (1998) *Ecotourism in the Less Developed World*, CAB International, Wallingford
Academic, but very susceptible to useful 'dipping'. Ranges over many countries represented in this book.

Weeden, C. (2000) 'Ethical tourism: an opportunity for competitive advantage' 7th International Conference on Retailing & Services Science, 7–10 July 2000 at Sintra, Portugal (Conference Proceedings)

Weeden, C. (2002) 'A qualitative approach to the ethical consumer: a debate on the use of focus groups for cognitive research in tourism', Tourism Research 2002, 4–7th September 2002 at Cardiff (Conference Proceedings)

Weeden, C. (2004) 'Ethical tourism: an exploration of the concept and its meaning for ethical and responsible tourists'. Tourism: State of the Art II Conference, June 2004 at Strathclyde University, Glasgow (A paper)

Wroe, M. and Doney, M. (2004) *The Rough Guide to a Better World*, Rough Guides Ltd, London
Produced in partnership with the UK Department for International Development (DFID) and made available through Post Offices this again speaks for itself through its title.

Magazines and Journals

Contours
Published quarterly by the Ecumenical Coalition on Tourism and reflecting its aims (see the entry on ECOT in Organizations and Websites below).

Ethical Consumer
Published in Manchester, this is the UK's only alternative consumer organization looking at the social and environmental records of the companies behind the brand names. The website address is: www.ethicalconsumer.org/

In Focus
Published by Tourism Concern in London this appeared as an academic quarterly for many years. It was relaunched in summer 2005 with a new format and aimed at the tourist and traveller who shared the aspirations of Tourism Concern.

Reports and articles

Badger, A. et al (eds) (1996) 'Trading places: tourism as trade', Tourism Concern, London
Examines the growth of tourism as a traded commodity and recognizes that it shares all the normal attributes of a traded good, with the addition that it impacts on human beings and a 'people or a culture once exploited and subverted to the needs of the tourist industry, can never be replaced' (Cecil Rajendra, 1992, quoted on page 9).

Goodwin, H. and Francis, J. (2003) 'Ethical and responsible tourism: consumer trends in the UK', *Journal of Vacation Marketing* vol 9, no 3
Examines the growth in the numbers of people prepared to pay a little more for an ethical holiday and the evidence for increasing demand for responsible tourism.

Kalisch, A. (2001) 'Tourism as fair trade – NGO perspectives', Tourism Concern, London
Without fair and ethical trade practice it is not possible to achieve sustainable tourism – host communities must have a fair return on their investments so as to be able to reinvest in the social and environmental regeneration of their communities.

Mintel (2003) 'Eco and ethical tourism', Mintel International Group Ltd, London
Among other topics, Mintel's report researches the growth of the ethical consumer movement, the increasing choice of ethical holidays and the future of responsible tourism.

Mintel (2005) 'Ethical holidays', Mintel International Group Ltd, London
This report offers the user a way of fully understanding the UK ethical holidays market. Mintel estimates that in 2005 the UK ecotourism market added up to about 450,000 holidays a year.

Stancliffe, A. (2000) *Don't Forget Your Ethics!*, Tearfund, Teddington
A Tearfund guide to tourism written by the founder of Tourism Concern - and her title again says it all.

Tearfund (2000) *Tourism – An Ethical Issue*, Tearfund, Teddington
Tearfund (2001) *Tourism – putting ethics into practice*, Tearfund, Teddington
In both cases the title is self-explanatory.

Tearfund (2002) *Worlds Apart: A Call to Responsible Global Tourism*, Tearfund, Teddington
A report from Tearfund. 'Tourism is like fire. You can cook your supper with it, but it can also burn your house down' – this anonymous aphorism emanating from someone in Asia conveys the philosophy of the report.

Tourism Concern (2005) 'Behind the smile: the tsunami of tourism', Tourism Concern, London
A booklet that accompanied the photo exhibition of the same title and which was part of the Tourism Concern campaign Sun, Sand, Sea and Sweatshops, which revealed the poverty trap in which so many hotel workers around the world are caught by reason of their poor working conditions.

Codes of behaviour for the traveller

Mason, P. and Mowforth, M. (1995) 'Codes of conduct in tourism', Department of Geographical Sciences, University of Plymouth, Plymouth (Occasional Papers in Geography, No. 1)
An academic paper – but one which succeeds in surveying its field of interest in a manner that is interesting in its content and accessible in its language. Not to be sought out but if encountered worth the time and trouble.

World Tourism Organization (1999) 'Global code of ethics for tourism', UNWTO, Geneva
A code adopted with the 'wish to promote an equitable, responsible and sustainable world tourism order'. See www.world-tourism.org for more information.

Statistics

The principal statistics published in the tourism field emanate not surprisingly from the World Tourism Organization (UNWTO) in Madrid. Chief among them is the Yearbook of Annual Statistics; like all such yearbooks its 'fault' is the time-lag in publication – the 2004 edition has data for 1998–2002.

The UNWTO also publishes a statistical series entitled Tourism Market Trends within which data are published for the following areas of the world: Africa, Americas, Asia, East Asia and the Pacific, Europe, Middle East, and South Asia. The caveat about publication time-lag applies also to these publications.

Health matters

Beeching, Dr and Lorie, J. (eds) (2000) *The Traveller's Healthbook*, 2nd edition, WEXAS International, London
All the nasties are here but to quote the first words of the introduction, 'don't panic' because so are the ways to avoid them.

Rough Guides (2004) *The Rough Guide to Travel Health*, Rough Guides Ltd, London
Written and researched by Dr Nick Jones and others, this covers all the basics – as do all their publications.

Wilson-Howarth, J. (1999) *Bugs, Bites & Bowels*, Cadogan Guides, London
Written with humour but an efficient survey of the field.

World Health Organization (2005) 'International travel and health', WHO Press, Geneva
'...intended to give guidance on the full range of significant health issues associated with travel'. A printed edition appears every second year but an internet version allows ongoing updating and has links to other information on, for example, disease outbreaks (www.who.int/ith).

Finally do not forget that as from 1 January 2006 the Form E111 has been replaced by the European Health Insurance Card. Further information is available from any branch Post Office. The URL for information, which incorporates the facility to apply online, is www.dh.gov.uk/PolicyAndGuidance/HealthAdviceForTravellers/fs/en

Organizations and websites

Notwithstanding the daily miracles worked by search engines, such as Google, some websites merit a place in even such a brief survey as this.

ACTSA (Action for Southern Africa) www.actsa.org/campaigns.htm
ACTSA is the successor organization to the Anti Apartheid Movement and campaigns among other things for tourism that brings real benefits to communities, workers, and local economies.

Association of Independent Tour Operators (AITO) www.aito.co.uk/
AITO has over 150 members and is the first tourism industry association to incorporate a commitment to responsible tourism in its business charter. Its five key objectives are: protect the environment, respect local cultures, benefit local communities, conserve natural resources, and minimize pollution.

Bluewater Network bluewaternetwork.org/campaign_ss_cruises.shtml
Bluewater works to move the cruise industry to protect the oceans and to take responsibility for the pollution and waste created by cruise liners. They have also led an environmental coalition in campaigning for new regulations to monitor cruise ship waste.

Carbon Neutral Company www.futureforests.com/
A company campaigning to help everybody, from the individual to large corporations, to reduce their carbon emissions.

Climate Care www.climatecare.org/Partners/index.cfm
Climate care works to help people offset greenhouse gas emissions.

EcoTravel.com www.ecotravel.com
This is a searchable directory of travel organizations with information about their eco-philosophy and practices. Their mission is to build a community of 'eco-travellers' wedded to responsible tourism.

Ecumenical Coalition on Tourism (ECOT) www.ecotonline.org
ECOT is a Hong Kong-based coalition seeking to unite people around efforts to negate the undesirable effects of modern tourism by putting in its place socially responsible and ethically oriented tourism. It believes that justice and sustainability for host communities are paramount and campaigns for the human rights of women, children, indigenous peoples and workers in the tourist trade. ECOT also opposes tourism projects which create environmental devastation.

responsible and ethically oriented tourism. It believes that justice and sustainability for host communities are paramount and campaigns for the human rights of women, children, indigenous peoples and workers in the tourist trade. ECOT also opposes tourism projects which create environmental devastation.

ECPAT www.ecpat.net/eng/index.asp
ECPAT is an international network of organizations and individuals bent on eliminating the commercial sexual exploitation of children, including within tourism. The acronym stands for: End Child Prostitution, Child Pornography and the Trafficking of Children for Sexual Purposes.

Equations www.equitabletourism.org
Equations is an Indian non-profit organization established for research, training and the promotion of holistic tourism. It questions the real benefits of tourism to host communities as well as the socio-cultural economic impacts. This is a vision of tourism that fits within a world structure within which wealth and benefits are distributed more equitably between North and South and in which tourism is just one more way to work towards a more just world.

North South Travel www.northsouthtravel.co.uk
North South Travel is a travel agency offering worldwide discounted fares, but unlike others the profits are all channelled to projects in Africa, Asia and Latin America through the charity, the NST Development Trust.

Planeta www.planeta.com
Planeta is a 'Global Journal of Practical Ecotourism' and Planeta.com is a virtual library that archives thousands of pages about ecotourism and conservation. It looks at the whole world of practical ecotourism. The mantra is: Think smart. Travel slow. It is the first website to focus on ecotourism, conservation and conscientious travel around the globe.

Responsible Travel.com www.responsibletravel.com
An excellent website for anyone interested in 'holidays that give the world a break'.

The Travel Foundation www.thetravelfoundation.org.uk/00_home.html
The Foundation is a UK charity that aims to help the tourism industry arrive at a happy marriage of profitability and sustainability. It hopes to safeguard both the environment and the well-being of host communities.

The Travel Foundation Tobago www.thetravelfoundation.org.uk
The Travel Foundation Tobago is supporting a number of community and environmental projects. Contact the office for details of the current programme:
Programme Coordinator, The Travel Foundation Tobago, 11 Cuyler Street, Scarborough, Tobago, Tel: 868-635-0032; Cellular: 868-620-4676

Third World Network www.twnside.org.sg/
The TWN is an independent non-profit international network involved in matters relating to development, the Third World, and North–South issues.

Tourism Investigation and Monitoring Team (tim-team) www.twnside.org.sg/tour.htm
An independent research and monitoring initiative founded in 1994 to provide information for public use and to campaign for social and ecological justice in tourism and development. It publishes New Frontiers, which highlights issues of tourism, development and the environment in the SE Asia Mekong subregion.

INDEX

Aboriginal communities
181–7
Aboriginal Cultural Tours
181
accessibility 6
accreditation schemes 44–5
Action for Tourism
Development
(AFTOD), Uganda 69
ACTUAR, Costa Rica
108–13
Addai & Dwumah Tour,
Ghana 93–4
Adria Adventure, Croatia
195
Africa 56–97, 204, 206, 208
East 57–71, 206
North 72–4
Southern 75–90, 216
West 91–7
African Legacy, Nigeria 96
African Pro-Poor Tourism
Development Centre
(APTDC) 58
agritourism
Costa Rica 108, 111–12
Guatemala 115
Peru 141
Portugal 199
Thailand 158
Uganda 69
Agua Blanca Lodge, Bolivia
126
Akha Hill Tribe, Thailand
158
Albergue-Campemento
Kennedy-Tateje,
Mexico 119
All Way Travel, Peru 139
Alok Holistic Health
Community 210
Alternative Tourism Group
(ATG), Palestine 177
Alternative Tours, Palestine
177
Alternative Travels, India
163
Amahoro Tours, Rwanda 64
Amazon region
Bolivia 25
Colombia 133
Amazonas Lodge, Peru 140
Amboro, Bolivia 126
The Americas 98–145
Caribbean 99–105
Central 106–21, 207, 212
North 122–4
South 125–45, 207

Ammarin Bedouin Camp,
Jordan 175–6
Anangu Tours, Australia 181
Anapia & Yuspiqui, Peru 140
Andes Tropicales, Venezuela
145
Annapurna Conservation
Area Project (ACAP),
Nepal 168–9
Aracari Travel Consulting,
Peru 140
Asia 146–79, 214
Central 148–50
South 161–74
Southeast 151–60
Southwest 175–8
Asociacion de Desarollo San
Jose Rural
(ADESSARU), Costa
Rica 108
Association Akhiam,
Morocco 73
Association Ak'tenamit,
Guatemala 114
Association of Small-Scale
Enterprises in Tourism
(ASSET) 91
ATEC (Talamenca
Discovery), Costa Rica
108–9
attitudes of tourists 33
Australia 181–7
authenticity 27, 31, 50
Aventura Maya K'iche,
Guatemala 114
awareness 36–7
Ayers Rock resort, Australia
182
Azafudy, Madagascar 63,
214

backpackers see budget
accommodation
Baikal, Lake 199–200
Bali, Indonesia 153–4
Baobab Travel 204
Basata, Egypt 72
Basecamp Explorer, Kenya
59
batteries 7
beach cabins
Jamaica 105
Kenya 59–60
Mexico 119
Bedouin communities
Egypt 72–3
Jordan 175–6
Bees Abroad 204

Belize 106–7, 212
Bellavista Cloud Forest
Reserve, Ecuador 134
Beyond Borders, Haiti 103
Bhutan 161–2
Billion Star Hotel, India 163
biosphere reserve, Honduras
118
birdwatching, Guatemala
114
Black Sheep Inn, Ecuador
135
Blue Mountains Aboriginal
Walkabout 182
Blue Ventures, Madagascar
63, 214
The Boat Landing Guest
House, Laos 155
Bocobonet, Botswana 76
Bolivia 25, 125–8
Bonani Our Pride Tours,
South Africa 81
Bookabee Tours, Australia
182
Borneo Adventure, Malaysia
157
Borneo Touch Ecotours,
Malaysia 157
Bosnia & Herzegovina 193–4
Bosque Alegre, Costa Rica
109
Bosque Nublado, Santa
Lucia, Ecuador 135
botanical gardens, Hawai'i
122
Botswana 75–6
Brazil 128–32
budget accommodation
Malawi 78
Mexico 119
Morocco 73
New Zealand 189–90
Buenaventura's Mangrove,
Colombia 132–3
Buffalo Ridge Safari Lodge,
S.Africa 82
Bulungula Lodge, South
Africa 82
Bungoolee Tours, Australia
182–3
Bush & Beyond Guided
Walks, N.Zealand 188
bush culture, Australia
183–4

Calabash Trust and Tours,
S.Africa 48–9, 82
Caledonia Languages 99,

205
Calentura & Gualmoreto
    Foundation, Honduras
    117
Cama e Cafè, Brazil 128–9
Cambodia 34, 151–2
camel safaris, India 163
Camp Coorong Centre,
    Australia 183
Campi Ya Kanzi, Kenya 59
camps
    Botswana 76
    India 166
    Kenya 59, 60–1
    Mexico 119
    Mozambique 79–80
    South Africa 86–7
    Swaziland 88
    Uganda 69, 70
    see also safaris
Camps International, Kenya
    59
Cape Capers Tours, South
    Africa 83
carbon-neutral flights 6
Caribbean 16, 21–3, 42,
    99–105
Carpe Diem Travel,
    Cambodia 34, 151–2
Casa Calateas, Costa Rica
    109
Casa Grande, Nova Olinda,
    Brazil 129
Casacode, Costa Rica 109
Catlins Wildlife Trackers,
    N.Zealand 186
Cave Hill Safaris, Australia
    182
Cayaya Birding, Guatemala
    114
Cegonha Branca, Portugal
    198
Central America 106–21,
    207, 212
Central Asia 148–50
Cerro Escondido Lodge,
    Costa Rica 109–10
certification schemes 44–5
Chalalan Ecolodge, Bolivia
    25, 126
Chole Mjini, Tanzania 65–6
Chumbe Island Coral Park
    (CHICOP), Zanzibar 71
Civil Society Green Life,
    Peru 140–1
climate change impacts 38–9
clothing 7
coastal protection, Brazil 132
Cockpit Country Adventure
    Tours, Jamaica 104
Coco Planet Tours & Travel,
    India 163–4
Colombia 132–4

Community Action Treks,
    Nepal 169
community tourism
    Bolivia 126–7
    Colombia 133–4
    Gambia 3
    Jamaica 14–15, 105
    Peru 142–3
    projects 46–9
    South Africa 85–6
    see also host accommoda-
        tion; indigenous
        communities
Community Tours,
    Nicaragua 120
Comunidad 'Nueva Alianza',
    Guatemala 115
Coorong Wilderness Lodge,
    Australia 183
coral park, Zanzibar 71
Costa Rica 45, 49, 107–13,
    212
Countrystyle Community
    Tourism, Jamaica 105
crafts, Bali 153
Crete's Culinary Sanctuaries
    (CSS) 196
Croatia 194–5
Crooked Trails 210
cruise-ship tourism 21–3, 26
Cuba 99–100
culinary experiences, Crete
    196
culture 9, 27, 99

Daktari Wildlife Orphanage,
    S.Africa 83
Damaraland Camp, Namibia
    80
Dantica Lodge & Gallery,
    Costa Rica 110
Diamond Beach Village,
    Kenya 59–60
The Different Travel
    Company, Sri Lanka
    172–3, 214
disabled visitor facilities
    Australia 186
    Dominica 101
    Hawai'i 123
    Portugal 199
    South Africa 83
Discovery Initiatives 205
displacement of people 23–4
Diverse Travel, Australia
    183–4
Djuma Game Reserve,
    S.Africa 83
Dominica 10, 100–1
Dominican Republic 14–15,
    18, 102–3, 214
Doro Nawas Camp,
    Namibia 80–1

Dragoman Overland 205
Dream Nepal Travel & Tours
    169
DREAM Project, Dominican
    Republic 102, 214
drinking water 7
Duba Plains Camp,
    Botswana 76
Duma Explorer, Tanzania 66

East Africa 57–71, 206
Eastern Europe Holidays,
    Bosnia & Herzegovina
    193
Ebenezer Campsite, Kenya
    60
Echoway 212
Eco Hotel Uxlabil, Atitlan,
    Guatemala 115
Eco Inn Experiences 211
Eco-Kerala, India 164
ECOCLUB, Greece 195–6
Ecomaya, Guatemala 115
economic development 8
economic leakage 17–19
ecotourism
    camp, Gambia 1–3
    certification 44–5
    growth 10, 26
    Sri Lanka 173–4
Ecotourism Kazakhstan 148
Ecovillage Torri Superiore,
    Italy 197
Ecuador 134–8
education see schools
Egypt 72–3
El Copal, Costa Rica 110
El Encanto de la Piedra
    Blanca, Costa Rica 110
El Nagual Reserva, Brazil
    129
El Yue Agro-Eco Farm &
    Lodge, Costa Rica 111
employment 20–3
environmental impacts 9, 26
environmental protection
    13–14, 42
Equatorial Travel 205
Escazu Mountains, Costa
    Rica 110
ethical consumers 29–30
ethical tourism 2, 14, 31–7
Ethiopia 22, 57–8
Europe 192–203
Expert Africa 206, 207
Explorandes/Titikayak, Peru
    141
Explore! 206
external events 11, 20–1

fair trade 5, 34
Fair Trade in Tourism,
    S.Africa 84

farms *see* agritourism
Favela Tour, Brazil 129
Fazenda Rio Negro, Brazil 130
Fiji 187–8
Fijian Village Homestays 187–8
Finca Esperanza Verde, Nicaragua 121
Finca Sonador-Longo Mai, Costa Rica 111
Firn Travel, Russia 199–200
food imports 18–20
Footprint, Vietnam 160
Foundation International Shiwiar Sin Fronteras (FUNSSIF), Ecuador 135–6
French Pass Sea Safaris, N.Zealand 189

The Gambia 1–3, 91–3
Gecko Villa, Thailand 158
Ghana 93–5
Ghana Tourist Board 94
Ghanadventure 94
global citizenship 13
Global Vision International 216
globalization 11–14
Go Native America, USA 124, 211
golf course construction 24
Golondrinas Foundation, Ecuador 136
GoXplore 216
Granja Porcon, Peru 141
Greece 195–6
Green Visions, Bosnia & Herzegovina 194
greenhouse gas emissions 38
GSE Ecotours, Kenya 60
Guatemala 113–16
Guerba World Travel 206
Guludo Base Camp, Mozambique 79
Guurrbi Tours, Queensland, Australia 184

Haiti 103
Hana Maui Botanical Gardens, Hawai'i 122
Hawai'i 15–16, 122–3
health tourism 210
Herzegovina *see* Bosnia & Herzegovina
hill tribes, Thailand 158, 159
Hiluvari Lakeside Lodge, S.Africa 84
Himalayan Homestays, India 164
Himalayas
   Bhutan 161–2

Nepal 168–72, 208, 209
   tourist code 167
Hog Hollow Country Lodge, S.Africa 84
Hohoe District, Ghana 94
holidays
   costs 5, 17–18
   enjoyment factors 32
homestays *see* host accommodation
Honduras 117–18
host accommodation
   Bosnia & Herzegovina 194
   Brazil 128–9
   Cuba 99
   Ecuador 137–8
   Fiji 187–8
   Ghana 93–5
   Haiti 103
   India 163–5
   Kazakhstan 148
   Kenya 60
   Kyrgyzstan 149
   Nicaragua 121
   Peru 139–41
   Rwanda 64
   Senegal 97
   Solomon Islands 191
   South Africa 86–7
   Sri Lanka 174
   Tanzania 66, 67
   Thailand 158–9
   Uganda 69–70
host countries 8–11
Hotel dos Lunas, Guatemala 115–16
Hotel Mar de Jade, Mexico 119
Hotel Mocking Bird Hill, Jamaica 105
houseboats, India 163–4
Humacchuco, Peru 142
human rights abuse 23–4

Ibike Tours 211
Iga Warta, South Australia 184
Iguana Mama Tours, Dominican Republic 102–3
Iguana Research & Breeding Station, Honduras 117–18
Iko Poran, Brazil 130
imported foods 18–20
Imvubu, South Africa 84–5
income 8, 27
   see also revenues
Independent Trekking Guide Group (ITGG), Nepal 169
India 48, 162–6
Indian Country Tourism,

USA 124
indigenous communities
   Australia 181–7
   Bhutan 158, 159
   Costa Rica 112
   Ecuador 135–6
   Egypt 72–3
   Guatemala 114–16
   Jordan 175–6
   Kenya 18, 23, 59, 60–1
   Mongolia 150
   New Zealand 189–90
   survival 19
   Tanzania 66
   USA 124, 211
Indonesia 152–4
informal economy 21
information 9
Insider Tours
   India 48, 164
   Sri Lanka 43, 173
International Centre of Bethlehem (ICB), Palestine 177–8
International Porter Protection Group (IPPG), Nepal 169–70
IntoAfrica UK 206
Intrepid Travel 207, 212
Isla de Chira Lodge, Costa Rica 111
Italy 197, 213

Jack's Tour & Story Telling, Australia 184
Jamaica 14–15, 104–5
Jan Harmsgat Country House, S.Africa 85
jobs in tourism 20–3
Jordan 175–6
Journey Latin America 207
Jovenes Agro Ecologista de la Zona Norte (JAZON), Costa Rica 111

Kabani, India 165
Kahawa Shamba Community, Tanzania 66
Kai Eco-travel, Colombia 133
Kaie Tours, Botswana 76
Kandora Lodge, Indonesia 153
Kapawi Ecolodge & Reserve, Ecuador 136
Kart, Gambia 91–2
Kasapa Centre, Ghana 95
Kasbah du Toubkal, Morocco 74
Kawaza village, Zambia 28–9, 89

Kazakhstan 148
Kecobat, Kenya 60
KEEP - Kathmandu Environmental Educational Project 170
Kekoldi Indigenous Reserve, Costa Rica 112
Kenedy-Tateje Campemento, Mexico 119
Kenya 17–18, 20, 23, 58–62
Kerala, India 164, 166
Kilimanjaro Native Cooperative Union (KNCU 1984) 66
Kilimanjaro Porters' Assistance Project (KPAP) 66
Klippe Rivier Country House, S.Africa 85
Knapdale Eco-lodge, N.Zealand 189
Koiyaki Guilding School, Kenya 60–1
Kolam Responsible Tours, India 165
Kooljaman at Cape Leveque, Australia 184–5
Kuku Yalanji Dreamtime Walks, Australia 185
Kumanii Lodge, Ecuador 136–7
Kurmanchal Seva Sansthan (KSS), India 165
Kwahu Tourism Project, Ghana 95
Kyrgyz Tourism Association (KCBTA) 149
Kyrgyzstan 149

La Casa de Don David, Guatemala 116
La Estancia Ecolodge, Bolivia 126
La Laguna del Legarto Lodge, Costa Rica 112
La Selva Jungle Lodge, Ecuador 137
Lake Bunyonyi Development Project, Uganda 69
Lama Trek, Peru 141
Lamai Homestay, Thailand 11, 158–9
Landcruiser Tours, Nicaragua 121
Laos 154–6
Last Frontiers 208
Lesotho 77
Levendis Estate, Greece 196
Lewa House, Kenya 61
Lewa Safaris Camp, Kenya 61

libraries, Nepal 171
Llachon, Peru 142
local knowledge 7, 9
local ownership and control 48
local skills 11, 196
lodges see rainforests
Lombadina, Australia 185
Los Campesinos, Costa Rica 112
Luwawa Forest Lodge, Malawi 78
luxury accommodation
  Botswana 76
  Gambia 92
  Indonesia 154
  Kenya 61
  Mozambique 79–80
  New Zealand 189
  South Africa 83, 86
  Zambia 89

Maasai Conservation & Development Organisation (MCDO) 61
Maasai Mara Reserve, Kenya 60–1
Maasai people, Kenya 18, 23, 59, 60–1
Madagascar 10, 63, 208, 214
Madidi National Park, Bolivia 126
Madidi Travel, Bolivia 128
Makasutu & Mandina River Lodge, Gambia 92
Malawi 78
Malaysia 24, 156–7
Maldives 19
Malealea Lodge & Pony Trek Centre, Lesotho 77
Mallku Cueva/Villa Mar, Bolivia 127
Mamiraua Reserva, Brazil 130
Manda Wilderness Project (MWP), Mozambique 80
Maori culture 189–90
Mapajo Ecolodge, Bolivia 127
Maquipucuna Ecolodge, Ecuador 137
marine conservation, Madagascar 63
marine tours, New Zealand 189
Masakala Guesthouse, S.Africa 85–6
Mayan community, Guatemala 114–16
Mekong Tourism Development Project,

Laos 155
Mexico 118–19
Michael Blendinger Nature Tours, Bolivia 127
Mila Restored Cretan Settlement 196
Mimili Maku Tours, Australia 185
Mitra Bali, Indonesia 153
Momopeho Hacienda, Ecuador 137
Mongolia 150
Montana Verde, Costa Rica 112
Montenegro see Serbia & Montenegro
Morocco 73–4
The Mountain Institute, Peru 142–3
Mozambique 78–9
Muir's Tours 208, 213
Multi-Environmental Society (MESO), Tanzania 67
Myanmar 23–4

Nakapalayo Tourism Project, Zambia 90
Nam Ha Ecotourism Project, Laos 156
Namibia 80–1
Native American tours, USA 124, 211
The Native Hawaiian Hospitality Association (NaHHA) 122–3
native peoples see indigenous communities
Naturally Morocco 74
Nature Tourism, Bhutan 162
Neat Safaris, Uganda 69
negative impacts 15–16, 23–4, 29
Nepal 168–72, 208, 209
The Nepal Trust 170, 209
New Zealand 188–90
Nicaragua 120–1, 212
niche products 37
Nigeria 95–6
Nihiwatu Resort, Indonesia 154
Nipbamjen Aboriginal Tour 186
Nkwichi Lodge, Mozambique 80
nomadic herders, Mongolia 150
North Africa 72–4
North America 122–4
North South Travel 208
Nuqui, Colombia 133–4

Oceania 180–91
Of Road & Sea,

Mozambique 79
Ol Pejeta Conservancy Laikipia, Kenya 62
Olive Cooperative, Palestine 178

Pacaya Volcano National Park, Guatemala 116
packing list 6–7
Pafuri Camp, South Africa 86
Palestine 176–8
Papillote Wilderness Retreat, Dominica 101
Pedras Negras, Brazil 130
People to People Safaris, Tanzania 67
Peru 139–44, 210
Peru Verde 143
Petra, Jordan 175
Phaphama Initiatives, S.Africa 86
photography 7, 9, 29
Phumulani Lodge, South Africa 86
planning 6
Ponta Grossa, Brazil 131
Pooh Eco Trekking, Thailand 159
population displacement 23–4
The Portal to the Mayan World, Guatemala 116
porters' rights 46–7
Portugal 198–9
Pousada Aldeia dos Lagos, Brazil 131
Pousada Uacari, Brazil 130
poverty alleviation 49–50
Bees Abroad 204
Nepal 172
Prainha do Canto Verde, Brazil 131
preparation for travel 6–7
Projeto Bagagem, Brazil 131

Quinta da Comenda, Portugal 199

Rainbow Serpent Tour, Australia 186
Rainbow Tours 208, 210
rainforests
Australia 185
Belize 107
Bolivia 126–7
Brazil 129–31
Colombia 132–3
Costa Rica 109–13
Ecuador 134–8
Guatemala 114–15
Honduras 117
India 166

Malaysia 156–7
New Zealand 189
Nicaragua 121
Peru 140
Ram (Italy) 212
Ranweli Holiday Village, Sri Lanka 173
Real Africa Excursions, Uganda 69–70
Reality Tours & Global Exchange 211
Red de Desarollo Sostenible (RDS-HN), Honduras 118
REDTURS, South America 125
Regional Tourism Organization of Southern Africa (RETOSA) 75
Reliance Travel & Tours (RTT), Nepal 170
Relief Riders International 211–12
Responsible Ecological Social Tours (REST), Thailand 159
responsible tourism 3–4, 40, 43–4, 50
revenues 5, 8, 10, 16–20
Rio Platano Biosphere Reserve (RPBR), Honduras 118
Rolwaling Ecotourism Development Project (RETP), Nepal 171
Rooftop Retreat Guesthouse, India 165–6
Royal Society for the Conservation of Nature (RSCN), Jordan 176
Ruboni Community Centre, Uganda 70
Runa Tupari Native Travel, Ecuador 137–8
Rural Education and Development (READ), Nepal 171
Rural Organization for Social Elevation (ROSE) 165
Russia 199–200
Rwanda 64, 212
Rwenzori Mountaineering Tours, Uganda 70

Saddle Skedaddle 209
Safari Garden Hotel, Gambia 92
safaris
Australia 182
Botswana 76

India 163
Kenya 58–62
Mozambique 79
New Zealand 189
South Africa 82–3, 86, 87
Tanzania 67
Zambia 89
see also trekking; wildlife reserves
St Dominic's Rural Training Centre, Solomon Is. 190
St Lucia 15
San Christobal Lodge, Bolivia 127–8
San Ignacio Resort Hotel, Belize 107
Sandale Eco-Retreat, Gambia 92
Santa Isabel, Cuba 100
Santawani Lodge & Kaziikini Camp, Botswana 76
schools
Gambia 92
Ghana 95
Mexico 119
Solomon Is. 190
sea kayaking, Croatia 195
sea safaris, N. Zealand 189
Selva, Nicaragua 121
Senegal 96–7
Senevolu 97
Serbia & Montenegro 200–1
Serere Sanctuary, Bolivia 128
Sewalanka Foundation, Sri Lanka 173
sex tourism 28, 151
Shiwiar people, Ecuador 135–6
The Silent Way, Sweden 203
Simply Tanzania 67
Slovakia 201–2
Slovakia Green Tours 202
smiling 14–15
snow tours, Sweden 203
Snow White Treks & Tours, Bhutan 162
social impacts 28
Socialtours.com, Nepal 171
Solomon Islands 190–1
South Africa 81–7, 216
South America 125–45, 207
South Asia 161–74
Southeast Asia 151–60
Southern Africa 75–90
Southwest Asia 175–8
Soweto Nights, Safari Days 87
Sri Lanka 43, 172–4
Sri Lanka Eco Tours (SLET) 174
Sri Lanka Ecotourism

Foundation (SLEF) 174
Stibrawpa Casa de las Mujeres, Costa Rica 113
Stormsriver Adventures, S.Africa 87
Sua Bali, Indonesia 154
Sumburu people, Kenya 23
Sunderbans/Manas Jungle Camps, India 166
sustainable tourism 42, 133–4
Swaziland 88
Sweden 202–3
Symbiosis Expedition Travel, Cambodia 152

TALK Tourism, South Africa 86
The Tamarind Tree, Dominica 101
Tanzania 64–8
Tanzania Journeys 68
Telepare Ecolodge, Solomon Is. 191
Tell Tale Travel, Thailand 159
Tenmala Ecotourism, India 166
Terra Incognita Ecotours 212
Terramar, Brazil 132
Tesoro Verde, Costa Rica 113
Thailand 11, 157–9
Three Camel Lodge, Mongolia 150
Three Rivers Eco Lodge, Dominica 101
Tiger Mountain Pokhara Lodge, Nepal 171
Titicaca, Lake 126, 139, 140, 142–3
toiletries 7
Toledo Ecotourism Association (TEA), Belize 107
tour operators 16–17, 37–43
  other countries 212–13
  UK 16–17, 40–3, 204–10
  USA 210–12
  volunteering 213–16
tourism, statistics 5–6
Tourism in Ethiopia for Sustainable Future Alternatives (TESFA) 22, 57–8
Tourism for Help, Cambodia 152
Tourism for Rural Poverty Alleviation Programme (TRPAP), Nepal 172

tourist code, Himalayas 167
tourists
  ethical attitudes 33
  requirements 32, 50
Traidcraft 209
travel codes 9, 167
travel companies 16–17
  see also tour operators
Travelroots 209
The Treasure of Winaymarka, Peru 143
tree house hotel, Tanzania 65–6
Tree Top Walk, Australia 186
trekking
  Ethiopia 22, 57–8
  India 163, 166
  Indonesia 153
  Kazakhstan 148
  Kyrgyzstan 149
  Laos 156
  Lesotho 77
  Nepal 168–72
  Peru 141
  Tanzania 68
  Thailand 159
  tour operator 208
  see also safaris
tribal peoples 19
Tribal Warrior Association, Australia 186
Tribes (travel company) 209
Trinity Tours & Safaris, Kenya 62
Tropic Ecological Adventures, Ecuador 138
tsunami (Asia 2004) 11, 20, 157–8
Tuku Wairua Centre, N. Zealand 189–90
Tumani Tenda Ecotourism Camp, Gambia 1–3, 93
Twin Buffalos Safaris, Kenya 62

Uganda 68–70, 212
Uganda Community Tourism Association (UCOTA) 70
UK tour operators 204–10
Ulu Ai Project, Malaysia 157
Uluru (Ayers Rock), Australia 181–2
Umlani Bushcamp, South Africa 87
UNORCAC Community Lodge, Ecuador 138
UNPD Lo Podgorica, Serb.& Mont. 201
US tour operators 210–12
USA 123–4

Valley of the Giants Walk, Australia 186
Venezuela 144–5
Vicos, Peru 143
Vietnam 160
Vision du Monde 213
Volcano Guest House, Hawai'i 123
volcano national park, Guatemala 116
volunteering
  Brazil 130
  Costa Rica 111
  Dominican Republic 102
  Ecuador 134, 136, 137
  Ghana 93–4
  Kenya 59
  Madagascar 63
  Nepal 169, 170
  New Zealand 189
  organizations 213–16
  Senegal 97
  South Africa 83
  Sri Lanka 172–3
  Tanzania 66
  Zambia 90
VSO (Voluntary Service Overseas) 40, 43

Wardan Aboriginal Cultural Centre 186–7
waste dumping 26
water filters 7
water supplies 25
West Africa 91–7
Wild Kerala Tour Company, India 166
wildlife reserves
  Honduras 117–18
  India 166
  Kenya 62
  Peru 143
  South Africa 83
  see also rainforests; safaris
Wind, Sand & Stars, Egypt 72–3
Woodlands, Sri Lanka 174
Woza Nawe Campsite, Swaziland 88

Yachana Lodge, Ecuador 138
Yachaqui Wayi, Peru 144
Youth Association of Zambia (YAZ) 90, 216

Zambia 28–9, 89–90, 216
Zanzibar 71
Zion Country Beach Cabins, Jamaica 105

I would like to support **TourismConcern**

☐ **By becoming a member:** Waged £24 / Non-waged £12

☐ **By making a donation:** I am happy to set up a regular monthly standing order of £3 / £4 / £5 or £_____ to Tourism Concern and have completed the standing order form.

☐ **Gift Aid Declaration** I am a UK taxpayer and wish to make this and all other future donations as Gift Aid so that Tourism Concern may reclaim 28p for each £1 given at no extra cost to me.

Full name _____ Title _____

Address _____

_____ Postcode _____

Telephone _____ Email _____

Signature _____ **Date** _____

PAYMENT METHODS (payment in Sterling please):

▸ By **cheque** or **Postal Order** made payable to Tourism Concern
▸ By **Standing Order** (UK only):

Please pay Tourism Concern £_____ a month, each month until further notice

My Name _____

Name of My Bank _____

My Bank's Address _____

My Sort Code _____ My Account Number _____

Standing Order to begin on ___ / ___ / ___ until further notice

(please allow 1 month from signature date. You may cancel this at any time by informing Tourism Concern or your bank).

To your bank: Please pay the above amount each month to Tourism Concern, Sort Code 08 92 99, Account Number 65130397, Co-Operative Bank, Community Direct Branch, PO Box 250, Delf House, Southway, Skelmersdale, WN8 6WT.

Signed _____ **Date** _____

▸ By **Visa** or **Mastercard** **Amount:** £_____   Expiry Date ____

Card Number ⬚⬚⬚⬚⬚⬚⬚⬚⬚⬚⬚⬚⬚⬚⬚⬚   ⬚⬚ ⬚⬚

Address the card is registered to (if different from above): _____

Please **COMPLETE** and **RETURN** this form to:
Tourism Concern, FREEPOST LON 18202, London N7 8BR
or Fax to: 020 7133 3331

TourismConcern

Avoid Guilt Trips

Buy fair trade coffee + bananas ✓

Save energy – use low energy bulbs ✓
– don't leave tv on standby ✓

Offset carbon emissions from flight to Madrid ✓

Send goat to Africa ✓

Join Tourism Concern today ✓

Slowly, the world is changing.
Together we can, and will, make a difference.

Tourism Concern is the only UK registered charity fighting
exploitation in one of the largest industries on earth: people forced
from their homes in order that holiday resorts can be built,
sweatshop labour conditions in hotels and destruction of the
environment are just some of the issues that we tackle.

Sending people on a guilt trip is not something we do. We know as
well as anyone that holidays are precious. But you can help us to
ensure that tourism always benefits the local communities involved.

Call 020 7133 3330
or visit **tourismconcern.org.uk** to find out how.

A year's membership of Tourism Concern costs just £20 (£12 unwaged)
- that's 38 pence a week, less than the cost of a pint of milk, organic of course.